# THE PSYCHOLOGY
# OF HAPPINESS

## Understanding
## Our Selves and Others

ROBERT NAJEMY

D1567573

# THE PSYCHOLOGY OF HAPPINESS

## Understanding Our Selves and Others

### ROBERT NAJEMY

I would like to offer this book to all of humanity
as well as to our brothers the animals and plants,
and all the elements of nature.

**You are all my teachers.**
I am grateful to you.

**ISBN** 0-9710116-0-5
United States Copyright Office no. 068722878 Sept. 07, 1994
Library of Congress Control Number: 2001091866

Published by: **Holistic Harmony Publishers**
(www.HolisticHarmony.com)
P.O. Box 2504, Worcester. Mass. 01613-2504, U.S.A.

Cover Photograph: Rena Papadopoulou
Cover Design: Uranus

# Table of Contents

# INTRODUCTION

**Dear Reader,**

I offer you this book, with the hope that material presented here will help you as much as it has helped me in my life. This is not an ordinary book on psychology. It is a handbook for **self-transformation.** Its purpose is to open the way for a new, more positive, more joyful view of life.

The concepts and techniques found in this book, come from a very wide variety of sources, including:

**1. Psychological** approaches such as Humanistic Psychology, Transactional Analysis, Effective Communication Training, the Twelve Pathways to Higher Consciousness of Ken Keyes, Body Centered Psychology, Eye Movement Desensitization and Reprogramming.

**2. Philosophical** and spiritual concepts from various sources that supplement the psychological point of view.

We might call this **spiritual psychology**, the **psychology of transformation, the psychology of happiness**, or the **psychology of evolution.**

I have preferred to express these concepts in a simple way so that all can work effectively. Do not let this simplicity cause you to underestimate the power of the material presented here. Literally hundreds of thousands of people have used these systems to create emotional peace and mental equilibrium. Many of them did not stop there, but went on to develop themselves spiritually, experiencing higher states of consciousness of increased peace and love.

**This is a practical book**, a handbook for a new way of perceiving ourselves and the world; for a new way of feeling, loving and acting.

Before each chapter, we have placed **Life Stories** that describe various situations that we are likely to encounter as well as a list of lessons we might learn from them. After each chapter we have placed **techniques** which we hope you will employ and benefit from.

The previous editions of the book were abundant with questionnaires and sample answers to those questions that allowed the reader to work on him or her self.

Because we have added here many more chapters as well the **Life Stories** and **Techniques**, we have decided to place those questionnaires on our web site (www.HolisticHarmony.com) for those who really are seeking to understand and transform themselves.

I would suggest that you read the book twice. Once before you answer the questionnaires and employ the various techniques described and then again as you are employing them.

It is not necessary for you to have emotional problems to gain from this book. The book is based on the **psychology of evolution.** Applying these principles can open us up to ever greater inner peace and unconditional love for all beings. We are lead to higher states of consciousness, and prepared for more advanced spiritual techniques, such as meditation.

Some basic points are repeated, as these truths need to be encountered many times, in order for them to sink deeply enough into our subconscious mind. This repetition also enables us to see how these truths apply to various aspects of our lives.

This work has actually been divided into two books. The one you are holding addresses it self to **"Understanding Ourselves".** The second volume investigates **"Creating Conscious Love Relationships."**

## I WENT OUT TO END MY LIFE AND FOUND IT

I would like to briefly share with you how I came to write this book.

I was 22 years old and had followed the socially dictated path towards happiness. I graduated from university and was working as a chemical engineer making plenty of money. What else could I want? I had all "ingredients" for happiness; a car, stereo, nice looking apartment, a girl friend or two. "Well, what else could you want, young man?"

I was never more miserable in my life. I was experiencing a **crisis in identity and life values** during my first year out of engineering school, while working for an international chemical company.

Although, I had done everything society told me to do in order to be happy; **I had no reason for living**. I had no idea why I was living or what was important. My life had no meaning for me.

This crisis of doubt and confusion began to permeate every aspect of my life. I had thoughts like, "Is life completely relative? Is this all there is; fifty to eighty years of momentary happiness and unhappiness, working, sleeping, eating, enjoying sensual pleasures and then it's finished, as if it never ever existed?"

"If so, then why go through it all? Why not commit suicide and finish it now, as there is no purpose to life? Why struggle, why be good, why take care of my health, why make any effort whatsoever to succeed if everything, that I would do and become, would sooner or later be consumed by the river of time?"

Soon it became unbearable, and I decided that life really wasn't worth living.

While sitting at a lake thinking about how I was going to finish my life, a strange set of experiences, which I have never clearly understood, involving a friendly snake which appeared and looked into my eyes for a considerable time before passing on, deterred me from my decision.

Something was happening within me. A whole new world opened up. Suddenly I saw the world in a different light and a new hope had sprouted within me.

The next day I informed my boss that I would be leaving in a month's time. He was shocked and wanted to know what I was going to do. The only answer I could think of was, «I'm going to take a year off and search for a meaning in life».

What was I searching for? The answers to some extremely important but seldom asked questions such as:

**1.** Who or what exactly am I?
**2.** What I am doing here on this earth, in this body?
**3.** Why was I born in America and not in Africa or on some other planet?
**4.** Why was I born at all? For what reason?
**5.** Who or what is controlling the circumstances of my life?
**6. What is the purpose of my life?** What should I do with my life?
**7.** What happens after I die? Is that the end?
**8.** Is there such a thing as good and bad? Is life simply a chemical phenomenon or is there some spiritual entity behind all this?

I will throughout this book refer to the answers which I have received concerning the above mentioned questions, but here let me simply categorize the meaning of life into four headings; Relationship, Creativity, Service and Evolution.

These constitute the basic focal points that give meaning to most lives.

**1.** We find meaning in sincere loving **relationships** in which we transcend our fears and alienation and open our hearts to others unconditionally. These people give us a reason to live, and this is why departure from them is so painful. Our ultimate relationship, however, will be with the Divine.

**2. Creativity** is our basic nature. As expressions of Universal energy we are co-creators here on the earth level and creative expression is essential for our balance, happiness, self esteem and well being.

**3. Serving** or being useful to others gives is a reason to exist. We feel that our existence counts, that our life has a meaning.

**4. Evolution** or **Self-Actualization** is evident in all creation. We can improve our selves physically and psychologically, increasing our love, creativity, inner peace and happiness and live in greater harmony with our environment.

We all experience within us forces pushing us to improve our selves. We clearly know that we can be happier and more loving than we are. **We can manifest greater portions of our inner potential.**

We also experience the same inner pressure towards relationship, creativity and service.

The ultimate meaning of life, however, will be found in the **fullness of existence it self**, without any other reason. However, as this requires an extremely high state of consciousness that few of us experience, this book shall investigate these more tangible sources of meaning and happiness.

## MORE HELP

Throughout the last 33 years I have been investigating human psychology from many different aspects, through personal appointments, classes, seminars and workshops. This has resulted in a volume of information and techniques much too large to present in this book.

Much of that extremely useful material which has to do with relationships will be coming out in my next book., **Conscious Love Relationships**.

However, in order to allow those interested to access so many more beneficial articles and chapters, we have placed them on our web site for your perusal. We hope that you, your family and friends will benefit from the web site and also the books and cassettes described therein.

The site address is:   *www.HolisticHarmony.com*


I wish you happiness.

May you always be well.


Robert  Elias Najemy Jr.



Athens, Greece
March , 2001

*Life Story no. 1*

# COMMUNICATION PROBLEMS

Anna enjoys sharing her feelings with her husband Paul. She also needs to know what he is feeling and thinking in return. When she is unable to communicate with him, she feels neglected and unloved.

Although Paul does love Anna, he does not enjoy communicating as much as she does and feels very uncomfortable sharing his feelings, mostly because he is not very familiar with them. Also, when he **is** aware of his feelings, he is ashamed to share them because he fears this will lessen his "manhood".

This constructs a conflict of needs. The more Anna pressures Paul to open up and communicate, the more he withdraws and avoids her. If she pressures him too much, he angrily pushes her away.

As a result, Anna feels rejected and unloved, while Paul feels pressured and suppressed. The more Paul avoids Anna and does not fulfill her needs, the more negative, critical and accusatory she becomes. In response to Anna's negative reactions, Paul avoids her even more.

He feels she does not understand his needs and refuses to accept him as he is. She feels he does not love her and that he rejects her as a woman and a partner in life.

Anna is unhappy and completely unsatisfied with her marriage. Her needs are not being fulfilled. Paul directs his attention to other activities, such as work, sports and recreation with friends.

Both are susceptible to others of the opposite sex who they believe will truly "understand" them.

In this case, two individuals, who actually love each other, have become victims of their own programming and needs. Their attachments, fears and lack of communication skills are destroying their relationship and their happiness.

They both need to understand the beliefs creating their fears and attachments in order to put themselves in the other's position, understand the other's needs, and communicate more openly and clearly.

This book is dedicated to our freedom from such mechanical robot-like interactions.

## Belief Analysis

**Anna might be limited by some of the following beliefs:**

**1.** I need to share my feelings with people I love in order to feel safe and also to feel close to them.

**2.** In order to feel close to others, I must know what they are thinking and feeling.

**3.** If others do not want to share with me, there must be something wrong with me.

**4.** If others do not want to communicate with me, I feel that they do not love me.

**5.** I cannot feel safe with someone I do not know emotionally.

**6.** I must share my problems with my loved ones and receive their input and support.

**7.** I am the victim and have suffered a great injustice.

**8.** I am responsible for Paul's happiness.

**9.** My self worth and security are dependent upon how much my husband cares for me and shares his feelings with me.

**Paul might be limited by some of the following beliefs:**

**1.** I am in danger when communicating feelings.

**2.** Emotions are for women. Action is for Men.

**3.** I am in danger if I have feelings of weakness.

**4.** I must never show weakness.

**5.** She is suppressing my personality and I am losing my freedom.

**6.** She does not accept me as I am. I am in danger because she wants to change me.

**7.** I am the victim of her criticism.

**8.** I must avoid her in order to preserve my freedom.

### Anna might benefit from developing some of the following beliefs:

**1.** I feel close to my husband regardless of how much he can share with me.

**2.** I am safe and loved even when my husband is unable to communicate.

**3.** Life provides me with exactly what I need in order to learn my next lesson.

**4.** I dynamically create my reality with or without my husband.

**5.** I accept and love myself regardless of his behavior.

**6.** I understand his difficulty to communicate and love him as he is.

### Paul might benefit from developing some of the following beliefs:

**1.** I feel safe and comfortable communicating my feelings to my wife.

**2.** I accept my feelings and share them with my loved ones in order to create deeper love relationships.

**3.** I am free to be myself in every situation.

**4.** I enjoy sharing my inner world with my beloved wife.

**5.** In each moment life provides me with exactly what I need to learn my next lesson.

# CHAPTER 1

# HOW OUR
# PERSONAL REALITY IS CREATED

## A CHANGE OF ATTITUDE

I was sitting on a bench in the National Park in the center of Athens, Greece while three children played nearby. They were playing "basketball", trying to throw a ball into a garbage can. The older boy, about seven years old, had thrown the ball in four times, and his young girlfriend had thrown it in twice. His little sister, however, who looked to be about five years old, had not been able to make even a single basket. The game continued with great earnestness, with exciting joys and devastating disappointments. Every time they tossed the ball into the can, they immediately looked over to see if I had been watching. I became very emotionally involved without saying a word, but was rather worried about the attitude of the youngest girl, who still hadn't managed to put the ball in. The score was now 6 to 5 to 0.

I noticed she was more concerned about the fact that she wasn't getting the ball in the can and the disappointment involved, than she was in concentrating on the aim of her toss. **She had come to believe that she couldn't do it, and didn't even take the time to seriously look** at the basket she was shooting for. Instead, she was already prepared to show her disappointment, which usually consisted of jumping up and down two or three times with both feet, and banging herself on the head. Sometimes she spun around in a circle (which, by the way, was similar to the way her brother acted when he was successful, only his hands would be raised in the air in triumph).

The little girl was becoming more and more desperate, even resorting to kicking the ball away, so the others would have to chase after it. That made them angry and they retaliated by telling her how bad she was at the game. At other times, she would grab the ball and run away with it, making her brother chase after her and forcibly snatch the ball away from her.

I was practically in tears by now, although not one word had passed between us. I then closed my eyes and focussed my thoughts on the little girl, mentally communicating to her that she must concentrate and think positively. I continued doing this for about three minutes.

Then I opened my eyes and kept this idea in my mind and my eyes on her. Her next try was another failure, but she didn't seem quite so upset.

The very next time she did something completely different. She took the ball in her hands, and looked at it closely, and **began to talk to it with conviction and authority, telling it that it MUST** go into the basket and that if it didn't, it would be punished. Then she looked lovingly at the ball and kissed it, turned toward the basket and threw it directly in.

I was so happy for her that I could hardly remain seated. I actually started to cry.

The little girl continued with this more positive technique for the rest of the game, and the final score was 10 to 8 to 6. My little friend had 8.

Now, it is not difficult to understand the point. **The little girl lacked confidence and concentration, and because of this, she set herself up for failure.** When she failed, she became even more convinced of her inability, and set herself up physically and psychologically for each successive failure. She stopped making a serious effort. She simply went up to the line with failure in mind and threw the ball without trying.

Perhaps my concentration and prayers were picked up by her subconscious. Perhaps they weren't. Then, for some reason, she changed her behavior and employed more concentration and optimism. She told the ball what it had to do and she became very sure of herself. The ball went directly in, guided by her positive and convinced state of mind.

When the ball went into the can, **the little girl's opinion of herself completely changed; now she was a success**. Her entire physical reality changed, and she made more baskets in the remaining time than the other two children combined.

Children can alter their reality relativity easily through a change of attitude and behavior because of their less rigid belief system. For us adults, who have many more years of conditioning, such a change might take more time. **But it can be done** and more importantly, in many cases, **it must be done,** if we are to enjoy a life of happiness, success and growth.

Many of us set ourselves up for failure because of our habitual negative thinking and basic beliefs concerning our impotency. In the following pages, we will discuss the techniques by which we may recondition our thought processes and change our reality

## WE CREATE OUR REALITY

Most of us would like a happier, healthier, more harmonious reality. In order to improve our reality, we must understand the mechanisms of its creation. Most of us feel that "things simply happen in our lives" or that we just feel "this way" or "that way." Few of us actually investigate **how** our reality is created.

We might say that our reality is constructed of two basic factors:

**1.** What is **happening** or has happened.

**2.** What we **believe**, and consequently how we feel about ourselves, in relationship to what has happened, is happening or will happen.

This **belief system** or programming, which creates our subjective perception of reality, is a result of our past experience.

A description of how elephants are trained will help us understand the relationship between our past, our beliefs and our reality.

## SELF LIMITING ELEPHANTS

Elephants born in captivity are restrained by a chain that attaches one leg to a metal spike driven into the ground. This prevents them from roaming. They become accustomed to the fact that, as long as the chain and spike are next to them, they are unable to move.

As they grow older, their minds become programmed. When they see the spike and chain, they "believe" and accept that they will not be able to move. They become so conditioned that when their owners place a small **rope** and **wooden peg** next to them, they make no efforts to step away from it, because they "believe" they are unable to.

In truth, their actual power as adults is so great that they could easily pull up a chain and spike of any size. Their programming or "belief," however, allows this tiny rope and wooden peg to limit their movement.

We are all very much like these elephants. We allow the weaknesses, fears and rejection we experienced as children to program us into a life in which we lack power, peace, love and happiness. We become controlled by false childhood assumptions we have made about our ability, strength and self worth.

We **can** move away from these "pegs" of self-limitation, but we must **chose** to do so.

This is a very simple description of an extremely complicated and intricate process, which we will analyze in greater details throughout this book.

## THE STIMULUS

The first factor in the creation of our reality is called the **stimulus**. This is an event that we **observe** or perhaps even **fanaticize** or **project.**

**1.** Some **external stimuli** include events such as the following:

We receive love, admiration, attention, gifts, money or success at some effort, or we are rejected, falsely accused, suffer a loss of someone or something important to us, or experience failure at some endeavor.

**2.** We might also be affected by **internal stimuli,** such as thoughts about the past or future.

**3.** Our **emotions** or **thoughts** may become stimuli for other emotions, such as when we feel anger or self-rejection when we observe that we have allowed ourselves to become aggressive or fearful.

**4.** Other more subtle stimuli might be the state of our **hormones, chemical balance** or **energy state.** We have all experienced days when we were more emotionally vulnerable, perhaps due to low energy. This is especially but not exclusively so for women, because of hormonal changes.

## THE EVALUATION OF THE STIMULUS

As these stimuli pass into the mind, it evaluates them seeking to determine whether they are **supportive** of or **endangering** to our basic needs.

**1.** If our subconscious programming determines them to be supportive, we feel relaxed, happy and loving.

**2.** If we conclude that they are endangering, we experience fear as well as and a wide variety of other emotions, such as pain, disillusionment, bitterness, injustice, depression, jealousy, envy, anger, hate, etc.

Our emotional state constitutes the greater portion of our subjective personal reality. It is not so much what happens in our life that creates our reality but how we perceive and react to what happens or to what we imagine is happening or will happen.

This is the first basic premise of what we might call the "**Psychology of Happiness**" or the Psychology of Evolution or of Transformation. **We create our own reality by the way we interpret and react to the events and other stimuli mentioned above.** Many might think of situations in which this might seem false or difficult to perceive, however, deep examination of this concept will prove that it is true in all cases. **Our belief system creates our reality.**

## AUTOMATIC PROGRAMMING

If we want to be happy, we need to transcend our automatic, mechanical emotional reactions. We need to **understand** why we automatically react in certain ways, such as with fear or anger, and **how** we can begin to **free** ourselves from undesirable emotional responses. Otherwise we are not free. We are under the control of the programming of our childhood, our past, our lack of clarity, and our lack of awareness. We are "asleep" to our real personal nature, and the true nature of the reality surrounding us. This book is intended to serve as a "wake-up call".

We are in a state of evolution from our animal nature through our human nature to our divine nature. In reality, our essential being is beyond this temporary body and mind. We are aspects of Divine Creation, and thus we embody love, knowledge and power. Mistaken conditioning has caused us to lose contact with this inner nature.

## THE LION CUB

The story about the lion cub more graphically describes this process.

Once there was a great lioness who went hunting with her newborn cub. While chasing and attacking a flock of sheep, the lioness made a wrong move, fell off a cliff and died.

The cub was left without a mother and grew up in the midst of the sheep. As the years passed, the cub became a full-grown lion, but it was instinctually conditioned to behave as a sheep. It ate grass, made a bleating sound, and developed a fear of all other animals, just like the sheep.

One day, another lion attacked the flock, and in the chase, was shocked to see the ridiculous sight of a full grown lion running away with the sheep bleating "bah bah" in fear.

He caught up to the sheepish lion, and asked, "What are you doing? Why are you acting in this ridiculous way? You a great, powerful lion acting like a lowly powerless sheep? What has come over you? You should be ashamed of yourself."

The sheepish lion explained that he was a sheep, and that the flock had taught him to fear and bleat and run in horror from the powerful lions.

The adult lion took the sheepish lion down to the river and asked him to look at the reflection of his own face. He saw that he was like the lion and not like the sheep. The lion then woke up from his ignorance and discovered his previously ignored inner courage, strength and majesty.

We are like the sheepish lion. The sheep represent our human nature, our personality, which moans, fears, complains and worries. The Lion is the spiritual aspect of our being, which is a source of great power, wisdom, creativity, goodness and love.

Great spiritual teachers have appeared throughout history with the same message of our "LION NATURE", the untapped spiritual power and greatness that dwells within us.

## OUR MISTAKEN IDENTITY

All our problems are simply the result of our mistaken identity.

We have learned to suppress what is naturally good within us. We have learned to mistrust others and compete against them, rather than cooperate and share with them. We have learned to be neurotic and fearful of new persons and situations. We have lost the ability to be open and loving, as we were when we were children. We have been taught that we must fight for what we need even at the others' expense.

Such beliefs have been instilled into us, as a way of "being smart", or "being successful". Many of us who have followed this philosophy find ourselves isolated, secluded and lonely. We may have everything that society programmed our minds to believe was important, but do we have love, health, peace of mind, self-understanding, harmonious relationships or happiness?

One natural disaster, such as an accident, fire, earthquake, war, or death of a loved one, can destroy our happiness instantaneously when it is based on external factors.

## EFFORT WITHOUT ATTACHMENT

This in no way means we should not seek to create the reality we desire for ourselves, our loved ones and our community. It means we need to make our best effort towards a better life, but **without attachment** to the results of our endeavor.

This requires a delicate balance. Some of us make very little effort to improve our selves or our lives, and thus we obtain limited results. Others try extremely hard, but are so greatly attached to the result that they experience anxiety, fear and stress. **Attachment to some particular source of happiness is often our main obstacle toward the happiness we seek**. In this book, we shall learn to understand which attachments limit our happiness and how we can transform them into preferences.

Technique no. 1

# BREATHING OUT TENSION

### Why this technique is useful

**1.** Breathing is an extremely powerful and effective key to the nervous system, energy and mind.

**2.** By controlling the breathing process, we can release tension that might be accumulating in the muscles.

**3.** As we relax these muscles, our energy flows and the mind becomes more peaceful

### A simple technique for handling tension is to:

   **1.** Inhale slowly and deeply,
   **2.** Hold your breath for about 5 seconds and focus on the area where the tension is accumulating.
   **3.** As you exhale, feel that tension flow out with the exhalation.

### This technique can be performed:

   **1.** In the morning upon waking in order to vitalize the body for the day.

   **2.** In the evening in order to release stress, relax and rejuvenate the mind for evening activities.

   **3.** Any time you feel tense or tired in order to release stress, relax, and /or rejuvenate.

### Note:

This should not be done for more than 5 minutes at a time
without the assistance of an experienced guide.
Never hold the breath for more than 5 seconds.

*Life Story no. 2*

# ANXIETY ABOUT GRADES

John and Barbara have three children in junior and senior high school. Their house is the site of frequent battles concerning how much the children need to study and what grades are acceptable. The main battle is with their youngest child, Peter, who refuses to study. The more they pressure him, the more rebellious he becomes. He now perceives them to be his enemies, and a great power struggle takes place between them.

Peter lacks self-confidence and self-acceptance, and is tired of being compared to his older sisters. He would like to have good grades, but the fear of trying and not succeeding is unbearable for him, and thus, he prefers not to try at all.

He would much rather play at the computer or search the net than study subjects he feels have nothing to do with life. He prefers to partake in activities he can control and succeed at, rather than those which hold the risk of failure and create anxiety.

John and Barbara attach great deal of importance to grades, success, economic status, and most of all, to how they and their children compare to other families and what others think of them.

They find it difficult to decide how much responsibility they have for Peter's future, and whether it is their duty to pressure him. Still, what creates even more anxiety for them is the fact that they are programmed to believe his "failure" is their "failure." They measure their self worth as persons and parents by their children's grades and accomplishments.

They are ashamed to admit to others that Peter is not doing well. They feel lessened in other's eyes.

Peter realizes this and is hurt by the fact that they are allowing what other people think to be more important than how he feels. He feels misunderstood, rejected, and unloved. His parents feel the same.

He needs to be accepted and loved for the person he is, regardless of his grades. His parents do love him, but their fears concerning his future, their own self worth as parents, and what others think of them, prevent them from expressing their love without inhibitions.

Peter would like to make them happy, but his fear of failure and need to protect his freedom and self worth by rebelling against their pressure, become obstacles in his ability to do so.

They all need to analyze and free themselves from the beliefs and attachments preventing them from experiencing and expressing the love they have for each other.

### Belief Analysis

Their beliefs cause them to be caught up in this situation.

**John and Barbara might be limited by some of the following beliefs:**

**1.** Our child is our creation. We are totally responsible for what he becomes.

**2.** Our self worth depends on how he turns out: his grades, his health, his success, his behavior, etc.

**3.** Others will judge us according to our children's success or failure.

**4.** Our self worth is dependent upon what others think and say about us.

**5.** Our child will be able to succeed and be happy only of he obtains high grades and a university degree.

**6.** This is a difficult world and we must protect and prepare our child for it.

**7.** Later in life, our child might hold us accountable for the fact that we didn't push him enough.

**Peter might be limited by some of the following beliefs:**

**1.** I am not smart; I cannot succeed at school.

**2.** My self worth is dependent upon my grades.

**3.** My self worth is dependent upon how I measure up to my sisters and others.

**4.** My parents will love me more if I have high grades and less if I do not.

**5.** I will probably not be happy or successful in life if I don't get good grades.

**6.** I am a failure and no one loves me.

**7.** I am living in a prison and have no freedom to live my life I as I chose.

**8.** My parents want to control me in order to satisfy their own needs.

By adjusting their belief system, this family could solve many of their problems.

**John and Barbara might find peace in some of the following beliefs:**

**1.** Our child is God's creation and has within him the blueprints of his life. We are here to aid him in his search for himself.

**2.** Our child is like a seed that knows what it needs to become.  We are here simply to water the seed and nourish it, not to tell him how to live his life.

**3.** Our self worth depends solely on our motives and effort to help our child, not on the result.

**4.** We are worthy of love and respect regardless of our children's grades.

**5.** We are worthy of love and respect regardless of what others think or say.

**6.** Our child has the ability and inner guidance to create success and happiness regardless of his education.

**7.** Life gives us and our children exactly what each of us needs for his/her growth.

**8.** We offer love, guidance and support to our child, but allow him to make his own choices and grow through living the consequences of those choices.

**9.** We understand and respect our child's fears and seek to help him believe in himself.

**Peter might be helped by some of the following beliefs:**

**1.** I am intelligent and totally capable of succeeding in school and life.

**2.** I deserve love and respect regardless of my grade level.

**3.** I am special and unique from my sisters and all others.

**4.** I will create success and happiness in my life.

**5.** I am worthy of love and respect exactly as I am.

**6.** I understand my parents' anxiety and need to pressure me to study, and feel their love behind those actions.

**7.** I understand their fears and accept them as they are.

**8.** Real freedom is the freedom to intelligently direct my energy in ways that benefit my life and future.

**9.** My parents love me and are trying to help me in their own way.

# CHAPTER 2

# ATTACHMENTS
# ADDICTIONS
# PREFERENCES

**Happiness exists within us.** We cannot experience it, however, as long as we are searching for it outside of ourselves. When we are unable to manifest that to which we are attached or addicted, our minds experience pain, fear, jealousy, self-rejection and even anger.

## CAPTURING MONKEYS WITH BANANAS

The following true facts about how monkeys are captured in Africa, India and South America will allow us to understand the power of attachment.

A narrow-neck bottle is tied to a tree. A banana (or some peanuts) is placed in the bottle. The monkey sees the banana and very intelligently manages to squeeze its hand through the bottleneck and slip its fingers around the banana.

When it tries to pull its hand out in order to eat the banana, it won't come out because its hand, which is now holds the banana in the form of a fist, cannot pass through the narrow bottleneck. It pulls and pulls, but cannot get its hand out. It sees the trapper approaching him and tries to get away, but cannot, because its hand is wrapped around the banana and thus unable to get free from the bottle.

Although it is obviously going to suffer under the hands of trapper, and the bottle and the banana are the cause of its demise, it never crosses its mind to let go of the banana so it can extract its hand and be free.

The monkey literally becomes attached to the banana, and the banana, which was previously a potential source of happiness, has become a source of its suffering.

We are like those monkeys. We have a variety of "bananas" in our lives to which we are attached, and although they create much suffering for us, we cannot allow ourselves let go of them.

## TYPES OF ATTACHMENTS

The words addiction and attachment refer to any object, person, experience, role, quality or even idea that we believe we cannot be happy without. Unhappiness ensues when we do not have that particular thing we are attached to. We also experience unhappiness when, although we have what we want, we fear that we will lose it. For example, we might fear losing our love partner to someone else, or losing our health or money.

We might be addicted to:
receiving other people's attention,
being accepted,
being loved exclusively,
being cared for and protected by others,
possessing power over others,
being rejected,
pursuing professional success,
being the prettiest or the smartest,
being spiritual,
being right,
maintaining order and or cleanliness,
acquiring money and material possessions
being the victim
being in control
being right
being better than others
being strong
being weak
and many other possibilities.

We might be addicted to coffee, cigarettes, sweets, food, and sensual pleasures.
Some of us are addicted to affirming our "freedom" in peculiar ways, such as shunning any disciplines, being unfaithful to a lover, or ignoring others' needs.
None of these are wrong or bad. However, our attachment to them will create suffering whenever we cannot have what we desire.

## A CHOICE

When we are attached to something we have not yet been able to manifest, we have two choices.
**1.** We can **suffer** because we cannot get the banana out of the bottle, and thus get trapped in a vicious circle of suffering and unhappiness.
**2.** We can allow our attachment to become a **preference** for the "banana" (any

banana) which we will enjoy having but can live without.

We can get so caught up in trying to force a **specific** "banana" out of a specific bottle that we become blind to the fact that there are hundreds of "bananas" lying around for our taking, if only we could just muster up the intelligence to let go of that which we are trying to force life into giving us.

A good example of this is when we become attached to acceptance, approval or love from a specific person such as a parent, spouse or child. When we cannot get their affirmation, we feel hurt and angry. In our obsession for recognition from these specific persons, we lose sight of the fact that we have love, acceptance and approval from so many other persons. We are so focused on that which we cannot get that we are blind to what is offered so abundantly to us from other sources.

## AVERSIONS

An addiction can also be expressed in the negative as an **aversion** towards something. That is, we can have an addiction to something **not** happening, such as the loss of some object or relationship, or receiving disrespect from our child, or being caught in a traffic, or being kept waiting at the bank, at the doctor or the bus stop.

Addictions, aversions and attachments are the cause of our suffering. When we feel unhappy we can be sure that there is some attachment preventing us from feeling well. We believe we must have something we do not have, or get rid of something we do have. Simply put, **we cannot accept what life is offering us.**

As we often do not have the power to change the world or the people around us, we are inclined to become unhappy, depressed, angry, jealous, fearful, hateful, bitter, etc. It is important to remember that it is **not the life event** that causes our negative feelings, but rather **our addictive programming** which prevents us from accepting that which we cannot change.

## PREFERENCES

We do have a choice. We can change our attachments into preferences. We can prefer something to happen, but if it doesn't, we can accept that and be happy without it. This does not mean we should not try to change whatever we can in accordance with the way we prefer things to be, but while we do this, we must accept the ultimate result.

This is clearly a **practical** solution that needs to be employed once we have done everything within our power to improve our external circumstances. Thus the only lasting way to find inner peace and happiness is to change our internal programming.

Remembering the following prayer by St, Francis will help. **"Lord help me to change what I can, to accept what I cannot, and to know the difference between the two."**

## THE BIRD ON THE BRANCH

The following example might help us understand this balance.

A tired bird rested on a branch for support. It enjoyed the view as well as the safety it offered from dangerous predators. Just as it had become accustomed to that branch and the support and safety it offered, a strong wind started blowing, causing the branch to sway back and forth with such great intensity, that it seemed it was going to break. The bird, however, was not at all worried, for it knew two important truths:

The first was that even without the branch, it had its own power to fly and thus remain safe through the strength of its own two wings. The second was that there were many other branches upon which it could temporarily rest.

This small example represents our ideal relationship with our possessions, personal relationships, and social and professional positions. We have the right to enjoy all these things. We can enjoy their support and comfort, however, we need not fear when they seem to waver under us and appear to be disappearing.

All things in life are in a state of change and can disappear at any time. Our real strength lies not in those external ephemeral things, but rather in our two internal wings, LOVE and WISDOM. These will eventually become our security bases, our source of enjoyment and happiness.

We can enjoy this material world without being suppressed by it because of our fear and dependence upon it.

When we are dependent upon someone or something, we eventually become their slave and sacrifice our freedom.

## SECURITY ADDICTIONS

There are basically four categories of addictions, which are related to our four basic needs: security, pleasure, freedom and affirmation - power.

Our **security attachments** are relics from the thousands of years as primitive human beings. In those days, security in terms of food and shelter was not as easily fulfilled as it is today. Satisfying those needs occupied a great portion of our time, energy and thought. Instincts developed for the sake of survival of the individual and the species.

If we were to once again find ourselves living in jungles, we might find these instincts useful. Few readers of this book are likely to be in danger of starvation or lack of shelter. Rather the opposite is more likely to be true. Most of us are unhealthily over-fed and physically weak from too much shelter from the natural elements.

Yet, although these needs are satisfied beyond healthy limits, we continue to be preoccupied with them as addictions, accumulating more and more possessions, and eating far beyond our physical necessity. This creates weak and «dis-eased» bodies and minds.

## RELATIONSHIPS AS SECURITY

We live in **fear of losing** those things upon which we depend for our feeling of security. This is especially so in the case of relationships. Relationships with spouses, parents, children, siblings, friends and employers or employees can offer us emotional and sometimes financial security.

Many women, especially in the East, have been programmed to believe they cannot exist alone without their husbands or families, thus they live in constant fear of that possibility. When we are attached to someone or something, we become willing to suffer abuses and hardships because we are afraid of giving up whatever security we «think» we are receiving from them. We accept injustices through fear of losing our security base.

Separation from all and everything is not only **definite** (at least at death), but even more probable when we are attached because we tend to attract what we fear through our continually thinking about it in a negative way. We can attract exactly that which we fear by having it so constantly in mind. If, in our insecurity, we fearfully believe someone will steal our possessions, we send out clear and strong subconscious messages into our environment and consequently attract thieves.

We do not, however, create the others' reality through our fears. We do not cause loved ones to suffer or die because we fear that. Of course, by projecting such negative thoughts we do not help them either.

When we feel weak and insecure, we deny our true inner immortal nature. We make ourselves weak and feel helpless to change our unhappiness. This seriously inhibits development and keeps us lost in negative emotional states like frustration, depression, anger, bitterness, hate, envy, jealousy and fear. We might then over-eat, smoke, drink, or take tranquilizers or other drugs in order to escape from the anxiety created by our unfulfilled security addictions.

The truth is that total inner security can only be achieved by developing self-confidence and faith in our spiritual existence beyond the death or suffering of the personality and body. This will be discussed later. A first step towards reaching that stage is to discover our security addictions and transform them into preferences.

## PLEASURE ADDICTIONS

All that we have said concerning security addictions also applies to **pleasure addictions**. The focus or motive may be different, but the result is the same. Our sensation addictions cause us to attempt to control the situations and people around us so we may obtain the sensual pleasure we desire.

We are seldom successful in obtaining **all** the sensations we "need." We can rarely control circumstances so as to have all sensual stimuli, such as tastes, sexual experiences, or the specific visual or audio inputs, as frequently as we would like them. Even when we can, the pleasure we receive from having them is short lived.

There is a saturation point after which the stimulus ceases to create pleasure. We then feel aversion toward the stimulus until our desire surfaces all over again. This keeps us constantly dissatisfied and unhappy, wasting considerable amounts of thought, energy, action, money and time on superficial pursuits.

It also causes us to perceive people as **objects of pleasure** or **threats to our pleasure**. As in the case of security and power addictions, our love will be self-seeking and conditional. If those we "love" do not supply what we want, i.e. security, pleasure or obedience, we stop loving them and feel hurt and angry. Much of what we call "love" is actually addictive attachments motivated by needs for security, sensation or power. Very few of us, if any, love selflessly and uncondi-tionally without looking for something for ourselves in the relationship.

Sensation addictions are the cause of much unhappiness and conflict with our environment and others. We will be much happier when we transform these de-sires into preferences, when we prefer certain tastes, or experiences, or comforts. Then we are happy when we have them, but can accept not having them, if that is the situation life is offering at the moment. Then we will not become depressed or angry with those around us, when our pleasure needs are not fulfilled.

It is natural that we need to find a balance between satisfying sensual needs and being free from them. This is not a matter of good and evil, right and wrong, or purity and sin. It has to do with freedom from mechanisms that limit our freedom, love and happiness. If we try to deny ourselves the pleasure we seek, we may be-come dry and lifeless in many ways, pursuing balance in perhaps other even less healthy ways. If, on the other hand, we are slaves to our desires, we can easily lose our health and happiness.

## POWER AND AFFIRMATION ADDICTIONS

**Power** and **affirmation addictions** can also provoke emotions such as anger, fear, bitterness and conflict within ourselves and others. We seek in many subtle ways to manipulate others into behaving as we would like or as we need them in order to feel affirmed and powerful. We may do this with angry, aggressive words, with soft cajoling or by appearing weak, hurt, ill and helpless. The goal is to get things to be the way we want them to be, as opposed to the way the others would like them to be.

When functioning under the control of such attachments, everyone is seen sub-consciously as an entity to be controlled, or as a threat to our power. In such cas-es, true love is not possible. We can easily feel attached to a person who increas-es our feelings of power or self worth, but if that person decides to rebel, change, give affirmation to others, or prefer them to us, we might then suffer and lose our feelings of "love" for that person.

Money is often used as an instrument of control. Parents often control their chil-dren by bribing them or withholding money. They may also withhold love and acceptance from the children as a way to manipulate their behavior. This results in negative consequences for both the children and the parents.

It is simply impossible to love steadily while playing power games or being motivated by power addictions. It is also difficult to be happy, for there is no love or peace in such motivations. The result is argumentation, hurt feelings and alienation.

On the other hand, As Ken Keyes, the author of the **Handbook to Higher Consciousness**, appropriately points out, it is important to remember, "You create as much suffering in the world when you take offence as when you give offence."

In other words, we can play the power game from the other end by becoming the victim and wallowing in feelings of helplessness, bitterness and hate. This is an addiction to powerlessness, which becomes a good excuse for not taking responsibility for our own lives.

## FREEDOM ADDICTIONS

A number of us fear that our freedom is in danger. This is a natural result of the fact that we have in fact experienced a lack of freedom at times in our lives or witnessed others who have.

We have various ways of satisfying our freedom addictions. Some people feel "free" because they can smoke or eat or take drugs, others because they can have multiple sexual partners, others because they can buy whatever they like, others still because they refuse to do what others want or because they are rebelling towards the social norms.

We seldom ask ourselves whether, in fact, we are free to be happy in all situations. Whether we are happy not to eat excessively, not to smoke, and not to take tranquilizers. Whether we are free to be true to one love partner or free to cooperate with others when we would like to. Whether we are free to employ the disciplines which will create the health, vitality and peace of mind we are seeking.

Obviously, freedom to one part of our being might be slavery to another. We usually seek freedom from external obstacles rather than from internal ones, such as fears, attachments and addictions that limit our love, peace and happiness.

Consequently our happiness is basically obstructed by our attachments. These attachments are created by certain beliefs we need to change in order to transform our attachments into preferences.

Only then we will be able to seek and enjoy what we desire without losing our peace, love and happiness if we do not succeed.

**We also need to think seriously about the difference between attachment and love,** between being with someone because we need them or being with someone because we love them. This is the essential difference between relationships based on **co-dependency** or **co-commitment**. We will investigate this later on.

### Technique no. 2

# A HOT BATH and / or A MASSAGE

These two external aids can effectively help us
to relax and release negative energy.

When all else fails, we can resort to a relaxing salt bath
or treat ourselves to a massage.

## WE DESERVE IT.

### Note:
Sometimes we do not care for ourselves
with the idea that doing so would be "selfish."

Consider that the greatest gift we can
offer our loved ones is
a happy and well person.

If, in order to serve them,
we become easily irritable, negative
and perhaps and even angry,
our offering may actually be unpleasant.


We **do** have time to both **serve the world**
and **take care of ourselves.**

# *FEAR THAT HE IS HAVING AN AFFAIR*

Wendy is sure that her husband Mark is having an affair. She has no concrete proof but she just knows it in her heart. She is afraid, deeply hurt and disappointed. She feels rejected, demeaned, betrayed, and quite insecure, not to mention angry.

Mark is not actually having an affair yet, but **is** interested in another woman. Until now, they have had long conversations, but both are very hesitant to make that step of coming together physically. Mark wants to continue to see Marsha without Wendy. He does not even want her to know about this "contact." He wants to be with someone who "understands" him.

Wendy frequently complains to Mark about family problems and how she is the victim of this situation in which she is sacrificing her time and her professional satisfaction to be with the children.

She feels hurt that Mark does not appreciate her sacrifice and needs him to show her more love and affection.

Ever since the children were born, it has been difficult for Mark to see Wendy sexually, and she is not receiving the affirmation she needs from him as a woman. She feels used.

Also, her incessant nagging makes her even less inviting to him. Now he avoids her, physically and emotionally.

She perceives this as rejection, and now that she suspects he is seeing someone else, her need for affirmation is even greater. She has become increasingly critical, accusing and demanding.

The further she pressures him for attention and love, the more he feels the need to avoid her. The more he avoids her, the more rejected and betrayed she feels.

In her own way, she is pushing him away from her. By not giving her what she needs, he is augmenting her negativity, which then bounces back at him.

They are growing further apart and no longer enjoy each other's company.

### Belief Analysis

Both need to look at and transform their belief systems in order to create a more lively and truthful relationship. Each needs to take responsibility for his and her reality. They can help each other create happiness.

**Wendy may be limited by some of the following beliefs:**

**1.** My self worth is dependent upon being loved exclusively by my husband.

**2.** I am not enough for my husband.

**3.** I am the victim in this situation.

**4.** A wife should sacrifice her career for her husband.

**5.** I have lost something important in life by leaving my professional life. I am a victim of social programming.

**6.** My husband does not love me.

**7.** If my husband does not love me, I am not worthy

**8.** I am not safe in the world by myself and especially with the children.

**9.** I am in danger of being alone.

**10.** I need my husband in order to feel safe and worthy.

**Mark may be limited by some of the following beliefs:**

**1.** My wife doesn't understand or accept me.

**2.** When she complains, she is rejecting me and I am demeaned.

**3.** I cannot feel my self worth when she is rejecting me.

**4.** My freedom is in danger.

**5.** I might be happier with someone else.

**6.** I need someone who accepts me as I am and doesn't complain.

**7.** I cannot be happy when suppressed by this family situation.

**8.** I cannot feel sexual with my wife when she is trying to control me.

**9.** I cannot see my wife sexually when I think of her as the mother of my children.

Some beliefs which each could develop in order to free up their love and solve the problem:

**Wendy might benefit from some of the following beliefs:**

**1.** I am worthy of love and respect regardless of my husband's interests or behavior.

**2.** I am a vital and interesting woman, enough for any man.

**3.** I create my reality and life gives me exactly what I need to learn my next lesson in my growth process.

**4.** My husband and I have equal rights and responsibilities toward work and the family.

**5.** Whatever I do with love cannot be a loss. I have lost nothing by giving myself to my children. The highest profession on the planet is that of the mother: our future depends upon it.

**6.** My husband loves me, but is controlled by inner obstacles towards expressing that love.

**7.** I am worthy of love and respect regardless of my husband's feelings or behavior.

**8.** I am safe in the world as I am.

**9.** There are millions of beings with whom I can connect if I feel the need.

**10.** I am safe and worthy in my self.

### Mark might benefit from some of the following beliefs:

**1.** I want to understand and respond lovingly to my wife's insecurities at this time.

**2.** I recognize her complaints as an expression of her unfulfilled needs and seek to fulfill them as much as possible.

**3.** I am worthy of love and respect regardless of my wife's satisfaction or behavior.

**4.** I am a free soul.

**5.** Happiness exists within me and does not come from an outside source.

**6.** I accept and love myself as I am.

**7.** I love my family and gladly surrender my other needs for their welfare.

**8.** When I focus on my wife, I perceive the being I originally loved on all levels, even physically.

**9.** I love my wife. I want her to be happy and I behave accordingly.

## CHAPTER 3

# HOW TO ANALYZE EMOTIONS

In order to create happiness, inner peace and harmony we need to develop more positive ways responding to the various events and stimuli, which presently stimulate within us negative and unpleasant feelings. To do so, we need to investigate more deeply the mechanisms generating these emotions.

### THE BASIC PREMISE OF THIS SYSTEM

This whole process of self-analysis, self-knowledge, self-improvement and self-actualization is based on one basic concept: that **" our beliefs create our reality."**

Whatever happens in our lives is:
**1.** Received by our senses and
**2.** Then interpreted by our belief system.

Depending upon our beliefs, **we will interpret each event uniquely** from others who have different beliefs. Our belief system creates our emotions.

The following figure (taken from Ken Keyes' *Handbook to Higher Consciousness*) helps us comprehend how our programming affects our inner reality. The mind functions, in many ways, just as a computer does. It does with any input exactly what we program it to do. Our mind has been programmed throughout our childhood to perceive ourselves, others and the physical world in very specific ways that limit our joy, love and peace.

We can use the following diagram in order to analyze our feelings.
After observing and analyzing any experience, which concerns us, we can place its various aspects into these boxes above.

# SQUARES FOR ANALYSIS

| | |
|---|---|
| **The Stimulus:**<br>(What happened or is happening,<br>An event external or internal)<br><br><br><br><br><br><br><br>**No. 1** | **Programmings - Beliefs**<br>(What I believe about what is hap-<br>pening in box 1 which creates my<br>feelings written in box 3) |
| **Reaction:**<br>(How I react - behave- internally<br>and externally)<br><br><br><br><br><br>**No. 4** | |
| **Emotions:**<br>(How I feel when presented<br>with the sitmulus in Box 1.)<br><br><br><br>**No. 3** | **No. 2** |

## THE STIMULI

In **block 1** we enter the **external event,** i.e.:

1. Our spouse is paying attention to someone else.
2. We are given a gift that we really like.
3. Someone rejects us or our beliefs.
4. We are falsely accused.
5. We enjoy a wonderful evening with a loved one.
6. We achieve an important goal.
7. Our child does poorly at school.
8. Someone important to us does not agree with what we have done.
9. Someone intimidates us.
10. We have to speak to a large group of people.
11. We are informed that we have a serious illness.
12. We remember a painful event from the past.
13. We think about how secure we will be when we grow older and less capable.
14. We are confronted with something we fear.
15. We have not yet been able to have a baby.
16. We have been given a pregnancy we do not want at this time.
17. Our child is taking drugs.
18. A loved one is very ill.
19. Our partner is cheating on us.
20. We notice that we are feeling fear.
21. We win the lottery.

Others...............

## OUR BELIEFS

The stimulus is then perceived and evaluated by our **programming (block 2)** which interprets the act as either threatening or supportive to our security, self-affirmation, pleasure or freedom. Depending upon our beliefs concerning these stimuli and ourselves we create a wide variety of emotions. What is "small stuff" for some is "crisis material" for others. We subjectively create our reality by the way we are programmed to feel and react to these stimuli. (You can download a large list of possible beliefs from our web site www.HolisticHarmony.com)

## OUR EMOTIONS

This creates our **inner emotional experience (block 3).** We can create any variety of emotions and responses. As many of us are not particularly aware of our emotions, we include the following list of emotions that we might have in response to some event or thought.

**UNPLEASANT**
Fear
Discouragement
Rejection
Anxiety
Demeaned
Hurt - pain
Worry
Disillusionment
Insecurity
Victimized
Anger
Hate
Depression
Frustration
Loneliness
Bitterness
Jealousy

Envy
Unworthiness
Rage
Guilt
Self rejection
Self doubt
Shame
Injustice
Disappointment

**PLEASANT**
Love
Happiness
Compassion
Understanding
Affection
Brotherhood
Unity

Security
Peace
Courage
Encouragement
Joy
Patience
Gratitude
Acceptance
Respect
Fulfillment
Faith
Hope
Peace
Affirmation
Respect
Satisfaction
Pride
Esteem

## OUR REACTIONS

Our emotions cause our **reactions** to that stimulus (event or thought) **(block 4)**. Reactions can be internal, external, physical, emotional, mental and spiritual. We might subconsciously tighten muscles in our abdomen, chest, legs, arms, arteries, throat or head. Various reactions will take place in our nervous and endocrine systems as they prepare for "fight or flight" responses. If the emotions are positive, all of the above will be reversed.

We might cry or laugh. We might become defensive, antagonistic, critical, interrogative or intimidating. We might become aloof and alienated. We may or may not express what we are feeling to others. We might put on an emotional mask that prevents others from seeing how we feel. We might fall into depression.

In the case of positive emotions, we may become joyful, exuberant, more loving and open. We might also simply relax.

## THE REACTION TO OUR REACTION

Our reaction now becomes a new stimulus to our environment. This is true whether we express our real feelings of not. Others perceive even the emotions that we hide either consciously or unconsciously. Our "reaction" now becomes their "stimulus", and they now react according to their beliefs, programming and resulting emotions.

Their reaction then becomes a new stimulus for us, which passes into our programming and returns again back to them.

## PROGRAMMED INTERACTING ROBOTS

Essentially what we have here are programmed robots interacting in mechanical ways, none of them capable of controlling in any way how he or she feels or reacts. Our subconscious belief systems are interacting.

We are generally not free to select how we will react to people who "press our buttons". When we have "sensitivities" towards certain types of stimuli or behaviors, we are at the mercy of those sensitivities and lack the clarity and strength to feel and react differently.

We all experience certain behaviors on the part of others as threatening to our security, self worth, power, freedom or pleasure. Some of those might be found in the following list.

**We might feel fear, hurt or anger** at someone when that person:

**1.** Does not agree with us.

**2.** Does not understand us.

**3.** Obstructs us from satisfying our needs. (Remember: a need could be psychological, such as the need for acceptance, respect or self-esteem.)

**4.** Does not respect us.

**5.** Thinks that he or she is superior.

**6.** Tries to control or suppress us.

**7.** Criticizes us.

**8.** Tells lies or gossips about us.

**9.** Harms us or someone close to us.

**10.** Has evil intentions or ulterior motives.

**11.** Is negative, complaining, whining, critical, etc.

**12.** Thinks he or she knows it all.

**13.** Gives us advice we have not asked for.

**14.** Plays the role of the victim, the "poor me", and demands attention.

**15.** Does not take care of him or her self or does not pull his or her weight.

**16.** Makes mistakes

**17.** Does not keep his or her promises or appointments.

**18.** Is weak and dependent

**19.** Acts in an egotistical and selfish way, disregarding others' needs.

**20.** Uses us or others.

**21.** Is cold and insensitive

**22.** Is not responsible to his or her word, or commitments.

**23.** Is lazy

**24.** Ignores our needs

**25.** Rejects us.

Other reasons_____

When we react to such stimuli in mechanically programmed ways, we often create the exact circumstance we are trying to avoid. A classic example is the case in which we are afraid that our loved one might be interested in someone else. In such a case, we would logically become more demanding, suppressive, interrogative, and jealous. This will obviously push our loved one away, possibly into the arms of another.

We try to force the other to act in such a way so that we may feel secure, rather than analyze why we feel so insecure, and make an effort to free ourselves from that programming.

Another common case is when we take responsibility for our children's performance in school. The more we pressure them, the less they develop inner discipline and the more they rebel. Eventually, we may even push them into reacting in ways that bring about the opposite of the result we are seeking.

## CHILDHOOD CONCLUSIONS

We are each conditioned to misperceive various situations because of our childhood subconscious programming. Thus we must place another square in our diagram to the right of box number 2. This represents childhood experiences that have caused us to form certain "conclusions" about our security, self worth, freedom and other important factors. These conclusions then become our belief system, which controls our emotional life and subsequently our experiential reality.

The problem here is that we as children often make incorrect assumptions. As children, we feel responsible for how everyone feels and have very little sense of our power and our self worth.

A child can feel responsible for:

**1.** The parents' anger.

**2.** The parents' pain, suffering, illness or even death.

**3.** The parents' separation or divorce.

**4.** What happens to siblings and friends.

We, as children, tend to develop the following false conclusions:

**1.** We are weak and vulnerable, and need others to protect us.

**2.** We are not okay, not worthy of love, affection or respect.

**3.** Others know better than we do and we need to listen to them rather than ourselves.

**4.** We must be like others in order to be accepted by them.

**5.** We must do what others ask of us in order to be accepted and loved by them and not be punished.

**6.** We are sinners, unloved by God.

**7.** Others are responsible for our reality and how we feel.

**8.** We are responsible for the others' reality and how they feel.

**9.** Life is difficult and dangerous.

**10.** We should not have faith in anyone or place our trust in him or her.

**11.** Our freedom is in danger from those who want to control us.

**12.** We do not have the right or the ability to satisfy our needs.

**13.** God's love is conditional and we will be punished if we are not "good."

**14.** Our self worth is dependent upon how we compare to others in terms of appearance, wealth, strength, knowledge, "goodness," and professional success.

**15.** Our self worth is dependent upon acquiring the acknowledgement, acceptance and respect of others.

Although we now consciously realize that these beliefs are false, they thrive in our subconscious, or in what we call our "inner child," and they subsequently control our emotional reality and reactions.

## METHODS OF SELF TRANSFORMATION

The purpose of the work we will be doing here is to recognize and free ourselves from these false perceptions of ourselves, others and the nature of the universe in which we live. This can be achieved in various ways, including:

**1.** Self **observation**
**2.** Self **analysis**
**3. Positive thinking** and positive thought projection.
**4.** Childhood regressions with the purpose of **releasing** through cathartic techniques hidden pain, guilt and anger.
**5.** Childhood regression with the purpose of reprogramming or **transforming** the assumptions made in the past.
**6. Logical** and **spiritual concepts** designed to free us from negative self-limiting beliefs and mechanisms.

These and many other techniques and concepts will be simply described in this book.

Many other techniques will also aid in the process, such as creating a healthy and vital body and mind through natural eating, exercising, breathing techniques, relaxation and meditation techniques, as well as expanding one's faith, love and religious life.*

Here, however, we will deal mainly with the psychological approach.

### Note:

Most people will benefit from professional guidance in this work. Those who have a history of clinical therapy with drugs should consult their doctor or professional counselor before digging deeply into the subconscious.

Working with a group is almost always more beneficial, supporting and productive.

* The author offers books on these subjects also.

These can be viewed on our web site.

Technique no. 3

# DANCING OUR EMOTIONS

## Why this is useful

Creative self-expression helps to channel emotional energies in creative and useful ways.

All forms of creative expression are healing and very effective in helping us regain harmony with ourselves.

Dancing, drawing, painting, singing, chanting, acting, writing, cooking, flower arranging and even cleaning or gardening, or any other type of creative expression, will allow our energies to flow, breaking up the emotional energy blockages.

We are simultaneously put in touch with our creative center, which is directly associated with higher levels of our being.

Creative activity also enables us to focus on the present, thus helping us to let go of the past and present, which are the sources of our problem.

The result is a general sense of well being and fulfillment. We then love more easily.

## A simple technique for releasing tension:

Of all these forms of expression, dancing is perhaps the most immediate and powerful in its effect, as it requires no materials or special place, involves all the body, and powerfully releases the emotional energy blockages as we move to the rhythm.

If we are experiencing negative emotions, we can dance to music which allows us to connect with the emotion we are feeling, explore it and express it. Or we can put on music that stimulates in us the opposite positive feelings and connects us with those positive energies through moving to this music.

## Note:

We will benefit greatly physically, emotionally and spiritually by setting aside a certain amount of time for daily or at least weekly creative expression.

*Life Story no. 4*

# ALCOHOLIC FATHER
# AND HUSBAND

Mary's father was an abusive alcoholic. Her husband Tony is following in his footsteps. As is quite common, Mary has selected a husband who is simply a continuation of her father. When Tony is not drunk, he is self-demeaning and quiet. He prefers to be at home and avoids contact with others. When he is drunk, he becomes aggressive, violent and threatening. He is verbally abusive toward her and the children, and has on a few occasions, become physically violent.

Tony does not love himself, so he naturally feels that Mary and the children do not love him either. His parents were abusive to him and he is unconsciously carrying on the tradition. He does love his wife and children, and feels tremendous remorse for his behavior, although he denies it to others. It is too painful for him to see himself. He is self-destructive and in denial.

Mary feels hurt, disappointed, abused, humiliated and angry. She is also very much into the roles of the "savior" and the "victim". She is a "savior" because she knew Tony had this behavioral problem and thought she could save him. She is a "victim" because she feels unjustly abused by him and life. She also wonders at times if God is punishing her for something she has done.

Mary has not been able to communicate with Tony. When he is sober, he denies the problem, although, occasionally, he will ask forgiveness. When he is intoxicated, he is blind and deaf with anger.

Mary feels responsible for healing Tony and feels that she has failed. Both of them and also the children are suffering in this situation.

What might Mary's lessons be in this situation?

## POSSIBLE LESSONS:

**1.** To realize she deserves respect and love.

**2.** To free herself from childhood experiences in which she was conditioned in some way to believe she is not worthy of love, and affection, happiness or freedom.

**3.** To learn to love and accept Tony despite his weakness and negativity.

**4.** To see that he is suffering and to seek to help him without losing her self-respect, and without indulging him, thus, allowing him to be responsible for his own therapy.

**5.** To free herself from the idea that she is responsible for creating his reality or finding his cure.

**6.** To allow him to maintain total responsibility for both his unhappiness and his therapy.

**7.** To realize she has the right to be happy even if he is not.

**8.** Not to take what he does personally, to realize that her self worth is not diminished by his actions, and to understand that the problem is his.

**9.** To search for what she may not be giving him, which he may need, such as love, acceptance and affection.

**10.** To relieve herself of the role of the parent or savior.

**11.** To learn to express her needs and rights clearly, lovingly and assertively.

**12.** To overcome any shame she feels toward others because of his problem. To free herself from worrying about how others perceive her and her family.

**13.** To behave assertively (not threateningly) so as to inspire respect from him and others.

**14.** To work on her relationship with her father so as to forgive him and find her own self-respect and inner strength.

## The following beliefs night help them out of this situation

### Maria may be helped by some of the following beliefs:

**1.** I love and accept others and help them while allowing them to retain total responsibility for their reality.

**2.** I help others more with my happiness, than with my pain.

**3.** I am worthy of love, affection and respect exactly as I am.

**4.** Life gives me exactly what I need every moment for my evolutionary process.

**5.** I assertively and lovingly protect my rights and needs.

**6.** I am worthy of love and respect regardless of others' behavior.

### Tony may be helped by some of the following beliefs:

**1.** I am a creation of the Divine.

**2.** I deserve love and respect exactly as I am.

**3.** I accept and love myself as I am.

**4.** I deserve and create a happy and harmonious reality.

**5.** I love my family, want them to be happy and will behave accordingly.

**6.** I am an expression of divine energy on earth. I am good and lovable being.

**7.** I recognize and admit my problems as I simultaneously seek to solve them.

Of course, Tony will probably also need to participate in a detoxification and group support program such as Alcoholics Anonymous.

# CHAPTER 4

# THE PSYCHOLOGY
# OF EVOLUTION

The word "psyche" comes from the Greek word for "soul." Psychology, then, should mean the study of the **soul**. As a science, however, it has given much more attention to the mind, which is merely an instrument for the soul, rather than to the soul itself.

When psychology began as a science not so long ago, the most well known name for some years was Sigmund Freud. Freud postulated the theory that man is motivated by various basic drives and needs, mostly sexual, which cause him to behave in the manner in which he does.

Psychologists now understand that man has other needs, which also motivate him and influence his behavior. The newer theories of psychology do not contradict or negate previous theories, but rather include them, while at the same time reaching out to a greater and more encompassing truth.

This trend of thinking, called **Humanistic Psychology,** takes into account healthy people and deals not only with illness, but with our individual and collective need **for self actualization**, or for **manifesting greater portions of our inner potential.**

## THE EVOLUTION OF DESIRE

Why do we do what we do? Our basic needs motivate us to think, speak or act in the way we do? These needs become desires, which then evolve into motives, which finally express themselves in the form of thoughts, words and actions seeking to satisfy those needs and desires.

These needs have been arranged into a **hierarchy of needs** by Abraham Maslow, a renowned professor of psychology at Harvard University. The pyramid below clearly depicts this evolution of desires.

**1.** At the bottom of the pyramid we find our most basic needs which we share with all other life forms. Unless we are able to satisfy these needs for food, air, water, clothing, warmth, sex and whatever else we may need in order to preserve our life in the body, we will not feel free to pursue other more evolved urges.

**2.** Once we have satisfied these basic physiological needs, we then become concerned about **shelter** and **safety**. It is no longer enough to simply have a full stomach, air to breath, liquid to drink, and a comfortable temperature. We now want to create safety for the future. We create homes seeking to establish "safe" environments that we can control.

**3.** After fulfilling these two basic needs, we feel the urge to **belong** to some type of group. Marriage and family fulfill this need, as do all types of groupings, such as religions, organizations, cults, teams, sports groups, clubs, associations, societies, cities, countries and groups of countries. Each of us seeks various groupings through which to satisfy this need to belong with others in some way.

**4.** We then feel a need for **self-esteem**. We are no longer satisfied with simply belonging. Now we want to be known and respected by others. Our needs for self-esteem and self-confidence cause us to develop talents and abilities, and expand our physical and mental powers. This evolution of needs stimulates a corresponding evolution in our abilities and powers.

Each need serves to stimulate growth at each particular stage of evolution. Thus, we have evolved through the following stages.

**1.** Wandering food seekers,

**2.** Settlers and home builders,

**3.** Creators of families, societies, cities, and nations,

**4.** Creators of arts, sciences, technology, religion and philosophy.

This same evolutionary process occurs within each individual today as he or she matures from a helpless little child into a capable **self-esteemed** member of society.

**Diagram: HIERARCHY OF NEEDS**

## NEEDS AND DESIRES

Let us distinguish a "need" from a "desire". Others may define these words in other ways, but for the purpose of this discussion, let us define a **need** as something that in reality is **necessary** for the maintenance of the body-mind balance and the spiritual evolution of the individual. A **desire** is a **sense of lacking** based on a previously existent need or the anticipation of a future need.

For example, the **need** to have enough food for the survival of the physical body can develop into a **desire** for more food than is necessary for that purpose. A habit is then created and we seek the food for other subconscious reasons, such as anxiety, boredom or sensual pleasure. Thus the need has become a desire.

The desire itself is **not** inherently negative. Whether or not a desire is useful, neutral or destructive is relative and personal. For example, an undernourished body will perish if not motivated by the need to search for food. Another individual may have found a **healthy balance** between his body's needs and his eating habits. Still another may be overcome with an abnormal desire for food, seeking security, meaning, pleasure, or relaxation through it to such a degree, that eating may become harmful to both the body and the mind.

Such a desire may monopolize such a high percent of an individual's thoughts, words and actions that it generates guilt, a poor self-image and frustration as well as ill health. Ultimately, he or she lives to eat, rather than eats to live.

The same example may be applied to any other need-desire, i.e. sex, a particular relationship, family situations, professional success, acceptance, esteem, etc. Each need has its function in propelling us forward in our evolutionary development, but when it stagnates into an endlessly reoccurring desire that knows no satisfaction, it becomes destructive.

These desires can become obsessions when we believe that there is a danger of them not being fulfilled. Such negative programming that cause us to believe we will not be able to satisfy our needs is formed from our experiences starting in our mother's womb until about the age of 8 years old. Experiences we have after this age will affect us, but our basic subconscious programming and original life view is fairly well formed by the age of 8 years.

## SOCIAL PROGRAMMING

Unfortunately, because of the lack of awareness on the part of our well-meaning parents and teachers (and society as a whole), most of us have been conditioned in such a way as to lack **self-love, self-acceptance, self-confidence** and **inner security**.

We have been programmed to believe that we do not deserve to be loved, and that we are weak and incapable. We have learned that the world and people are not to be trusted, and that we must be sly, hard and very cautious in order to protect ourselves and "get ahead" in the world. We have been conditioned to believe we will find happiness and contentment in money, a spouse and children, a highly respected profession and plenty of material possessions. We have learned that we should not express what we truly feel for fear of being hurt.

Instead of being motivated by **actual natural needs**, we are controlled by a false perception of reality based on this programming, which was recorded into our subconscious during those very impressionable and vulnerable years. We are motivated by a desire-based belief system which was founded on false perceptions of ourselves, others and reality itself.

Our goal now is to objectively analyze and understand this programming and reprogram ourselves with a more objective perception of ourselves and our reality so we may develop into the full happy, secure, content beings we have the potential to be.

## SELF-ACTUALIZATION

Eventually we will feel the need for growth and freedom from the limitations of these old programs and will become motivated by the highest need of Maslow's pyramid, the need for **self-actualization.** We have fulfilled, to a certain extent, our lower needs but still remain unsatisfied. We have everything we "should" have in order to be happy according to society's programming, but we still feel "empty". We have an abundance of food, air, shelter, safety, a sense of belonging and the respect of those around us, but we still crave something more. We become aware that we have **untapped resources latent within us** and begin to work toward their manifestation.

Our need for **growth** overcomes our need for **safety or to belong.** Or perhaps we realize that we are safe, and that we do not need to spend so much time, thought, energy and money on satisfying these illusory desires, which are the result of early childhood programming. We begin to spend more time, energy and thought on overcoming our fears and weaknesses, and manifesting our inner beauty.

On the other hand, if we do not first feel secure, we are unable to grow. These states will alternate cyclically in our lives. There will be times of growth, followed by times in which we establish security at the new level. Then, often a state of confusion or conflict will emerge in order to create the necessary flexibility for further growth. Over and over again, these three states flow through our being.

**1.** First we are **restless and confused, or in conflict**.
**2.** Then we make an **effort toward growth or change**.
**3.** Finally, we experience the **satisfaction of success** in that effort.

In order to achieve inner peace, we must accept all three states (restlessness, effort, satisfaction) as **equally necessary** in our evolutionary progress.

When we feel insecure because of various life changes, we might revert to the more basic needs, focusing on food, sex, emotional interaction, smoking, drinking, etc. We all have our own ways of recapturing that secure feeling through such familiar activities.

Freud pointed out that the mouth is a security center for many people. The first form of security is the mother's breast from which we suck our first life-sustaining food, without which we would die. Later, the mouth is used for eating, smoking cigarettes, drinking and talking; all of which can be forms of security seeking.

**When our basic safety needs (including a sense of belonging and self-esteem) are fulfilled**, there awakens within us our first **"meta-need"** or the **"the need to go beyond."** According to Maslow, the "meta-need" is the need for self-actualization. We begin to feel the need to know ourselves more deeply, and eventually to transcend ourselves.

This is often a very difficult and crucial milestone. At this point, many of the previous activities and interactions, which used to fulfill us and give us pleasure now, seem meaningless. We may feel depressed and confused. Much of that upon which we had based our life may now seem trivial and unimportant.

Eventually, we place one foot in a new world of seeking self-actualization to test it out. With one foot standing in our newly found way and the other holding onto old concepts and habits for security, we often experience conflict with ourselves, our environment, and especially with families and close friends.

It does not have to happen this way, but it often does. Eventually, the transition is made and we find a new security based on our own inner Self.

## OUR INNER NATURE

Let us examine what Abraham Maslow has to say about man's **inner nature**. If we replace the phrase "inner nature" with "soul" it will be much like reading a description of the soul, or higher self, as it is described in various philosophical and religious texts.

Here is a concise explanation of his "psychology of health" as expressed in his book *Toward a Psychology of Being*.

*"There is now emerging over the horizon a new conception of human sickness and of human health, a psychology that I find so thrilling and so full of wonderful possibilities that I yield to the temptation to present it publicly even before it is checked and confirmed, and before it can be called reliable scientific knowledge".*

(Various philosophical and spiritual systems have confirmed these same concepts for thousands of years).

*"The basic assumptions of this point of view are:*

*"1. We have, each of us, an essential biologically based inner nature, which is to some degree 'natural' intrinsic, and in a certain limited sense, unchangeable, or at least, unchanging".*

*"2. Each person's inner nature is in part unique to himself and in part species wide".*

(This is similar to the understanding that in one sense the soul is individual, and in another, it is one with the Collective Soul or "Oversoul", which is the unification of all souls).

*"3. It is possible to study this inner nature scientifically and to discover what it is like - (not invent - discover)."*

(This is the purpose of the various systems of self-discovery such as meditation and self-reflection).
"

*4. This inner nature, as much as we know so far, seems not to be intrinsically or primarily or necessarily evil. The basic needs (for life, for safety and security, for belonging and affection, for respect and self-respect, and for self-actualization), the basic human emotions and the basic human capacities are on their face, either neutral, pre-moral or positively good! Destructiveness, sadism, cruelty, malice etc. seem so far to be not intrinsic but rather they seem to be violent reactions against frustration of our intrinsic needs, emotions, and capacities. Anger is in itself not evil, nor is fear, laziness or even ignorance. Of course these can and do lead to evil behavior, but they needn't. This result is not intrinsically necessary. Human nature is not nearly as bad as it has been thought to be. In fact, it can be said that the possibilities of human nature have customarily been sold short".*

(This is a direct comment on the way Freudian psychology, as well as the concept "original sin," have planted in so many of us a lack of trust in our inner nature. We have been conditioned to believe that we are intrinsically bad and helpless, that we must be controlled and guided by external forces rather than listen to our inner voice. It is when we ignore this inner voice that we lose our way.)

*"5. Since this inner nature is good or neutral rather than bad, it is best to bring it out and encourage it rather than to suppress it. If it is permitted to guide our life, we grow healthy, fruitful and happy".*

*"6. If this essential core of a person is denied or suppressed, he gets sick sometimes in obvious ways, sometimes in subtle ways, sometimes immediately, sometimes later.*

*"7. This inner nature is not strong and overpowering and unmistakable like the*

*instincts of animals. It is weak and delicate and subtle and easily overcome by habit, cultural pressure, and wrong attitudes toward it".*

(This has happened in most of us. Because of habit, cultural pressure, and primarily, a lack of belief in our inner nature, very few of us find the inner peace and harmony we could have if we were guided from within.)

*"8. Even though weak, it rarely disappears in the normal person - perhaps not even in the sick person. Even though denied, it persists underground forever pressing for actualization".*

*"9. Somehow, these conclusions must all be articulated with the necessity of discipline, deprivation, frustration, pain and tragedy. To the extent that these experiences reveal and foster and fulfill our inner nature, to that extent they are desirable experiences. It is increasingly clear that these experiences have something to do with a sense of achievement and ego strength and therefore with the sense of healthy self-esteem and self-confidence. The person, who hasn't conquered, withstood, and overcome, continues to feel doubtful that he could. This is true not only for external dangers; it holds also for the ability to control and to delay one's own impulses, and therefore to be unafraid of them".*

Maslow made studies of people who were **more inner-directed** and had mastered themselves more than the average individual. These were people who had either fulfilled or had given up worrying about their basic needs and paid more attention to their need for self-actualization.

His psychological testing uncovered the following characteristics in these people:

*"1. Superior perception of reality (less distortion through fears and complexes).*
*2. Increased acceptance of self, of others and of nature.*
*3. Increased spontaneity.*
*4. Increased problem-centering (ability to go the center of a problem).*
*5. Increased detachment and desire for privacy.*
*6. Increased autonomy and resistance to enculturation.*
*7. Greater freshness of appreciation and richness of emotional creation.*
*8. Higher frequency of peak experiences".*

In peak experiences (that are actually beyond description) the ego is transcended, the sense of individuality is lost, and there is a feeling of oneness with the environment, whether it is with nature, with people or with God. It is a blissful experience that changes the person's life.

Peak experiences may come on the verge of death, or when a person thinks he or she is going to die. These experiences may also occur in nature, meditation, during an extreme emotional experience, during sexual orgasm, while creating intensively and in crisis conditions. They transcend the rational mind.

*"9. Increased identification with the human species". Consequently, less identification with the personality.*
*"10. Changed (the clinician would say, improved) interpersonal relations.*
*11. More democratic character structure.*
*12. Greatly increased creativeness.*
*13. Changes in the value system".*

Each of us possesses the capacity to further our self-actualization. Our lives will then be enriched in the above-mentioned ways and in many other ways that will allow us to experience greater peace, love, contentment and health in our lives.

## SEEKING SELF ACTUALIZATION

Let us now turn our attention to how we can begin our own evolutionary journey toward self-actualization and manifest the latent qualities and powers within us.

The **Eastern approach** is dedicated to creating harmony in body-mind-soul complex, and to eventually draw down super-mental spiritual energies into the personality. The personality becomes more relaxed, loving, selfless and creative. This is achieved through practices such as dietary discipline, bodily exercises, breathing techniques, relaxation, meditation, prayer, chanting, and self-study, as well as by other means. These practices develop clarity of mind, a positive attitude toward life, health and vitality, and the will power required to make the necessary changes in the personality structure.

In this book, however, we shall concentrate more on **the Western approach** of analysis and the eventual reprogramming of the personality structure. Whereas the Eastern approach focuses on relaxing the body and mind, thus opening up to the influx of higher energies which will transform it, the western approach focuses on mentally observing and reprogramming the personality complex and its conditioning and thus its resistance toward these same higher energies.

My personal experience is that the best results are achieved when the two approaches are **combined**. The first brings greater awareness, clarity, peace and willpower, while the second enables us to manifest those qualities in our practical everyday interactions. A combination of disciplined spiritual practices and self-analysis can bring about joyous changes in anyone's life. Here we shall look more deeply into the self-analysis and reprogramming approach.

Technique no. 4

# REGULAR EXERCISE

### Why this is useful

When we regularly exercise the body, in combination with deep rhythmic breathing, the energies of the body are freed from their blockages and are then kept in a harmonious flow.
A sense of greater well being and increased awareness and energy is created.
In this state, we are less likely to react negatively.
It is a fact that much negativity and depression is simply due to a lack of energy and a lack of proper flow of energy in the body.

When we feel run down, or imbalanced, we are obviously more susceptible to negative energies (people and events), and can be more easily upset.
When we have plenty of energy and feel well, we allow many stimuli which otherwise would bother us to pass by.

### A simple technique for releasing tension is to:

We can create a daily exercise program. There are an abundance of systems and groups that can guide us in this matter.

There are also a plentitude of videocassettes available to get us started.
A very simple and yet extremely effective and effortless exercise which rejuvenates the nervous system, and thus, the mind is the "half shoulder stand".
We lie on our back close to the wall with our legs raised resting on the wall.
We breathe slowly and deeply so that the blood will gather oxygen and flow into the brain, hypothalamus and pituitary glands. This can be done for 5 to 20 minutes.

This is a "savior" exercise whenever we are tired or upset. If you have high blood pressure or eye problems check with your doctor.

### Note:

A healthy body is the first step to a healthy mind.

*Life Story No. 5*

# MOTHER-IN-LAW

Phillip's mother-in-law Olga has moved in. She tends to intrude into their lives, telling them what they are doing wrong and criticizing their behavior; especially concerning how they bring up their children. She is an endless source of unasked-for advice. She also plays the victim and is very successful at making both Philip and his wife Kiki feel guilty that they are not making her happy. She is never satisfied and almost always finds reasons why she is being treated unjustly.

Phillip would like to make her happy, but she simply doesn't seem to want to. Fortunately both he and his wife agree that there is a problem. But neither knows what to do. The children are starting to rebel and have come into conflict with her a number of times lately.

If in fact life gives us exactly what we need, what might he and his wife and children be able to learn from this situation?

**Possible Lessons:**

**1.** To love and accept Olga as she is and forgive her for her weaknesses and negativity.

**2.** To express to her their needs and feelings more **clearly**, more **lovingly** and more **assertively**.

**3.** To free themselves from feeling guilty when they are not able to satisfy her needs or agree with her opinions.

**4.** To be able to say "no" without feeling guilty or believing that there will necessarily be a conflict, or that the she will stop loving them.

**5.** To cultivate the idea that the she can hear the truth and discuss any situation maturely like an adult.

**6.** To free themselves from childhood experiences in which they were programmed to believe that:

    a. Others would not respect their needs, or

    b. Would criticize them, or

    c. Would not be able to communicate peacefully.

**7.** To cultivate more positive feelings towards her.

**8.** To look for her positive qualities and see her as a test of their ability to love unconditionally.

**9.** To workout some types of practical agreements in which all feel that some of their needs are being fulfilled.

### Some beliefs that will help them cope with the situation:

### Phillip, Kiki and children may benefit from some of the following beliefs:

**1.** Each and every person is an expression of God sent to me to learn from and to love unconditionally.

**2.** Love requires honest communication.

**3.** I express my needs and feelings assertively, clearly and lovingly and deserve to be loved and respected when I do.

**4.** I am lovable and acceptable even when I cannot fulfill others' expectations.

**5.** Each is responsible for his or her own reality.

**6.** I am not responsible for her reality.

**7.** She is not responsible for my reality.

**8.** I love and help her as much as I can without getting caught up in how she responds.

**9.** I love her and understand her needs for attention and affirmation and give them to her in positive ways.

**10.** When she is negative, I perceive her need and fear and respond to them, and not to her negativity.

**11.** I am safe and worthy of love and respect regardless of her behavior.

### Olga may benefit from some of the following beliefs:

**1.** I deserve love and respect exactly as I am.

**2.** I feel safe and secure within my self.

**3.** I love and respect others and encourage them to follow their inner voice.

**4.** Just as I do not like to be criticized, I do not criticize others.

**5.** I feel my family's love even when they are not paying attention to me.

**6.** I fill my life with my own interests rather than with others' responsibilities.

**7.** I, and no one else, am totally responsible for my reality.

**8.** I allow others to maintain responsibility for their reality and their choices.

# Chapter 5

# THE SEVEN CENTERS
# OF CONSCIOUSNESS

**Note:** The concepts set forth in this chapter are ancient and agreed upon by many systems of philosophical and evolutionary thought, but this particular presentation has also been inspired by Ken Keyes, author of the *Handbook to Higher Consciousness*.

THE **COSMIC CONSCIOUSNESS** CENTER

THE **CONSCIOUS - AWARENESS** CENTER

THE **CORNUCOPIA** CENTER

THE **LOVE** CENTER

THE **AFFIRMATION - POWER** CENTER

THE **PLEASURE** CENTER

THE **SECURITY** CENTER

*THE SEVEN CENTERS OF CONSCIOUSNESS*

The life energy that flows through and sustains all beings is referred to by various schools of thought as bio-energy, cosmic energy, life energy, prana, chi, ki, orgone energy, etc. This energy is dispersed throughout the whole body, but is focused in the spinal column in various centers of energy according to the level of awareness and motives of the individual.

There are seven possible centers in which energy can enter, accumulate and function. Each energy center functions with a different set of needs, desires, motives and activities based the basic beliefs and thought-forms of that level of awareness.

Most of us experience predominately the lower three levels of consciousness, occupying ourselves with satisfying our basic needs for **security, pleasure, affirmation** or **power**.

As we evolve, we will begin to experience the "higher" more refined states of consciousness associated with the upper four centers. We can consciously facilitate this process of evolution leading to the higher centers, which will subsequently provide a more pleasant and fulfilling experience.

Let us briefly examine the seven centers.

## CENTER 1:
## THE SECURITY CENTER

We all require the basic elemental securities such as sufficient food, shelter, and safety from danger. As mentioned, it is unlikely that we face the danger of not being able to fulfill these needs. Yet, it is equally **unlikely** that we have relaxed our concern about our present, and especially our future security. We tend to continue accumulating money, objects and food **far beyond our natural needs**, often at the expense of health and harmonious relationships.

Security addictions dominate our emotional life. When functioning from this level, we become attached to certain relationships that we call "love" relationships, which are, in truth, "security" relationships. We can experience true unconditional love only when we are free of insecurity, fear, and from needing the other. **Love** gives and wants the other to be well. **Attachment** needs to depend upon and take from the other. These two often conflict when they coexist.

Ultimately, security can be established only from within, and must be based on an experience of or faith in our true spiritual nature. There can be no real insurance in the material world. There can only be the inner assurance that, no matter what happens, **we will continue** (even beyond death of the physical body).

A study of past fears and anxieties will probably prove to us that there is no need to fear whatever might be destined to happen. We have gone through so many situations where we feared, worried, and thought that the world might come to a crashing end for us, and yet here we are reading this text.

Everything in the past has passed, and everything in the present and all that we shall encounter in the future **will also pass** - both the pleasant and the unpleasant.

Life is change. **There can be no external security in a world of change.** Only the inner self, the soul, does not change. There lies our only true security - - **within us**.

When we are dominated by addictions based in the security center (which is associated physically with the bottom of the spine), even when everything is fine in our present, we will still find some imaginary future insecurity to concern us. Thus, the security center is, for most of us, a constant source of suffering and worry.

## CENTER 2
## THE SENSATION CENTER

This center is associated physically with the area some fingers below the navel. This is the center of our pleasure needs. We may enjoy various objects, persons, substances and situations as sources of our sensual pleasure. The most common are food, sex, cigarettes, drink and various chemical stimulants and relaxants, legal and illegal. Whenever these needs demand satisfaction, they have the potential to turn many of us into slaves, preventing us from relating freely and honestly to people and situations.

Our sex addictions prevent us from relating to others as souls or with pure selfless love. We tend to perceive them as possible objects of pleasure or threats to that pleasure.

Addictions to food, nicotine, alcohol and drugs obviously destroy our health, willpower, and self-confidence while they simultaneously distort our perception of reality. We become more interested in satisfying our addiction than enjoying the beauty and love within and around us.

Because we are often unable to fulfill our addictions, we tend to experience discontentment. On the other hand, even when we manage to satisfy a sensation addiction, the pleasure is usually short-lived and we quickly desire the same sensation. There is little potential for lasting happiness as long as these addictions absorb and monopolize our time, money, energy and thoughts.

At some point, we will become bored with this endless cycle of desire -- momentary satisfaction -- and reoccurring desire. We will then feel the need to free ourselves from this slavery and transform these addictions into **preferences**, or in some cases, rid ourselves of them completely if they are destroying our health.

When we prefer, we enjoy pleasurable sensations when we have them without becoming anxious when we can't.

Another interesting point here is that many of us have first indulged in some of these addictions as symbols of freedom. We interpreted our ability to smoke or drink as expressions our freedom from control by others. Ironically, in the end, we lose our freedom completely to these needs. We are free from control by others, but not from control by our addictions.

On the other hand, we also need to free ourselves from any guilt that may rise upon satisfying our needs. If we seek freedom from pleasure addictions motivated by feelings of guilt and shame, believing we are less worthy of love when we satisfy these needs, we face a probable backfire for a number of reasons which we will discuss later. Such changes are best made simply because we realize that they are **intelligent choices** that work for our benefit, and not because we feel guilt or perceive them as ways to be more loved or accepted by others, or by God.

## CENTER 3
## THE POWER CENTER

This center is located in the area of the solar plexus area. When we operate from this center, we are interested in **power** and **affirming** ourselves in relation to others, often by **manipulating** and **controlling** them.

We will find it difficult to give or experience love when we view each person an object to be manipulated or a threat to our control. Such games are played more intensely in political, business and sexual relationships, as well as in parent - child relationships.

In such a competitive atmosphere, there is little room for thinking about others. Pride, selfishness and egocentric behavior flourish. Instead of using the ego as a vehicle for our expression, we allow it to control us and create a false front, which, in turn, stimulates negative reactions in others.

This addiction to power can also be manifested in subtle ways, such as by appearing ill, weak or helpless in order to gain others' attention, sympathy, cooperation or even service.

If we observe when we are being controlled by power addictions and learn to change these addictions into preferences, we can allow others to be themselves and flow lovingly with what is happening. Our energies will then be free to rise into the next level of consciousness.

Our **need for affirmation** from others is perhaps the number one driving force in our lives. Most of our actions are based on this need. The importance which we give to our:

Physical appearance,
Professional position,
Knowledge and intelligence
Sexual virility,
Economic and social status,
Professional, social and family connections,
Professions,
How many books we have read,
How spiritual we are,
How many countries we have visited,
How "good" we are,
How many people we have helped in our lives.

All of these factors **can, in many cases,** be important to us because we **believe** they make others **accept us** more fully, **respect us** more deeply and **love us** more completely. We are very much controlled by the belief that our self-worth depends upon the way in which **others perceive us.**

Thus, most of our waking hours are spent doing whatever we believe may be necessary to do in order to make us acceptable to others, especially those who are important to us.

## CENTER 4
## THE LOVE CENTER

When our addictions are transformed into preferences, we can begin to experience **unconditional love**, in which we no longer need, seek or expect anything from the other person in return. We accept and love others, even when they are unable to comply with our preferences. Our feelings of alienation and defensiveness dissolve and we spend much less time and energy building up ego images to hide how we honestly feel. We sense a greater unity with others.

We understand that others are being dominated by their addictions and cannot help occasionally engaging in selfish behavior. We forgive them and feel compassion for them. We do not, however, feel superior. We feel neither superior nor inferior.

We play fewer games and are more honest. We are more relaxed in our relationships, which allows others to feel more relaxed, more accepted and more secure in our presence

Love flows more freely. Obviously, this center is associated with the heart center.

If you have ever been with a being who has loved you unconditionally, you will realize what a **healing and transforming experience it is**. We all deserve to be loved in this way and all others deserve that we love them in this way in return.

**Loving unconditionally does not mean** we must accept the others' negative actions or behaviors. We can accept them and love them as beings even when their actions are not acceptable. Thus, we can accept them, but assertively ask that their actions be more aligned with the truth that exists within them.

This is similar to the love of a mother for her child. The mother continues to love the child although she may be unable to condone certain aspects of the child's behavior. This is important for parents to understand. We can let the child feel that our love is continuous, but that certain types of behavior are unacceptable. Thus we make a distinction between the child and his or her behavior. The same distinction is also very helpful when dealing with adults, and also when confronting ourselves.

**Until now, our love has seldom been pure,** but rather love mixed with needs and attachments. We "loved" the other because he or she offered us security, pleasure or affirmation. If, later, he or she stopped fulfilling those needs, or started to obstruct our fulfillment of those needs or offered all they had offered to us now to someone else, does our love remain? Or do we feel hurt, rejected, betrayed, cheated, bitter, and perhaps anger, hate and a desire for revenge?

If this is so, then, what we were feeling, was not unconditional love. It was love mixed with needs and attachments that were being fulfilled by the other.

**The truth is that we can experience pure love only when we do not need anything from the other.** Otherwise, when he or she does provide us with what we need, our feelings will change, especially if he or she gives it to someone else.

## PURIFYING GOLD ORE

We need not feel guilty that our love is not pure. It is natural at this stage of our evolutionary journey. If we had already completed this lesson, it is likely we wouldn't have needed to incarnate. Our love now is like the gold ore when it is first taken out of the ground. It contains other impurities that must be removed. Our relationships are the crucible in which our love is heated, and its impurities come up to the surface. Our every love relationship, be it with spouse, child, parent or friend, gives us the exact stimuli we need in order to see the impurities which still exist in our love, and remove them, perhaps with the help of the techniques offered in this book.

We can recognize these "impurities" (our attachments, aversions and fears) by the **negative emotions** they provoke in us. Every time we feel negative emotions towards a loved one, let us ask ourselves:

**1.** "What is it that I want from him/her, that he/she is not giving me at this moment?

**2.** Can I love him/her in spite of his/her inability or refusal to give me what I want? Or is this a prerequisite I am placing on my love?

**3.** Can I love unconditionally?"

## CENTER 5
## THE CORNUCOPIA CENTER

The "Cornucopia" center is located in the center of the throat. Cornucopia means "horn of plenty". Ken Keyes has designated this name, because when we operate from this level of consciousness, we will find ourselves in a harmonious union with life. When this occurs, life itself provides all our needs without our effort.

Having satisfied our needs for security, self-affirmation and pleasure internally, our feelings of isolation from others and the world diminish. Everything that we need in terms of food, security, shelter, books, information, guidance, etc. is supplied through the **support of nature.**

This is a truly wonderful state in which life gives us exactly what we need at every moment. Life becomes a "continuous miracle" in which our needs are easily fulfilled, and feel deep gratitude for receiving so much grace in the form of even the simplest gifts.

As we are no longer wasting so much energy and thought on how to fulfill demanding addictions, we embody much more energy, love and clarity with which to live life and proceed on the evolutionary path. We have activated the heart center and will most probably be using our energies and power to make the world a better place to live, in whatever way we can.

This center may be identified with **Christ's promise** that if we live according to the Father's Will, then He will provide for all our needs just as He does for the birds and lilies in the field.

When we cease living only for ourselves, realize **we are all cells in the body of humanity** and begin to live like cells, serving the whole in every way we can, we will experience the miracle of material, emotional and spiritual affluence.

We will then **live lightly on the earth**, using and taking little while offering much to our fellow beings with whom we share this beautiful planet.

Rather than live like parasites, steadily devouring the planet's resources, we will **leave the earth a better place than we found it**.

We will be happy, content, fulfilled and at peace with ourselves.

## CENTER 6
## THE CONSCIOUS WITNESS CENTER

As this center gradually opens, we become increasingly **objective witnesses** to our life drama. We identify more with the soul and less with the particular personality and body, which we are momentarily occupying and expressing our Selves through. We experience a growing detachment and a calm, peaceful clarity in all situations. Although there is absence of codependent emotionalism, there is no lack of love.

We enjoy freedom from addictions and the particular life roles in which we had been imprisoned. While we may be engaged in many of the same activities, we are also simultaneously witnessing the whole drama in a detached way. We are not the doer, but the witness of the actions.

Many may say, "How boring! I would never like to be like that, so cold and unemotional." It is difficult to understand what it would be like while stuck in our present level of consciousness. When we were young, we had many toys, dolls and games, which we could never at that time have thought we would ever give up. But slowly we lost our interest in these objects and activities. If someone had told us then that we would lose our interest in them, we would not have believed them. Yet it happened.

It is very probable that, given time, we will also become bored with the suffering created by our present attachments and "games," and eventually prefer the detached peace and unconditional love of these higher centers.

In observing highly evolved individuals, I can certainly affirm that they experience and express much more love, peace and happiness than we do. They perceive individuals as parts of themselves and love all equally, while not demanding anything from anyone. Attachment and emotionalism are related to lower forms of selfish love. **Selfless love** is only possible from a self-fulfilled state of consciousness.

## CENTER 7
## THE COSMIC CONSCIOUSNESS CENTER

Our vocabulary has been developed based on the lower three levels of consciousness and miserably fails us when we try to describe this highest level. Here all separation is lost. We are the completion of the evolutionary process. There is **no other.** We are all. We are all beings and the entire world. We are the Divine. We are security, sensation, power, love, fullness of life and the witness of it all.

This state may be described by various names such as heaven, paradise, samadhi, nirvana, satori or liberation. Christ described this state when he said to his followers, "I am in you. You are in me. I am in the Father and the Father is in me".

In the remaining chapters, we will address ourselves to the process of freeing our minds and emotions from the lower centers of consciousness so we can begin to experience the higher centers of increased love, peace, clarity, vitality and unity with all.

Technique no. 5

# DEEP RELAXATION

## Why this is extremely beneficial

Deep relaxation in which we systematically relax the muscles and organs of the body can bring about a resolution of emotional tensions. This happens through a simultaneous balancing of the energy and emotional bodies.

This is an especially important technique to employ when our emotions are also creating psychosomatic illness because of unmanaged stress. The muscles, nerves, mind and all bodily systems are relaxed and rejuvenated.

When we are relaxed, those problems and stimuli, which would ordinarily disturb us, flow through us and we remain unaffected.

## A simple technique for relaxing the body and mind:

Deep relaxation is performed by progressively relaxing the whole body part by part starting with the feet and working upward through the ankles, calves, knees, thighs, buttocks, abdomen, lower back, chest, upper back, shoulders, arms, hands, fingers, neck, head, face, cheeks, eyes, forehead and top of the head.

This process of progressive scanning and relaxation of the body parts can be performed a number of times in one relaxation session which is usually done lying on the back on a firm but comfortable surface. We should be appropriately covered so as not to get cold as the metabolism drops.

The spine is kept straight with the head in a straight line with the spine and the arms and legs relaxed symmetrically on each side of the body. The palms are relaxed facing upwards towards the sky. The body and mind are progressively surrendered into relaxation.

In this relaxed state we can program positive thoughts and images into our minds.

For those who find this difficult, cassette tapes are available from various sources to help them get started. They are a helpful introduction to this technique.

We suggest, however, that you do not become dependent on a tape, but gradually learn to guide yourself into the relaxed state. Then pass the tape on to a friend who needs to relax or keep it for moments when relaxation is especially difficult. (Check our web site for cassettes)

## Note:

Resistance causes energy to stagnate as tension,
whereas relaxation allows energy flow without disturbance.

*Case History No. 6*

# *THE ABSENT SPOUSE*

Janice's husband Ted is seldom home. He prefers the office, the club and the bar. On the weekends he goes hunting with his male friends. She has made numerous attempts to get him to spend some time with her, but he does not respond. He doesn't say, "no", but always programs something else or tells her to stop suffocating him. It seems that he has some kind of aversion to being at home. Janice believes that he does not love her.

The fact is that he **does love** her and would not like to lose her, but cannot control his needs, which are to be with his friends and out of the home.

Ted had an extremely overbearing and controlling mother and didn't establish his freedom until he was about 22 years old. Although he loves Janice, he perceives her as an obstacle to his freedom. He has projected his mother onto her. He is unable to express this and simply avoids her.

She on the other had a father who abandoned her. And now Ted is doing the same.

The more he avoids her, the more demanding she becomes and then in turn, the more he fears being controlled by her.

They are reliving their childhood programming and will need to liberate themselves in order to heal themselves and their relationship.

**Some of Janice's lessons might be:**

**1.** To feel happy, fulfilled and worthy even when he is not there.

**2.** To communicate her need for him to be there more clearly, assertively and lovingly.

**3.** To love and accept him as he is, with his need to be away.

**4.** To search (perhaps with him) for what she might be doing which might be causing him to avoid her or his home.

**5.** Not to take this personally and realize that his need is not an expression of rejection nor a lack of love towards her, but simply his fear or need.

**6.** Not to measure her self-worth by the attention which she receives from him.

**7.** Not to nag about this, but to discuss it openly and without accusations.

**8.** To develop more personal interests to fill her own time.

**9.** Perhaps to join him in some of his activities that he feels comfortable sharing with her.

**10.** To get free from any beliefs that she does not deserve something better; or that this is the way it will be, because her father left her.

**11.** To express her needs more frequently and to think of interesting activities which they share.

**12.** To work on her relationship with her father, and the conclusions which she made as a child.

### Some of Ted's lessons might be:

**1.** To feel happy and fulfilled at home and with Janice

**2.** To be able to be himself with Janice and his mother.

**3.** To free himself from the fear of being controlled.

**4.** To realize that a relationship requires some energy and cannot be kept up in this way.

**5.** To focus on his love for Janice and express it in ways in which he feels safe.

**6.** To work on his relationship with his mother, and the conclusions which he made as a child.

### Some beliefs that will help them
### get free from these mechanical ways of interacting are:

### Janice might benefit from some of the following beliefs:

**1.** Fulfillment and happiness are within me and do not depend on anyone else.

**2.** I accept and love myself regardless of the other's behavior.

**3.** I express my needs and feelings assertively, clearly and lovingly.

**4.** Unity is not dependent on how much time we spend together, but how we feel towards each other.

**5.** Life gives me exactly what I need in each moment in order to learn and grow.

**6.** I feel safe and secure within myself.

### Ted might benefit from some of the following beliefs:

**1.** I love my wife and want to spend time with her and express my love to her.

**2.** I am free to be myself in every situation, even with my wife and my mother.

**3.** Freedom is an internal state. I am free to spend time at home and with my wife.

**4.** As I would not like to be alone at home, I choose not to leave my wife there alone.

**5.** I see all women as sister souls in the process of evolution.

**6.** I accept and love myself as I am.

## CHAPTER 6

# AN OUTLINE FOR
# MANAGING EMOTIONS

### WHAT ARE EMOTIONS?

We hear much talk about expressing our emotions, "letting it all out," "getting things off our chest."

What exactly are emotions? For the purpose of this discussion, we will be speaking about negative or unpleasant emotions such as fear, jealousy, anger, hatred, envy, bitterness, resentment, greed, etc. Positive emotions are essential for our relationships and inspirations, and will be discussed elsewhere.

One way of looking at negative or unpleasant emotions is to see them as thoughts that have been **energetically charged** primarily because we sense **danger**. Regardless as to whether we feel a sense of injustice, anger, hatred, jealousy, guilt or fear, we are feeling some degree of danger, some threat to our security, self worth, freedom or pleasure.

These emotions, or energized thoughts, then create physical, energy and psychological disturbances that can eventually lead to psychosomatic illness. They can also considerably deplete our vitality and immune system, and leave us exhausted on many levels of our being.

Negative emotions can also develop into a vicious circle of negativity. For example, we observe that we are feeling fear or anger and then feel guilt, self-rejection or frustration simply because we experienced those original emotions. We have emotions about the fact that we have emotions, thus we create even more fear and anger.

Such emotional states can distort our perception, cause us to make flawed decisions and perhaps even act against our true nature. They cause us to feel alienated from those who are, for us, the "cause" of our pain.

We use the words negative and positive to describe emotions out of convention. What we really mean by **"negative"** is **separating** or **alienating**. Separating emotions are those that cause us to feel alienated from and closed towards others.

**Positive** emotions are those that increase our feelings of **unity**, **love** and **one-**

**ness** with others. We can create a positive energy flow by experiencing and expressing our gratitude, good wishes, admiration and love.

We can also have emotions that **alienate us from our own selves**, such as guilt, shame and self-rejection.

Alienating emotions are based on identification with the ego. They inhibit our health, peace, happiness and spiritual development. Unifying emotions generate health, peace, harmony, mutual love and acceptance, as well as spiritual growth.

## DISCHARGING OUR NEGATIVITY ONTO OTHERS

Emotions are often expressed as uncontrolled words or actions. In such cases, we simply throw our emotional energy onto others by accusing, intimidating, blaming and generally bombarding them with this negatively charged energy.

For those who can do nothing else (for there are other alternatives), this is perhaps a preferable solution to suppressing feelings. There are, however, some disadvantages:

**1.** We lose **energy**, which we could have used for other, more creative or growth oriented processes.

**2.** This energy which is generally directed at others, in their presence or absence, affects them, becomes recorded in **their** emotional body, leaving **them** now to deal with it. This is true whether or not the negativity is actually verbally expressed.

Let me give an example of this. One day, I was visiting a friend who had a cat that was genetically related to the cat that belonged to my sister-in-law, with whom I was staying.

My friend's cat was dying of pneumonia and I had to hold the cat while it was given an injection. While holding it, I felt a great deal of the cat's negative energy flow into my hands. Then, when I returned home, as I walked through the door, my sister-in-law's cat sensed the energy and began howling and running around the house, often banging its head into the wall. The reason for this became obvious to me and I explained it to my sister-in-law. She understood, but confessed that the cat's actions were making her nervous. This negativity had traveled from one cat to me, to another cat, to my sister-in-law.

We can observe how negative emotions are transferred from one person to another, like a giant telephone network. The sales clerk receives negativity from one customer and passes it on to next. Most who come into contact with the public do the same. They receive from one and pass on to the next. Eventually, we spread these "emotional viruses" to our family and friends. Peace and happiness are rare in such an environment.

The negative energy, which we discharge to others, causes them to develop negative feelings towards us and this burdens and can even destroy our relationships.

Why do we allow this to happen? Because we have not learned to understand and deal effectively with our emotional nature. We are not interested here in suppressing our emotions, but rather in observing, analyzing, understanding, accepting and transforming them, usually in this order.

**3.** When we discharge onto others our emotional energies, we **do not get a chance to learn and grow** through those experiences, which are, in fact, opportunities through which we can develop inner strength and greater self-knowledge. When we blame others for our unhappiness, we lose opportunities for self-discovery.

Every present moment offers an **opportunity** to move forward toward our divine destiny. Mastering our emotional energy is one giant step in that direction.

## THE RESULTS OF SUPPRESSING EMOTIONS

Suppressing our feelings can have some of the following results:

**1.** We create **psychosomatic illnesses**, such as asthma, allergies, colitis, rheumatism, cancer, headaches, and hormonal imbalances, as well as a variety of other physical, emotional and mental imbalances.

**2.** Our **emotions are passed on to others any way**. They experience the subconscious effect of what we are feeling and actually react to that rather than to the mask we wear in an effort to hide what we feel.

**3.** We **lose the opportunity to communicate openly** and honestly so as to create sincere relationships.

**4.** We **fail to learn from the experience** as mentioned above.

## WHAT IS THE CAUSE OF
## OUR EMOTIONAL NATURE?

The ancient Indian sage Patanjali (300 BC) gives us a clear understanding of the human personality complex, its motivations, workings and relationship to the soul.

Perhaps a numerical approach will explain more clearly the generation of emotions:

**1. We are souls**. We exist as consciousness before the birth of the physical body and long after its death. We are divine consciousness that has no beginning and no end. We incarnate into a physical body.

**2.** This incarnation is part of an **evolutionary learning process.** We learn through the body and personality to experience more perfectly our true inner nature and express it externally in the material world.

**3.** The process of **discovering our real nature** is called enlightenment, self-realization, liberation or self-actualization.

**HOWEVER:**

**4.** Once in the body, we lose awareness of and are **ignorant of our true spiritual nature**, divine consciousness and energy.

**5.** This ignorance or amnesia of our true nature causes us to **identify with the body and mind** through which we are experiencing the world. This is roughly equivalent to our thinking that we are the clothing that we change on a daily basis. This identification generates a sense of ego or personality, which is similar to our clothes thinking that they are the real us. A sense of "I" and "mine" are generated, and the ego grows an illusionary power of its own.

This is also like the electrical energy, that passes through a light bulb, forgetting its nature as energy and believing it is the light bulb, thus becoming concerned with how it appears in relationship with other bulbs and what those other light bulbs think about it. Also there will be fear that perhaps the bulb might break, which would mean "death." Thus, our two main fears are of **death** and **rejection**.

But the electrical energy is one and the same in all light bulbs and does not perish with the death of the bulb.

**6.** This identification with the body and mind then **generates a variety of attachments and aversions.** Depending on our role-identifications, we will prefer some objects, people and experiences, and will want to avoid others.

For example:

**a.** When we identify with the role of the **parent**, we might be susceptible to the following **attachments**:

**1.** To being obeyed by our children.

**2.** To ensuring their health, happiness, grades and success.

**3.** To making sure our children are compared favorably to other children.

**4.** To being able to control them.

**5.** To their accepting our advice.

and the following **aversions towards**:

**1.** To our children's becoming ill.

**2.** To our children's keeping company with other children of whom we do not approve.

**3.** To criticism concerning how we are bringing up our children.

**b.** When we identify with the role of the **spouse**, we might be susceptible to the following **attachments**:

**1.** Exclusivity on our spouse's attention, love, affection and sexuality.

**2.** Our spouse's happiness and satisfaction

**3.** Our spouse's approval and acceptance.

**4.** Our spouse's health and success

and the following **aversions towards**

**1.** To being criticized or rejected by our spouse

**2.** Toward him or her paying attention to others of the opposite sex.

**3.** To our spouse becoming ill.

Each role creates a set of attachments and aversions that then limit our happiness and peace, creating negative emotions when they are not fulfilled.

Steps 4 through 6 show the evolution of emotional nature. When we fear that an attachment will not be fulfilled, we react with fear, anger, jealousy, hatred or perhaps depression. The same happens when we are presented with situations, people or objects that we would rather avoid.

Our uncontrolled negative **emotional reactions are proportional to our identification** with our ego roles and their attachments and aversions.

**We are creating our own hurt.** We are victims of our own ignorance and programming. Our suffering is created by our own beliefs, not by what others do or do not do. Others are the stimuli, which trigger our programming and cause our negative feelings.

We can begin slowly to work our way out of this darkness. It requires fortitude, perseverance and patience, but is there really any other viable alternative?

## HOW WE CAN MASTER OUR EMOTIONAL NATURE

Following are some techniques and concepts that may help us deal with and channel our emotional energies.

Of course, techniques are of no use sitting in our minds. They must be put into practice. Benefit will come from regular application of those that appeal most to each of us.

Techniques for mastering emotions can be divided into **five categories**:

**1.** Those that help **express or release** our negative energy in ways that do not harm others.

**2.** Those that **relax and release the tensions** on an inner level.

**3.** Those that **build our energy level** so that we have greater positive energy to deal with people and events.

**4.** Those that **transform** our emotional tension through **understanding** and **reprogramming** of subconscious conditioning.

**5.** Those which allow us to **transcend** our emotional nature.

Here we will list some of those techniques available. At the end of each chapter we have been and will be presenting you with a technique to study and perhaps employ. The idea here is that during the days you will be reading each chapter, you will have some time to absorb and try out the technique described before that chapter. Then you can regularly employ those techniques that suit you most.

**A word to those who have an aversion to techniques** and "recipes" as a way of transformation. Be careful that this is not a game played by your ego defenses to avoid painful changes. It is true that the final transformation is made without techniques or concepts. However, for most of us, such aids are not only useful but also indispensable, for success in the initial stages of this process.

These techniques may seem mechanical and non-spontaneous the first few times we employ them. But the reality is that, at the present, **the ways in which we think, speak and act are equally mechanical.** We are like robots reacting according to our subjective programming. Thus, by using such techniques, we "fight fire with fire" or "remove a thorn with a thorn". We use the programming possibilities of the mind to replace alienating, suffering-causing programs with unifying, happiness-producing ones.

## WE MUST ACCEPT WHAT WE WANT TO CHANGE

There is one **basic key** that we will need regardless of which techniques we decide to use. That is that, **in order to overcome or transform any emotion, we must first accept it.** Not accepting that we have a particular emotion, desire or fear, is a major obstacle towards transforming or changing it. We cannot change something that we deny exists.

Thus, the first step towards any change or transformation is to accept ourselves exactly as we are with all of our weaknesses, fears, attachments and desires. We need to first feel that we are worthy of love and acceptance exactly as we are. **Whatever we reject in ourselves or others will resist change**.

Also, some of us seek self-improvement with the idea that we will become more lovable to the Divine. I would suspect that in God's eyes we are all always lovable.  Better to avoid making these transformations in an attempt to make ourselves "good", or "better" than the others, or because we wish to become more lovable.

What is true is that **we will be freer, happier, and truer to our own inner nature,** liberated from mechanical emotional reactions, which destroy our health, happiness and freedom as souls in the process of evolution.

## COPING WITH EMOTIONS IN THE PRESENT

As some emotions may require time to be transformed or transcended, it is beneficial to be aware of various ways of handling those emotions in the present so they do not create problems in our bodies, relationships, or perhaps even in our work.

We must, however, remember that such techniques do not constitute a permanent solution, but rather a **temporary** means for maintaining our balance and harmony. We present you with this chart so that you may locate more easily the method that might help you or another.  They are described in small sections after each chapter.

**Some of the techniques that we might find useful, are:**

**1. Breathing and releasing.**

**2. Hot bath and massage.**

**3.** Total bodily expression through **dancing** and other forms of movement.

**4.** Regular **exercise** for the body and breath.

**5.** Regular **deep relaxation**

**6.** Expressing our emotions through **writing** in the first or third person.

**7. Channeling our emotional energy in various ways,** such as crying, laughing, working, playing, enjoying recreation, etc.

**8. Cathartic Release** of emotions through **crying, yawning,** shouting and /or intense movement, such as hitting a pillow, etc.

**9.** Learning to **deal more effectively with criticism** and differences in opinion.

**10.** Bringing to mind the **opposite positive emotion** of the negative one that is bothering us.

**11. Imagining that we are the other,** and trying to feel what he might be feeling in order to act in that way.

**12. Transferring attention to the physical body**

**13.** Daily **positive projection techniques.**

**14. Written Affirmations.**

**15.** Remembering that **life is a school,** which gives us exactly what we need at every moment in order to learn our next lesson on the path.

**16. Selfless service** toward those in need.

**17.** Directing our **Healing energy** toward those in need.

**18.** The continuous **repetition of a word,** phrase, prayer or sound which brings our mind to a positive state.

**19. Meditation.**

**20. Resolving emotions back to their source.**
(This is the basis of real transformation.)

Technique no. 6

# WRITING HOW WE FEEL

### Why this is beneficial

Writing is a very effective way to express, release and gain perspective on painful emotions.

Writing brings forth a higher part of our being that embodies greater objectivity and clarity.

Higher centers of consciousness and awareness are provoked when we write our thoughts.

We come into greater contact with our inner guidance.

This clarity relaxes us and allows us to reestablish our peace.

### A simple technique for releasing emotions and also gaining clarity about them is:

When we are stuck in an emotion, we can sit and simply start writing about what we are feeling, allowing our thoughts to flow freely onto the page in what is called flow of consciousness.

This may develop into a type of letter to someone in which we express to him or her how we feel. This letter might lead us to write to those who were important to us during our childhood years.

We also might find ourselves writing to God

The experience will be both releasing and clarifying.

### Note:

Writing is also a means of self -transformation.

*Life Story no. 7*

# SELF EVALUATION

Today Charles has discovered that his coworker Andy had a more successful professional year than he did. Andy sold more accounts and was commended and promoted by the company.

Charles is not happy about this. He feels jealous. Behind that jealousy are feelings of self-doubt, self-rejection and anger at himself for not being more productive.

He feels a failure. He was not feeling this way yesterday. His emotions are created by the fact of Andy's success, not by his own failure. No one in the company has said anything to him about not being productive. His employers are happy with him. Charles is creating his own negative emotions by comparing himself with Andy.

Charles' father was very demanding and often told him he would not make it the world and compared him to classmates who had higher grades. He never compared him to classmates who were less capable. His father was very successful professionally and Charles felt that his self worth depended on his equaling his father's success professionally and economically.

He gave up his interest in the arts to prove himself as a businessman.

As a result, he is continuously comparing himself to others, seeking to establish his self worth. When he finds someone whom he evaluates as less successful, he feels very good. When he perceives someone as being more successful he is plagued by self-doubt.

**Some of Charles' beliefs that might be obstructing his happiness might be:**

**1.** My self worth is dependent on how successful I am.

**2.** My self worth is dependent on how I compare to others.

**3.** My job will be in danger if I do not produce more.

**4.** I must be the best in order to be accepted and loved.

**5.** I must prove to others how worthy I am by being very successful.

**6.** I must prove to my father than I can make it in the world.

**Some beliefs that Charles could cultivate in order to find his inner peace are:**

**1.** My self worth is in me and has nothing to do with how much I accomplish.

**2.** I and all other beings are unique and cannot be compared.

**3.** I feel safe and secure in every situation.

**4.** I love and accept myself in every situation

**5.** I am lovable as I am.

**6.** My self worth is based on my being and not on how much I do.

**7.** I am a divine creation.

**8.** I am a beautiful and lovable aspect of Divine creation.

# CHAPTER 7

# CONCEPTS, TOOLS AND METHODS FOR SELF TRANSFORMATION

Our beliefs control the way in which we perceive and react to the world around us. Happiness can be experienced by adjusting and transforming our belief system. This process will be aided by contemplating the following:

## THREE CONCEPTS WHICH
## FACILITATE OUR TRANSFORMATION

**1. We are all responsible for our reality.** We are responsible for our happiness, our health and our transformation. We will benefit greatly by accepting the responsibility for our inner reality, which we have created up to this point, and that **only we** have the ability to transform.

We would do well to stop placing the blame for our problems on other people, our environment or society.

We also must realize that every situation offers us the choice to:

**a. Accept, change and improve,**
or
**b. Resist, resent and descend into negativity.**

It is seldom that someone else can make us happy by providing us with security, love and understanding. These are attributes we need to develop within ourselves. We cannot lay the responsibility for our health and happiness on our doctor, psychologist, priest or spiritual guide. They can help us, but they cannot do it for us.

We are responsible for learning how to care for our bodies and minds. We have the power to create health or suffering. The choice is ours.

We are not, however, at fault. There is a great difference between "**fault**" and "**responsibility.**" The word "fault" indicates there has been some wrongdoing or mistake. It is not our fault that we are not as well as we could be. It is a matter of evolution. We simply have not yet arrived at the level of personal and group awareness where we can create a more harmonious reality. We are presently in the **learning** stage.

A **flower bud** is not at fault because it has not yet blossomed. It will eventually bloom and become a flower. We do not look for the fault that has prevented it from becoming a flower. We do not reject the bud. We accept where it is in its evolutionary process. We know that it is only a matter of time.

Thus, taking responsibility for our life doesn't mean feeling guilty for what we have created. It simply means moving forward and **blossoming into the flower that we latently are.**

Just as others cannot create happiness for us, we cannot create happiness, health or success for others.

**2. We can change**. We have the ability and the right to change any aspects of our personality that we would like to improve. If we do not believe we can change, then we simply won't. Believing we can change allows us to **focus on what we have the potential to become** rather than remain lost in feelings of helplessness and hopelessness.

On the other hand, it is **essential that we also accept ourselves exactly as we are.** Acceptance and self-esteem are the first steps towards self-transformation, while self-rejection stands as a major obstruction to the process.

**3. We are all eternal souls in the process of evolution.** It is not mandatory that all accept this concept in order to benefit from this system of self-analysis. The belief that we exist as a spiritual consciousness beyond the body-personality complex does, however, offer us greater inner security and objectivity in our self-analysis process. Believing that we are separate from the personality, and that it is an instrument through which we are functioning, allows us to accept changes in the personality more easily. We can be more objective in analyzing the personality, because we can view it from the outside in a more detached way.

This identification with our spiritual nature offers us a **position of security** during this difficult period in which the personality may experience changes in its value systems, habits and belief systems. The personality seldom feels secure and safe for any period of time, unless it has contact with a frame of reference outside itself. We usually choose relationships, money, objects or even work as external frames of reference in order to feel secure and to identify our selves. Contact with our spiritual center, which is unaffected by the changing external world is an exceptional source of inner security, which liberates us from dependence on these external frames of reference.

We would do well to learn to feel this "I" who is beyond all these temporary, passing identifications and states of mind. When we identify with our true self, we can objectively observe and correct our personality.

## THREE TOOLS WHICH
## FACILITATE OUR TRANSFORMATION.

**1. I accept and love myself as I am**. Many of us do not accept and love ourselves, but instead feel we are unworthy and unlovable. The process of self-analysis is more painful without some degree of self-acceptance and self-love. Otherwise, as we discover the many weaknesses, attachments and fears from which we have been operating, we may begin to feel even more negative about ourselves, and our situation may worsen rather than improve.

We have had the "luxury" until now of blaming others for our unhappiness. Realizing that we ourselves create our reality can mistakenly lead towards self-rejection. This occurs because we are convinced someone must be wrong and at fault. When we realize that no mistake has been made and that all is happening in our lives in order to provoke our growth process, we will be able to accept and love ourselves and others exactly as we are.

For some, it may seem contradictory to accept and love ourselves as we are while, at the same time, we are seeking to change some of our behaviors and improve our attitude toward life. Deeper thought, however, will show that they are not contradictory when understood in the right sense.

**When we are in the fourth grade**, we do not hate ourselves and feel guilty because we cannot do what the tenth graders are able to do. We have patience with ourselves and know that someday we will arrive at that level as we grow and learn. At the same time, however, we would not like to stay in the fourth grade for eternity. Thus, we can accept ourselves exactly where we are, but also desire to keep evolving and improving ourselves.

When we speak of accepting and loving ourselves, we mean loving ourselves on three levels.

**a.** We love the true or **inner self**, which is constant throughout the years of growth and change.

**b.** We accept and love our **personality at its present stage of evolution.**

**c.** We accept and love our **body as it is**.

We accept and love the body and mind as **vehicles** through which we evolve. We accept them as we continue to perfect them.

**Our inner self** is the self which we call «I» throughout the various changes in our personality and body, such as:

**a. Age;** we referred to the same "I" when we were 2 years old, 15, 25 and now. We have different interests and beliefs and yet the same "I" is in there.

**b. State of consciousness** such as waking, dreaming, and sleeping. Although these three states are totally different, the same I is experiencing them.

**c. Roles;** we speak of ourselves as "I" when playing various roles, such as parent, child, spouse, friend, professional, etc. We manifest ourselves into so many different roles, such as mother, daughter, sister, friend, house cleaner, employer, employee, artist, cook, businessperson, driver, secretary, etc. All these roles are temporary and do not define what or who we are.

**d.** We pass through many **emotional states,** such as anger, fear, hate, joy, pleasure, pain, discontentment, contentment, love, peace, anxiety and depression, yet there is an «I» who remains constant throughout all the above mentioned changes.

This unchanging **witness** of all these roles and states is our **real "I".**

When a child is at fault or makes a mistake, we try to help the child by correcting him, but we do not stop accepting or loving him. We can treat our personalities in much the same way. When our car or camera breaks down, we do not feel badly about ourselves. We try to find out what is wrong with the machine or instrument and fix it. **The body and personality are instruments** that we use in our contact with and our evolution through the physical world. Thus, if we discover some weakness or faults within the personality complex, we do not need to feel self-hate or guilt, but rather consciously and clearly decide to remove whatever weakness or fault is causing the problem.

Thus **self-acceptance** and **change** are like the **two pedals of a bicycle** with which we progress through the fields of self-transformation.

**2. Honesty with ourselves and others.** If we hide the truth from ourselves or others, we will only delay our progress. We must be ready to see and express the truth about ourselves, no matter how uncomfortable or vulnerable we may feel in the process. The self-acceptance mentioned previously will help us discover the inner security necessary to re-cultivate this honesty.

**3. Practice - Persistence - Patience.** These are the three P's which will propel us toward success in our self-transformation process. Without **practice** of the various techniques offered, not much progress will be made. This practice must be **persistent** and regular. If we make effort for a short period of time, or only sporadically, we will not enjoy long-term results. **Patience** is absolutely essential, for we are not going to change 30, 40 or 50 years of conditioning in a few weeks, or even in a few months. Thus, we must make **continuous effort** and **be very patient** as we anticipate the results.

## THREE METHODS OF OBJECTIVE SELF-OBSERVATION

This process of self-observation can be facilitated in three basic ways:

**1. We can keep a daily diary.** Our observations will be much **clearer and more fruitful if they are written down on paper**. When we simply observe mentally, there is ample room for contradictions to coexist and details to slip by. Our problems breed in a confusion of unclear emotions and thoughts.

Writing down our thoughts helps us to perceive our personalities much more clearly. These observations are even more effective when written in the **third person** using the pronoun «he» or «she» or our first name, i.e. Mary or John, which allows for more objective observation.

If we use the pronoun «I», we might find it more difficult to write the truth. Also, we will be identifying with the wrong "I", that is, with the personality rather than with the soul, who is now observing the personality and writing about it in the third person.

In this daily diary, we can keep a record of the major emotional experiences and thoughts we experience each day. In this way, we will gradually uncover the basic **emotional patterns** that we have repeatedly created in our lives. We can then analyze the **inner causes** of these experiences, and record daily the major positive and negative emotions.

Each month, we can set aside a special time to read through what we have observed to draw conclusions and make some decisions about what we would like to do to improve our reality if we are not satisfied with it.

**2. We can work with questionnaires for more objective self-analysis.** In later sections, we will discuss some penetrating questions which will help us discover the attachments, aversions, fears, goals, values, talents and inclinations which motivate our thoughts, words and actions, and thus create our reality. It is best to answer these questions also in the third person for increased objectivity as explained above. (Check out such questionnaires on our web site)

**3. Psychologically oriented growth groups** can be very helpful in providing support and feedback to those who are going through this process. Being with others who have the same goal of self-discovery offers us strength and courage to continue and overcome the possible difficulties that may arise. The group may also offer objective insight into our problems.

Most groups have guidelines which discourage giving advice, since the basic premise is that we have our own particular answers within ourselves and it is best that we learn to dig within ourselves and find them. In such groups, the members learn **active listening** techniques through which they help each member through their **questions** and not through advice.

As the members of the group learn to trust each other more, they begin to open up and become freer and more honest in their communication. The group becomes a laboratory where we experiment with new ways of relating and being, as a step toward doing the same in society at large.

**Our results will be proportional to the
energy, sincerity and thought that we put into it.**

Technique no. 7

# CHANNELING ENERGY
# IN VARIOUS DIRECTIONS

### Why this is important

Channeling our emotional energy through various activities such as work, laughter and play in addition to crying, are all ways which many people have already found naturally to keep their balance.

When we are immersed in some unpleasant emotion, we can direct this energy elsewhere by working, cleaning up, being creative, serving others or even watching a comedy.

In this way, we direct our energy towards other activities and we are able to relax and find greater objectivity concerning what was happening.

### When we are controlled by unpleasant emotions
### we can try any of the following:

**1. Clean** out some closet, attic, garage or any area we feel needs cleaning. As we put order, we can imagine that we are also putting order to our emotions and mind.

**2.** Go to a **movie or theatre** that allows us to cry or makes us laugh.

**3. Play any sport** that engages our energy and attention.

**4. Work in the garden.**

**5. Any other activity** which engages us.

### Note:

Some of us can overdo this becoming workaholics or "laughers"
as a means of hiding from our pain.

### Balance is the solution.

*Life Story no. 8*

# SELF SUPPRESSION

Susan suppresses herself in order to be accepted and loved. However, those around her don't do the same. She feels mistreated and believes that she is being done an injustice to, but he never shares this with others. For her, the others are not correct, because they treat her unjustly. She feels hurt and mentally complains and criticizes.

She is very much in the role of the victim. On the one hand she believes that she must be the "good girl" who always says yes in order to be lovable and acceptable. On the other she also gets a feeling of self worth by being the victim and especially when the others are not "good". She feels her self worth when she makes sacrifices and others do not. She is the good one and the others are not.

This has become her identity, her life role. Because of this, she cannot allow herself to be happy or enjoy life's pleasures. If she were happy she would no longer be the victim and then she would lose her identity and her self worth.

She needs to be unhappy; only in this state does she feel safe and comfortable.

**Some of the beliefs that might be leading her into this role are:**

**1.** I am not worthy.

**2.** I am a victim.

**3.** I am not lovable.

**4.** Others will love me only when I do things for them and sacrifice my needs for them.

**5.** Whoever sacrifices for others is "good" and worthy.

**6.** The victim is "good" and the abuser is "bad".

**7.** I do not deserve to enjoy what I want, or express my needs.

**8.** The more mistakes and faults I can find in others, the more I am worthy.

**9.** My self worth is dependent on what others think of me.

**Some beliefs that might liberate her from this role are:**

**1.** I am worthy of love and respect exactly as I am.

**2.** I am the sole creator of my reality.

**3.** Others will love me even when I cannot respond to their needs.

**4.** A sacrifice with love is love. A sacrifice out of fear of rejection is no sacrifice. There are actually no sacrifices. There is only love and fear.

**6.** I am good as I am.

**7.** I deserve to enjoy what I like and to express my needs.

**8.** I accept and love all unconditionally - including my self.

**9.** My self worth is independent of what others think of me.

**10.** I am interesting and attractive without my problems

**11.** I communicate openly and sincerely in every situation.

CHAPTER 8

# OVERCOMING FEAR

### "WE HAVE NOTHING TO FEAR BUT FEAR ITSELF"
**Franklin D. Roosevelt**

Indeed fear is our greatest obstacle to happiness, peace and fulfillment on a personal, social and international level. All anger, hatred, prejudice, aggression, violence, and war can be ultimately attributed to fear.

### FEAR IS THE MOTHER OF ALL NEGATIVE EMOTIONS

From the moment we relinquished the security of our mother's womb and had our umbilical cord cut, we experienced separation, isolation, insecurity and fear.

We fear for our bodies and personalities because we know they are vulnerable and mortal. Out of fear, we seek to create some sense of security by ensuring that we have sufficient people, money, and objects, as well as a professional and social position, etc. in our lives.

Then we experience a **second level** of fear: the fear that we might not be able to hold onto everything we have acquired. We might lose them to death, decay or change.

We fear **not having** what we need in order to feel secure and happy.

We fear **losing** these things when we do have them.

We fear **others** who might take these things from us.

We fear **change** that might make them disappear.

We fear **death**, which means losing all this.

## SOME TYPES OF FEARS

There are literally thousands of various manifestations of fear. We can fear just about anything our imagination allows. Let us list just a few, while remembering that they all stem from the basic fear of pain, rejection or extinction of the ego or its various attachments.

Some of us are afraid of animals, insects, spiders, cockroaches, centipedes, snakes, birds and other wild animals. We fear each other and the opposite sex. The poor fear the rich and the rich the poor.

Movies, television and newspapers do much to increase our feelings of mistrust, vulnerability and fear, by concentrating on violence, both real and imaginary. We have learned to perceive our fellow beings as a threat to our safety and happiness. Some of us, for some irrational reason, choose to watch horrific and violent movies. After such an experience our imagination works overtime and creates fear at the slightest unexpected sound or experience.

Those of one race tend to fear those of another. Some nations create nationalistic feelings by generating fear of other countries.

Those, whose religious beliefs are weak, tend to mutate into fanatics out of fear of being wrong. The idea is that the more people you can get to believe what you believe, the more right you must be.

We may fear heights, confined spaces, open spaces, the ocean, fire, airplanes, trains, cars, elevators, or machines in general. Some fear lightning, thunder, storms, earthquakes or even strong wind.

We also might fear exams, classrooms or failing in general, or making mistakes, taking chances, letting go, expressing our real feelings or beliefs.

Many of us are afraid of telling the truth. We fear rejection and criticism, or not being loved or accepted. Some of us are afraid of falling "in love" or creating a love relationship because of the pain it may bring. Most fear speaking in front of large groups of people.

We fear not being loved if people really know us. We fear growing old and getting ill. We fear losing someone's love. We might subconsciously fear not having enough to eat.

We have learned to fear God, nature, and the elements. Most fear cemeteries and spirits of the dead.

Finally, there is the fear of all fears-- the fear of darkness.

**For many of us darkness offers a festive occasion for fear to play with our imagination**. A dark, unfamiliar room (or even a familiar one after seeing one of those horror films) becomes quite threatening. Darkness is the unknown and therefore is associated with danger and death. The mind can imagine anything hiding in the darkness. We are ignorant of what lies in darkness and thus identify it with danger and death.

Of all these fears the most common are of::
**1.** Rejection
**2.** Failure
**3.** Death of a loved one
**4.** Our own death
**5.** Illness and weakness
**6.** Physical and / or emotional pain
**7.** People and animals

## A QUESTIONNAIRE FOR DISCOVERING OUR FEARS

We can benefit more from our discussion concerning fear if we keep in mind our own particular fears. Take a look at the following list to see which stimuli or thoughts might sometimes cause you to feel uncomfortable. Basic fears can be expressed in an infinite number of ways according to each person's specific mental mechanisms. The various expressions of fear have different names, such as insecurity, anxiety, concern, weakness, worry, inability, confusion, fear itself, depression, denial, shock, hysteria, panic, paralysis, anger, hate, rage, aggressiveness, violence, jealously, etc.

Remember that sometimes fears can be subconscious, which means that we may not be aware that we fear something. Yet, although our basic emotion is fear, we might react with anger or crying. Even when we may not consciously fear, our inner child or subconscious may.

**Check on this list** whatever makes you feel uncomfortable and add anything else you discover.
1. Your own death
2. Sudden death by accident
3. Death of a loved one
4. Illness
5. Being paralyzed
6. Growing old
7. War
8. Earthquakes
9. Snakes, rats, mice, cockroaches
10. Dogs, cats
11. Failure at work
12. Failure in relationships
13. Failure at school,
14. Failure in life
15. Rejection from others
16. Being laughed at by others
17. Criticism

18. Loneliness
19. Financial insecurity
20. Others' aggressiveness
21. The dark
22. The unknown
23. God or his punishment
24. Losing your freedom
25. Losing your self worth
26. Conflicts with others
27. The sea, heights, fires
28. Cars, planes, boats
29. Elevators, confined spaces
30. Large gatherings of people
31. Travelling by your self
32. Losing your sanity
33. Being rejected in a love relationship
34. The opposite sex
35. Microbes and dirt
36. Others_____

Now keep in mind what you fear as you continue reading

## THE RESULTS OF FEAR

**1.** Fear and insecurity are synonymous. When we feel insecure, we naturally **become concerned and spend great portions of time**, energy, thought and money toward establishing external security. We focus on acquiring and protecting our sources of persons, food, shelter, sex, money, possessions, prestige or any other external factors which will help us feel secure.

**2.** This type of thinking and living is often, by necessity, **ego-centered** and maintained at the expense of others. We do not feel secure enough to love and give, but need to take. When such a psychology permeates our social and national psyche, it can lead to conflict and war.

**3.** When we feel insecure, we seldom have the confidence to try something new; we tend to stick to old habits and familiar ways. We fear the new and the unknown. **Our lives become stale, boring,** habitual, meaningless and without growth.
This boring, habitual kind of life leads to inertia; a waking sleep, a living death. Much time and energy are spent on satisfying our security addictions and there is little or no energy left for emotional, mental or spiritual growth.

**4.** Fear is also the **cause** and **result** of a feeling of **vulnerability** and **mistrust.**

When we feel insecure, we feel threatened by unfamiliar situations or people, thus explaining the development of racial hatred, religious intolerance, and international tensions and war. We mistrust each other and act in defensive and often offensive ways in order to protect ourselves from the imagined danger.

**5.** When we fear, **our reason is nullified** and our **imagination runs wild**, creating the worst possible scenarios, which are usually far from the actual reality.

**6.** Perception is distorted and **we misinterpret the others' intentions** and actions. When our reason is sufficiently overcome by a panicking imagination, we are moved to prejudice, narrow-mindedness, anger, hate, and in extreme cases aggression, violence, cruelty and war. Even in cases where we do not get carried to such extremes, our relationships usually suffer. **It is not possible to be open and loving when we are insecure and fearful.**

**7.** Such irrational behavior reaches its climax in the **mob mentality**. When many human beings gather into in a large group, their mentality often tends to be reduced to that of the lowest of the group's members. This can be likened to a chain, which is as strong as its weakest link. Large groups of people are not much different in their instinctual reactions from herds of animals and flocks of birds. If one panics in fear, all follow. We often hear of hundreds of persons injured and even trampled to death at soccer matches, demonstrations, and other large gatherings.

**8.** Living in fear means living with a constant underlying **tension**. There will be frequent secretions by the adrenal glands as unfamiliar persons and events will cause alarm and elicit the "fight or flight" response. This is exhausting for the nervous, immune and endocrine systems. The pituitary gland and hypothalamus are thrown out of balance, and the immune system becomes run down, setting the stage for **a variety of physical and mental illnesses**. Health and happiness flee from fear.

**9.** Perhaps the most unfortunate result of fear is that it acts like a **magnet,** literally attracting to us to the very things that we fear the most. Fearful thoughts are like magnetic waves which subconsciously interact with the world around us, attracting to us those exact situations and experiences that cause us to be frightened. If we fear thieves, we increase the possibility of encountering them. The same would be true of dogs, cockroaches, spiders, etc.

We do not, however, create the death of a loved one by fearing that. We do not create the others' reality.

Attracting what we fear is actually very useful for our growth process because it forces us to face and become familiar with the things that we fear, which is the first step towards overcoming them. Many of us have discovered by experience that our fear of an event had been out of proportion to the problem actually created by that feared event, and that our fear was entirely unnecessary.

**10.** Fear is also our greatest obstacle to moving forward in our lives. Every fear is like a closed door that **prevents us from researching, growing and developing** in many aspects of our lives.

## THE CAUSE OF FEAR

The prime and basic cause of all fear is our **ignorance** of our true nature. If we were convinced of our invulnerable eternal soul-nature, we would never experience any fear whatsoever. Because we do not, or cannot, believe this truth, we feel vulnerable, separate, isolated and susceptible to extinction or insignificance.

Because of this, we identify with the body and the complex of personality traits, which we call "I". All fears, no matter how specific they may appear to be, can be traced back to the basic fear of rejection of pain to or extinction of the "I", and the loss of any of its security attachments.

Some subordinate factors also contribute to fear:

**1. A feeling of separateness** increases our fear. When we feel close to people and nature we cannot easily fear them. Fear results from a feeling of alienation, which manifests a general feeling of suspicion of all and everything.

**2. Unfamiliarity** with people and things also causes suspicion and fear. When we come in contact with someone who dresses or behaves differently from what we are accustomed, our security base is undermined and we often react with caution and perhaps defensive or offensive behavior.

**3.** Those factors of mistrust and vulnerability function more intensely when we are **strongly attached** to certain situations, people and objects related to our security. We often play power games in order to protect our possessions, relationships or self-image when we suspect we are in danger of losing them.

**4.** When the above mentioned factors are present, they channel our **imagination** in negative ways, creating images of doom and suffering far beyond any physical reality or likelihood. Imagination in itself is not negative. It is misused by the fear complex of: alienation, unfamiliarity, vulnerability, mistrust and attachment.

**5.** Another factor is **memory** of previous negative experiences, where we have either witnessed or suffered harm, loss or death. Our subconscious mind stores memories of such unpleasant experiences from the past. We also carry within us instinctual fear complexes resulting from our evolution through the animal kingdom. Thus, we project onto the present and future what we have experienced in the past, generating a distorted perception of reality.

Also our memory is not quantitative but qualitative. It does not assign the same power to each memory. For example, we may have driven a car 3000 times without any problem, and then have one accident and fear driving after that. Thus we are allowing one experience weigh more than 3000. In the same way, we might have had hundreds of loving contacts with a person and then let one negative one cause us not to talk to this person and perceive him or her as evil.

## THE PURPOSE OF FEAR

Fear has its purpose in the animal kingdom, where the animal's low state of consciousness leaves little recourse but to fight or flee. As humans with higher consciousness, however, we have alternative methods for dealing with potential dangers. Clearer examination of the many situations which we feared as dangerous will reveal that they simply were not so. How many times have we been stricken with fear upon experiencing a sudden sound or sight, only to eventually realize we were completely wrong in our interpretation? How many times have we worried intensely about a future event, imagining the worst, only to have everything work out fine? And even if we could not, at first, accept how things worked out, everything was dissolved and forgotten in the ceaselessly flowing river of time.

Very few of our fears are based on our present reality, but rather are founded on a remembered but nonexistent past or an imagined future. Our fears seldom concern an immediate danger, such as a tiger attacking us or a bomb falling on our heads.

Even in the case that we are actually in danger at the present moment, fear will only cause us to become stiff in body and unclear in mind. We could deal with danger much more efficiently if we perceived and acted with clarity, self-confidence and courage.

## SOME WAYS IN WHICH WE CAN OVERCOME FEAR

As human beings in the process of evolution, it is imperative that we overcome the bondage of fear so we may experience the security, peace, love, courage, faith, wisdom, understanding and fulfillment which we desire, deserve and which is our destiny. Fear binds us to a lower level of consciousness with less love and happiness.

We can work on overcoming fear in the following ways:

**1.** Simply by having **contact,** in gradual but increasing doses, with that object or situation we fear, we will, by experience, learn that in reality it is harmless to us. Fear of the sea could be gradually overcome by immersing ourselves to increasing depths of the sea over a period of time. Fear of heights can be eventually conquered through exposure to gradually increasing heights.

This technique can be used with the fear of any real object or situation. The important factor to remember is to make the right dosage of contact. We should start slowly and bring ourselves just to the **threshold of fear**, just where fear begins and where we can still observe and work with the fear through breathing and relaxation.

Later, the experience can be repeated, this time increasing contact with that which is feared**, playing with our limits**, and learning to relax while in contact. We can relax by breathing slowly and deeply while reminding ourselves of the truth that we are not actually in danger, but that our mind is being controlled by some false conditioning, probably from some past experience.

At the moment we begin to feel fear, we can begin to **breathe more slowly and deeply, while concentrating on relaxing the body and mind.** We will notice that certain muscles begin to tense up. We can relax these muscles with the help of the breath and mental messages of relaxation.

We may remember **thoughts that help us to feel more secure** or bring to mind any frame of reference that allows us to feel security and protection, such as God, or various spiritual or logical truths. We can remind ourselves that our imagination is being exploited by our unfounded fears and that the danger we feel is not real.

**2.** Contact with the feared can also be made through the subconscious mind and the imagination. Through methods of relaxation, self-hypnosis, mind control, and positive projection techniques, **we can imagine having contact with the feared.** When we imagine ourselves in contact with the feared object or situation, we might find that we experience the same types of emotional and physical reactions as we do when actually in contact. We can then imagine alternative ways of feeling and reacting to that previously feared situation.

If we have feared certain animals, insects, or even certain types of people, we can imagine ourselves as feeling safe, secure and peaceful while in contact with them. We can imagine ourselves feeling safe, self-confident and courageous.

Such reprogramming of the subconscious mind will eventually alter our reactive mechanisms to life. Those who are already experienced in such techniques can do such reprogramming sessions alone, but many will need guidance in getting started.

Those who choose to can even imagine accepting (not desiring, but accepting) death. We can eventually reprogram ourselves to believe in our indestructible soul nature, thus removing all fear at the root.

**There are three approaches here.**
**a.** Some prefer to **project that nothing unpleasant will ever happen** to them. This is useful and will, to a large extent, send out positive energies to our envi-

ronment, creating a positive reality. Of course, we will all eventually die and all lose our loved ones at some point. No amount of projection will prevent this.

**b.** Others choose to **imagine all in God's light** and leave the specifics of what will happen to some higher and wiser power, such as God.

The first technique is an **active projection** of what we want to happen and the second is a **passive acceptance** of whatever is best.

**c.** A third possibility would be to **project what we prefer** in each situation and then **offer it to God**, placing it in light and completing our "prayer" with the thought, "May the Highest Good for all occur in this situation."

**3.** Memory **regression techniques** can also be used to expose to the conscious mind the hidden sources of fear locked in the subconscious mind. Individuals, who have been severely paralyzed by unreasonable fears, have been cured upon the release into the conscious mind of those hidden traumatic memories. Many case histories are available concerning those who had been affected by experiences from the past.

Through hypnotic regression and other techniques, memories of the past and birth experiences have been uncovered in hundreds of thousands of people. Such techniques are being used today by psychologists and other mental health professionals seeking to help liberate those suffering from inexplicable fears or guilt. Bringing these previously suppressed subconscious images into the light of the conscious mind helps to dissolve the problem.

**4. Relaxation and rejuvenation of the body and mind** through systematic practice of proper eating, physical exercise, breathing techniques and relaxation techniques or meditation, can release traumas, stresses and fears lodged in the body and mind.

As our whole being becomes more relaxed, tension and fear naturally subside, and inner peace and feelings of inner security develop.

Relaxation brings greater peace, and greater peace allows us to react with less fear and tension, thus allowing for more relaxation. The opposite is also true. Fear brings tension, in turn creating more fear.

When our energy level is higher, we are better equipped to deal with stress, challenges and difficulties. We feel stronger and more powerful, less fearful.

**5. A study of ourselves and the world** around will demonstrate that many beings, situations and events that we feared because of our unfamiliarity and ignorance are not actually harmful at all.

We tend to fear many types of animals, when the truth is that the animals have much more reason to fear us. We have caused harm to and killed many more of them than they have of us.

Often we fear others because **we project our own intentions onto them**. An aggressive person who wishes harm to others will also imagine the same intentions in the others. A simple peace loving person will have fewer fears.

A deeper study of our true nature will eventually guide us to the realization that our existence is not limited to our body and personality, which we are desperately trying to protect. Eventually, we will begin to perceive ourselves as eternal souls.

The more we understand, the less we perceive as unfamiliar, unknown and threatening. As our wisdom increases, we realize that we really have nothing to fear in this world.

**6. Growth groups** in which people come together to share honestly and openly for the purpose of self-improvement and self-understanding can be very helpful for those of us wanting to overcome fears and other negative emotions and habits.

**a.** We would become aware of the fact that others share many of our fears.

**b.** Talking about a fear makes it more objective and helps us to relate to it as something separate from ourselves the next time it arises.

**c.** A group gives us emotional support, and we can think of the group the next time we are faced with the fear-creating situation. In this way, we help each other grow more mentally and emotionally mature.

**d.** In addition, we get the benefit of feeling less isolated, less alienated, and more loved and understood.

**7.** We can develop separateness from our fear by objectifying the part of ourselves, which feels fear. This can done by:

**a. Drawing** how we imagine that part of our being to look,

**b. Writing** a letter to that part of our personality,

**c.** Engaging in a **written** or **verbal dialogue** with it.

In these ways, we are able to realize that we are not the part of ourselves, which is programmed to fear.

Then we can function parallel to it. Even though one part of ourselves does not want to proceed out of fear, we can **move forward in spite of those feelings.**

This is called **living parallel with the fear**. We observe it, recognize it, and accept it, but function parallel to it, doing what we actually fear to do. This is also very much like behavioral therapy in which we gradually come into contact with the aspects in life that we fear most.

The following is a letter written by a young man at the age of 25 after occasional periods of residing in a clinic for mental health. He has understood his fear well and his letter will help us also understand ours.

## A LETTER ADDRESSED TO FEAR

*"Dear Fear,*

*"I think I know quite a lot about you; with God's help, I more or less came to understand how you were born and how later you became so huge that you broke up my existence. The seed that bore you may have come from previous lives, but you fell on fertile ground, found the right conditions and grew so as to threaten everything inside of me. The ambience within the family, traumatic experiences, and perhaps things still unknown to me and yet to come, all served as food for you.*

*"Now that you have gone into orbit and are so low in the sky that soon you will sink, I can see you as a huge piranha with innumerable black tentacles, an entity close to the form of death.*

*I say that you are low in the sky because you still hold me captive, a prisoner. I know you originally came to protect me, but you hugged me dangerously tight, distorted my ideas, engendered violence and aggression, overfed my ego and almost destroyed me. You grew metastasis in every part of my being to such a degree that at the sound of your name alone I became terrified. I am afraid even when you are not there. In the end, like a ghost, you began to haunt me always and everywhere. In this ceaseless running you have imposed upon me, I have been running down many evil and dangerous roads.*

*"There is no doubt that if it weren't for you, I would not be escaping to find new horizons. Although I have tasted death because of you and am still in pain, I thank you for chasing me. On the dark paths I had taken, I suddenly saw in the sky a star, like a flickering candle, which began to guide me and determine my life. As time goes by, slowly but steadily, and this star shines more brightly and make my progress surer, I want you to understand that this light is divine and will gradually illuminate every nook and cranny of my being, the places where you are now.*

*"So I thank you for bringing me so far to protect me. Now I don't need you anymore. Go away. My real self is beginning to grow. That which fears nothing is strong and serene.*

*"As for you, the dwellings you find and the reality in which you flourish are all nothing but delusion.*

*"I thank God that, with His help, I dare to face you. With the ever- increasing light I shall beam onto you, you will begin to disappear, seeking another dark place in the shadows.*

*"I am already certain that you are low in the sky and someday will no longer exist. "*

This letter teaches some important points about fear and coming to terms with it.

**a.** The writer speaks of coming to understand **how** this fear was born in his mind. In this way, he objectifies it and can then perceive it as something separate from himself, which was programmed into him at some particular moment.

**b.** He gives it a **form**, a "huge piranha." This also facilitates objectifying and distancing it.

**c.** He understands that at first the **fear was a protective mechanism**, but it then got out of control.

**d.** He realizes now that he **does not need it** for protection, that he can find healthier forms of protection.

**e.** He also realizes he can heal this part of himself **by sending love and light**, for fear can exist only in darkness, ignorance and a lack of love.

**8. Faith in God** can be a great help in confronting any danger, real or imaginary. When we believe in a benign Divine Being whose presence and power permeates the universe, we feel protected. When we believe all that happens is in some way controlled or allowed by this benign and loving being, then we have faith that even seemingly accidental and unjust events have some higher purpose, and thus a higher justice, even when we are not able to understand it.

This is a matter of faith, which means we believe in a power or higher law that we cannot perceive or prove exists. If we could see the divine or its laws, we would call this knowledge instead of faith.

Faith and knowledge are the ultimate solutions to fear. No one can guarantee that something what we fear will not happen. It is probably very **unlikely**, but the possibility is always there.

Thus, the ultimate solution to fear is positive thinking:

**a.** A belief that **all will turn out well.**

**b.** But at the same time, we know that whatever happens will be the **best possible solution** for our growth process.

**c.** And that **we do have the power** to handle it.

The situations we fear offer us an opportunity to grow stronger and more self-confident. Faith in a Divine Justice allows us to enter openly into every situation knowing that we will encounter only what serves our own evolutionary process, whether it be pleasant or unpleasant.

Some of us who are ridden with unreasonable fears may be suffering from **subconscious guilt.** Often our fear is based on the belief that we will be punished in some way for "sins." We have been programmed to believe that we are not pure or good, and that because of this, we have lost divine protection and that we might be punished. Thus, guilt leads to fear. On the other hand, **recognizing our inner divine nature and our innate oneness with the universe will allow us to experience inner security.**

**9.** By practicing spiritual knowledge or **discrimination between our Selves and our minds,** we can observe fear functioning on its own. The idea here is that since we can observe the mind and comment on its activity, obviously, we cannot be the mind, but rather some higher entity that is observing it.

Thus, we can see that it is not our true Self that is expressing fear, but the mind, which is only an organ or instrument. We can watch the mind, the imagination and the whole passing drama of our lives as a witness.

We can reaffirm,

*"I am not this body.*
*I am not this mind.*
*I am not this fear.*
*I am the witness of all this."*

Those who believe so can add,

*"I am a soul in union with all other souls and with God."*

When we begin to feel the truth of these statements, we no longer fear others, because **there are no others.** We realize our oneness with all. We feel a loving union and thus security with all.

The fear created by the cut umbilical cord and the feeling of separateness is removed, because a **spiritual umbilical cord** has been reestablished to all of Creation.

**10.** The development of **pure love** is also an ultimate solution for fear. We cannot fear what we love. Love is based on unity and fear on alienation - separateness.

St. John the Evangelist wrote in one of his letters, **"There is no fear in love; perfect love drives out all fear. So then, love has not been made perfect in anyone who is afraid..."**

Swami Sarvananda agrees that, **"The basis of fear is the feeling of otherness. Love tends to union; separateness tends to fear".**

Love and understanding walk together hand in hand. We love when we understand others, and we understand when we love. When we are filled with love for all, we will not feel isolated and therefore intimidated by our environment. Many children and young animals feel this loving union with their environment, having not yet learned fearful reactions. A dog, cat, snake and lion all growing up together from infancy would feel no threat from, or fear of, each other.

This reminds me of a **true story** told to me by a friend. He was taking a hike in the mountains of Colorado and began repeating a prayer as he walked. The more he repeated the prayer, the happier and more in love he was with all he saw around him. He began running down the path in ecstasy feeling unity with all around him. As he turned a bend in the path, he found himself face to face with a mountain lion only two meters away. He looked into the lion's eyes and said with love, "Do not be afraid, I will not harm you."

**He could not feel fear in his state of love and unity.**

The lion turned and walked off.

Technique no. 8

# EMOTIONAL RELEASE

### Why this is important

Just as we clean our home, we need from time to time to clean out our "emotional closet" where we accumulate various emotions such as hurt, injustice, anger, guilt, bitterness and perhaps even positive emotions such as love, joy and creativity.

If we do not allow for this emotional catharsis occasionally, we will be much more vulnerable to negative emotions and psychosomatic illnesses.
After catharsis our energy flows, our heart is more open and our mind clearer.

### A simple technique for releasing emotions
### and also gaining clarity about them is:

Emotional release can be performed at any time we can be alone or with a person familiar with this process.

**Note:** This technique should not be practiced alone by those with a history of emotional imbalance or those who are taking medicines for their mental health.
**1.** We can sit or lie down, go inward and feel where our emotions are stored in our bodies. We can locate them by doing a **body scan** and noticing the areas which exhibit various **energy phenomena** such as: tension, pain, heat, cold, numbness, weakness, but mainly the feeling of energy or pain moving in that area.
**2.** We then **accept these emotions** and the **phenomena** that they create on the physical and energy levels.
**3.** We allow those phenomena and the emotions **to expand and express themselves** in various ways as they flow out. We might yawn, shake, cry, and shout or, in some cases, where anger is present, it may be useful to hit a pillow. We continue in this way until we feel that we have released whatever could naturally flow out in this session.
**4.** We can complete the exercise with about **20 minutes of relaxation** and connect with peaceful thoughts, truths, affirmations and emotions.

### Note:

It would best to have a guide for the first few times.

# *THE INTIMIDATOR*

Elias is an **Intimidator**. He seeks to control others by making them fear him. He obstructs them from asking anything of him or from controlling him, by making them afraid to approach. He does this by shouting, intimidating, accusing, threatening and occasionally even resorting to physical violence. He uses other people's fear and self doubt to control them.

For him the others are always wrong and, if they do not start "shaping up", he has every right to punish them. He is simultaneously the police, judge, jury and execution squad. Another benefit he gains from this role is that he never has to look at himself or change anything about himself, because "he is perfect" and the others are all wrong.

He is safe from them, but he is lonely and unhappy. He plays the strong one without needs, but the truth is that he is very afraid and needs love and acceptance. He is in reality a fearful child playing the role of the dangerous and fearsome intimidator. He is imprisoned in a defensive role that limits his freedom to be himself and is extremely unpleasant for others.

What can Elias do to get free from this way of communicating? How can he relax and open his heart? How can others deal with him?

**Some beliefs that might cause Elias to behave in this way are:**

**1.** I am in danger of not getting what I want.

**2.** I am in danger of not being in control of everyone, and if so, something horrible could happen. Something could go wrong.

**3.** If I am not in control and do not command everyone's respect even through fear, then I am not worthy.

**4.** I am in danger if others do not obey me or do not do what I say.

**5.** The only way to get people to do what I want is by making them fear me.

**6.** I am easily hurt and this is the only way I can protect myself.

**7.** The others want to control me and get things from me and this is the only way I can protect myself.

**8.** As a man I must be the king of my house and all must obey me. If they do not then I am a failure.

**9.** I must not let anyone see my weakness or fear.

**Some beliefs that could liberate him from this mode of functioning are:**

**1.** I am safe and secure in every situation.

**2.** My self worth is not in anyway dependent on how others behave towards me.

**3.** I can get what I need from people, by expressing my needs clearly and effectively.

**4.** We can find peaceful solutions to our needs or value conflicts.

**5.** I prefer people to cooperate with me out of love rather than fear.

**6.** I would not like others to intimidate or threaten me.

**7.** I trust in God's plan for me and my loved ones.

**8.** The others cannot learn through my experience, but only through their own.

**9.** Everyone deserves my respect.

**Beliefs that those around him can cultivate in order to be able to deal with him are:**

**1.** I am safe and secure in every situation.

**2.** Life gives me exactly what I need at every moment so that I can learn my next lesson in my growth process.

**3.** This person is my teacher which life has placed before me.

**4.** He is unhappy and afraid; or else he would not be acting in this way.

**5.** Behind his angry and threatening appearance hides a fearful and hurt child.

**6.** I deserve love and respect just as I am.

### A possible communication
with Elias by one of his close loved ones might be the following:

**"I need to discuss something with you**. You know, there are times when I am afraid of you. When you raise your voice and threaten me, you stimulate old fears from my childhood years. When that happens I retreat from confrontation with you, suppressing my needs and sometimes my values. When this happens I lose my self-respect, and feel abused and also anger towards you. My heart closes and my love for you diminishes. There are even times when I think of revenge.

"With the way you act, you may get what you want from me at that moment, but you lose my love and respect. I have decided to try to overcome my fears and be more honest with you. I am going to try to express my needs and values even when you shout or intimidate me. I would like to ask for your help with this effort.

**"I am very interested in helping you fulfill your needs.** I believe that we can both get what we want together. I would like to ask you to express your needs without threatening me. Simply tell me what you need from me. I, in response, will also express my needs to you. I believe we can find solutions without my fearing you and retreating when you threaten me. "How do you feel about this idea?"

# CHAPTER 9

# UNDERSTANDING EMOTIONS

In order to create the healthy, happy and harmonious reality we all desire, we will need to create **emotional harmony**.

This process can be divided into six basic steps:

1. **Recognize** our emotions.

2. **Accept** them as they are.

3. **Release** them.

4. **Understand** how they are created.

5. **Transform** them through understanding and create more positive ones.

6. **Transcend** them and our personality.

Here we will present a short profile of some of the basic emotions. We have developed specific questionnaires for understanding each one. As this book would have become prohibitively large if we included them here, those who are seriously seeking to understand themselves can download these questionnaires from our web site at **www.HolisticHarmony.com**. Answering these questions will help you discover how those emotions are created and how you might transform them.

## ANXIETY AND WORRY

**Anxiety** and worry, although obviously forms of fear, have become so common that it is worth looking at them separately. Anxiety often concerns the factors of **time** and **results**. We are anxious because we fear that we will not have enough time to complete all that we have planned, or that the result will not be successful, perfect or acceptable to the others.

We **worry** often for the same reasons, but also when we fear something may not turn out as we hope. That "something" may concern ourselves, our children, or our parents or spouse, which of course, ultimately, through our attachment to these people, has to do with ourselves.

We learn to worry as children, and this becomes a habit causing us to search for issues to be anxious or worrisome about, even when there is nothing really important enough to merit such a concern. We may wonder at times why our mind thinks so much about a particular matter, creating anxiety and worry, when in reality that matter is not so important to us.

For this reason, we would do well to employ a program of exercises, breathing techniques, deep relaxation with positive projection, perhaps meditation, and of course, a healthy diet and creative expression. These activities will help reorganize our energy patterns, freeing us from the hold of negative thoughts.

**Positive antidotes** to anxiety and worry could be:

**1. Faith** in divine wisdom and justice; that all will occur as is necessary and beneficial for our growth process.

**2. Confidence** in our ability to deal with whatever life brings us.

**3.** Realizing that we are **worthy of love** and acceptance as we are.

**4.** Living in and enjoying the **present moment.**

### HURT - BITTERNESS - INJUSTICE - ABUSED - PAIN

When we cannot get what we want or need, or what we feel we have the right to have, we feel pain, hurt, bitter, abused or injustice. We have not received the behavior we expected or believed we deserved. We also feel pain when we lose someone or something important to us.

The beliefs behind these feelings are that "we need to have that which we are not getting in order to be safe or happy." We have associated our security, satisfaction, self worth or freedom with something that we are not getting from persons, society, God, or life as a whole.

We feel hurt because we have not received the respect, love, affection, loyalty, truth, kindness and justice that we were expecting.

**Positive alternatives** to hurt, bitterness and feelings of injustice could be:

**1. Faith** in divine wisdom and justice;

**a.** That all, which has occurred, was allowed by God because it serves our evolutionary process;

**b.** That all that has happened or is happening is the result of natural and just laws of the universe.

**2.** Accepting that we are the **sole creators of our reality.**

**3. Forgiving** and forgetting the past.

## DISAPPOINTMENT - DISILLUSIONMENT - DISCOURAGEMENT

A wise teacher once said, " No appointments, no disappointments."

These emotions occur when we have created expectations concerning what we will receive from others, God and life. We might also feel such emotions concerning our own abilities or efforts when we are unable to achieve the goals we desire. We feel this way when things do not happen the way we expected, or more often, when others are not who we expected them to be. We develop expectations, and then feel cheated when we they are not fulfilled.

Also, when we do not achieve the results we desire, we feel disappointed and disillusioned in ourselves, others or God. When we succumb to such feelings, **we often give up making any further effort**, which in turn obstructs our growth.

**Positive alternatives** to disappointment and disillusionment could be:

**1.** An understanding that we are all in a **process of evolution** and that no one is perfect.

**2. Faith** in the flow of life.

**3. Confidence** that with patience, practice and perseverance, we can manifest the changes we seek.

**4.** A **larger sense of time**, in which we realize that, any efforts made for less than fifty years, are actually **small** in relationship to the immensity of our being.

## DEPRESSION

Depression is a state in which, as with the previous emotions, we are not getting what we want from life. Here we also feel unable to do anything about it. It is a combination of being **dissatisfied** with ourselves and/ or others, combined with feeling totally **powerless** to do anything about it.

There may also be a feeling that **nothing is important enough** to make an effort to achieve or that nothing will give us joy or satisfaction. All is meaningless.

We gradually give up more and more activities and responsibilities because we feel nothing is important. Disappointment, disillusionment and depression are sometimes **preparatory states** for change. Being dissatisfied with what exists is often the start of the conscious growth process and serves as a motivation for major changes. Many people have been led to a spiritual path through these emotions.

**Positive antidotes** to depression could be:

**1. Acceptance** of one's life and self as are.

**2. Confidence** that we can manifest the internal and external changes we desire.

**3.** Realization that our **lives have meaning** and purpose.

**4.** Seeking to be if **service and help to others.**

## JEALOUSY - ENVY

These two emotions are born from our lack of acceptance **of who we are** and **what we have**. When we do not accept ourselves, as we are, we envy others for traits or achievements that we wish we possessed. We probably believe we will be more respected and admired or considered more successful if we had those traits. On the spiritual path, we might envy the other for his ability to meditate, serve, fast, etc.

When we cannot accept what we have or do not have, we feel envious towards those who have it or perhaps are taking it from us (such as love or attention from our parents, spouse, children or friends).

Our most intense jealousy has to do with being given exclusivity of an important person's love and attention, and in the case of a spouse, sexual contact.

As children, jealousy is one of the major emotions we experience when a new-born sibling enters the family and our exclusivity, or percentage of attention, is lost or diminished. We might also feel anger at this other being who now receives what we had been getting and still desperately want. The same happens when we fear that our spouse may be interested in someone else.

We are more vulnerable when we have identified our survival, security, satisfaction and self worth with another person's attention. The fear that we may not be safe or worthy without them creates what we call jealousy.

**Positive alternatives** to jealousy and envy could be:

**1. Acceptance** of one's life and self as are.

**2.** Recognition of **our inner self worth.**

**3. Acknowledgement of** all that we actually do have.

**4. Faith** that we each create our reality and that we have exactly what we need for our next step in our evolutionary process.

**5. Loving others** and feeling happy for their successes.

## LONELINESS

Loneliness, like fear, is a deeply ingrained emotion that has to do with existence itself. Both emotions are based on the illusion of our separateness and identification with the body and ego.

For those of us who have not yet become aware of an inner source of security, satisfaction, self worth, love and purpose, facing loneliness is similar to facing death. Without a relationship with ourselves or with the divine, there is no life, no source, no happiness, no security, no purpose for living without others.

**We must distinguish between being alone** and **feeling lonely**. One can be surrounded by hundreds of friends, family and admirers and still feel lonely. Another can be alone on a mountaintop for years and never feel lonely. Feeling lonely means **not feeling connected** to others, to God, to nature or to life. We may be surrounded day and night by persons to whom we feel no connection, or be alone in a cave and feel connected to God and all of creation.

When analyzing the causes of loneliness, we should look specifically for feelings of **shame** and **pride**. These opposite emotions tend to separate us. When we feel shame, guilt or self-doubt, we cannot believe that others love us or want to be with us. Even when they do love us, we cannot feel their love.

When we are proud, we cannot keep company with" just anyone," nor can we be the ones who will express our need to be with others. We are too proud and want the others to ask us for our company.

Also susceptible to such thinking and loneliness are those of us who have been programmed to believe **that we must be perfect, strong** and never ask for or be in need.

**Positive antidotes** to loneliness could be:
**1.** Taking an **active interest** in others' needs or making an effort to serve others
**2. Opening** to others with love.
**3. Ceasing the comparisons of** ourselves with others.
**4.** Developing a **relationship with God.**
**5.** Finding a **meaning in life.**

### SELF DOUBT, SHAME, GUILT, SELF REJECTION, UNWORTHINESS, REJECTION, HUMILIATION

These various forms of self-doubt are, together with fear, the most basic of all emotions and the causes of most other emotions. They are all based on the belief that we are not good and lovable except under certain conditions. We have all been programmed with our individual conditions, which most likely concern two basic circumstances:

**1.** When our actions are not in alignment with our **conscience**.

**2.** When we do not fulfill, in our opinion, certain **social conditions** concerning who is worthy of love, acceptance and respect, i.e. appearance, wealth, intelligence, ability, professional success, physical strength, sexual attraction, acceptance by others etc.

Deeper research shows that behaviors, which are out of harmony with our conscience, are often created by fears that result from our social programming.

For example, we lie because we fear we will lose people's respect if we tell the truth.

We will dedicate an entire chapter to this subject.

## ANGER - HATE - RAGE

Rage is an advanced form of anger, just as panic is to fear, a state in which we are even less in control of our words and behavior. Hate is a condition in which we think very badly of someone, avoid contact with him, and probably wish the worst for him, perhaps even hoping he might experience a tragedy. All three of these emotions, which from here on in we will simply call "anger", are **secondary emotions** in the sense that they arise from other emotions, such as hurt, fear, guilt, injustice, disappointment, etc.

In general we are controlled by two thought-forms here:

**1. We must have something** that the other is obstructing us from having. This could be anything from sleep, food and shelter, to our peace of mind, our spouse or other persons to whom we are attached.

2. We believe this person toward whom we feel this anger **is responsible for our reality**. We believe that if it were not for him or her, we would not be unhappy. He or she is "responsible" for our pain and unhappiness.

Anger can also be a **starting point for major change** for an individual, or even an entire society. Anger can be a source of energy and dedication toward transforming the negative and unjust circumstances around us.

Many of us first need to learn to feel, accept and express our anger before we can regain our self-esteem and empowerment. (We need not vent our anger toward others. We can learn nonviolent ways to express this energy.)

Also, there are some cases in which we may need to express anger in order to get a result for which we are responsible. This can be done, however, without demeaning or hurting the other.

Hate, on the other hand, which is based on weakness, has few redeeming qualities. A strong person seldom hates.

Thus, we are not interested in suppressing our anger, but rather in recognizing it, accepting it, expressing it in non harmful ways, understanding it and focussing its energy in positive directions toward self empowerment and social change.

Here is a brief list of some **common reasons we might feel anger** towards someone: (You may want to check those which tend to bother you.)

**1.** When others do not agree with us.
**2.** When they do not understand us.

**3.** When they obstruct us from satisfying our needs. (A need could be psychological, such as the need for acceptance, respect or self-esteem)

**4.** When they do not respect us.

**5.** When they think they are superior.

**6.** When they try to control or suppress us.

**7.** When they criticize us.

**8.** When they tell lies or gossip about us.

**9.** When they harm us or someone close to us.

**10.** When they have evil intentions or ulterior motives.

**11.** When they are negative, complaining, whining, criticizing etc.

**12.** When they think they know it all.

**13.** When they give us advice we have not asked for.

**14.** When they play the role of the victim, the "poor me," and want attention.

**15.** When they do not take care of themselves or carry their share of the load.

**16.** When they make mistakes

**17.** When they do not keep their promises or appointments.

**18.** When they are weak and dependent.

**19.** When they act in an egotistical and selfish way, disregarding our or others' needs

**20.** When they use us or others.

**21.** When they are cold and insensitive.

**22.** When they are not responsible to their word or responsibilities

**23.** When they are lazy.

**24.** When they ignore our needs.

**25.** When they reject us.

**Other** reasons_____

It would be interesting to go through the same list replacing the word "they" with the word "I," making the logical changes in the rest of the phrase, so as to determine when we get **angry with ourselves**. This exercise may also reveal that some of the anger we feel toward others is actually a projection of anger that we feel toward ourselves. If we could understand and accept ourselves in those situations, we might also understand and accept others.

Positive alternatives to anger or hate could be:

**1. Understanding** others' weaknesses and negative traits.

**2. Having faith** that nothing happens by chance.

**3.** Realizing that **we are the sole creators** of our reality.

**4.** Directing our **energy toward changing** or correcting that which makes us angry.

**5. Recognizing and understanding** our own weaknesses and negative traits.

**6. Forgiving and loving** others as they are.

## REJECTING OTHERS,
## CRITICIZING, CONDEMNING, BLAMING

Rejecting or criticizing others is not actually an emotion, but rather a **reaction or behavior** caused by our emotions and beliefs. Being that they occupy a considerable place in our lives, both in the form of our criticism toward others and as the criticism we receive, it will be useful to examine this emotional reaction.

In general, we criticize, blame or reject others when they behave in ways that bother us or prevent us from fulfilling our needs.

Another reason we reject others is that because we believe that, in that way, we establish our own self worth in relationship to them. Still another reason is that by criticizing and finding fault in others, we can place the blame for our problems and our reality directly upon them. They are to blame and we do not need to look at what we might need to learn in a situation where we are not satisfied with what we are creating in our lives.

We might criticize others because they do things we do not allow ourselves to do, and thus we feel a type of injustice because we are trying so hard to be "good" or "correct" and the others are not. Thus, they are wrong.

We also often criticize whatever we do not understand, whatever we fear or whatever is different.

As Christ said, "Judge not, that you be not judged." " You will be judged by the measure with which you judge." "Let he who has not sinned, throw the first stone." "Look not at the sliver in the others eye, but the log in your own."

In other words, do not judge or criticize.

The following list may help some of us discover what we tend to criticize in others so we can then discover why we feel the need to criticize.

**Behaviors which we tend to criticize or reject in others or perhaps in ourselves:**

If we tend to be critical in any of these situations, we will want to ask ourselves what we believe causes us to do so:

**1.** For their egotistical behavior
**2.** For their immorality
**3.** For not being consistent with their word
**4.** For being late for appointments
**5.** For trying to control us or others
**6.** For telling lies
**7.** For being false or two faced
**8.** For wanting to be the exception to the rules
**9.** For being weak
**10.** For acting as if they are superior
**11.** For thinking they are very important
**12.** For not living by the rules

13. For being aloof.
14. For not acknowledging our presence
15. For rejecting us
16. For not being correct
17. For wanting to project themselves
18. For seeking affirmation through what they do
19. For being hypocrites
20. For not working conscientiously
21. For not keeping our agreements
22. For ignoring our needs or the needs of others
23. For being inconsiderate
24. For hurting or harming us or others
25. For gossiping about us or others
26. For the way they dress
27. For the way they express themselves
28. For the way they work
29. For the following behavior _____
30. Because they do not _____
31. Because in the past they _____
32. Other reasons _____

Now we can look through the same list and change the word "they" to "I" and discover which behaviors we reject in ourselves. In this way, we might search for answers to three questions.

**1.** Whether we tend to reject ourselves for the same behaviors and thus perhaps our rejecting the other is a projection of our self-rejection?
**2.** Whether we allow ourselves the freedom to do some things for which we reject others, and thus have a double standard?
**3.** Whether we reject in our selves aspects which we accept in others and why?

**Positive antidotes** to rejection and criticism could be:

**1. Understanding** and **accepting** others as they are.
**2.** Remembering that we are all in a **state of evolution** and that our fears and weaknesses control us.
**3. Loving** others and ourselves unconditionally.
**4.** Remembering that we **would not like others** to criticize or reject us.
Now that we have discovered the kinds of behaviors that annoy us, we can look at the possible reasons why they affect us this way. The idea here is that, since life is a process of spiritual evolution and each event and situation is a lesson in that process, each behavior, which bothers us or causes us to criticize, contains within it something we can learn.

# THE PSYCHOLOGY OF GRATITUDE

We have spoken here primarily about negative unpleasant emotions. What about positive ones? There is not much benefit from analyzing why we feel happy, as such an analysis will likely reveal that our sources of happiness are based on external factors which could easily change. We might also discover that we are dependent on external sources for our feelings of security, self worth and happiness.

**Faith** and **love** are the basis for positive feelings. We will discuss the various aspects of love and unity in a future chapter. Right now, however, I would like to briefly address one positive emotion; **gratitude**.

We have so much to be grateful for and yet gratitude is a rarely felt emotion. This is especially true if we compare our lives with eighty percent of those sharing the planet with us. We would all benefit by realizing how blessed our lives are. Sharing such positive feelings of appreciation, gratitude and joy also enriches and beautifies our environment and the lives of those around us.

A simple technique is to spend a few minutes each **day thinking of or even listing** those aspects of our lives for which we could be grateful. Even the most taken for granted simplicities of life, such as running water, a warm home, friends and family, can be sources of joy when seen through such eyes.

Some have even developed the ability to feel grateful for their unpleasant experiences and injustices because they often offer us the opportunity to develop inner strength and deep insight into ourselves and life itself.

When we worry about what we do not have or what we have lost, we neglect and thus, lose all those wonderful things we do have. Ken Keyes calls this **"The mosquito effect"**.

If we manage to eliminate nine out of ten mosquitoes in a room, we will still be annoyed by the remaining one. If we have ten problems and solve nine of them, rather than being grateful for the nine solutions, we obsess-over the remaining problem. If we own ten objects and lose one of them, rather than feel grateful for and enjoying the remaining nine, we will experience the pain of the loss of that one.

Where would you prefer to place your focus; on what you have or what you do not have? Would you prefer to see the glass as half empty or half full? Would you prefer to perceive the problem in every opportunity or the **opportunity in every problem?**

## GENERAL APPROACH FOR ALL EMOTIONS
### (Refer to this chart when working with emotions)

In addition to the various specific questions for each specific emotion offered on our web site, there are some universally beneficial techniques that can be employed. These techniques are described in more detail in the previous chapter on fear. They very briefly are:

**1.** Learning to **accept our emotions** as they are.

**2. Objectifying an emotion** by:
**a.** Writing a letter to it,    **b.** Dialoguing with it,
**c.** Drawing it,                **d.** Speaking to it,
**e.** Dancing it.
The same can be done by writing to or dialoguing with the **part of us** that feels that emotion, rather than writing to the emotion itself. There is a slight difference. Try it.

**3. Keeping up a high level of energy** through proper diet, exercise, breathing, relaxation, meditation, etc.

**4. Positive projection** regarding those matters which concern us.

**5. Making a more dynamic program for action** towards changing our external situation so that it is more like we would like it to be.

**6. Engaging in prayer, faith in God**, and belief in divine justice and in our own selves as immortal beings.

**7. Enjoying perfect spiritual love** without attachment.

The following will require an **experienced guide:**

**8. Discussion Groups** in which we share our thoughts with others and listen to theirs as we proceed together to free ourselves.

**9. Transforming the form of the emotion** in the subconscious.

**10. Transformation regressions** to past experiences, reliving past events with the knowledge of the present.

**11. Psychodrama** and reverse psychodrama with those who are related in some way to those emotions. **12. Dialoguing** with "personas" or parts of us that have these emotions.
. We suggest that you photocopy the above list and have it on you so that when you are controlled by a negative emotion you can refer to it for a technique to employ.

We remind you that you can find specific questionnaires designed to aid you in discovering the roots of each emotion at our web site
**www.HolisticHarmony.com.**

Technique no. 9

# DEALING WITH CRITICISM
# AND DIFFERENCE IN OPINION

## Why this is important

We often become emotionally disturbed during a disagreement, or an argument, or when someone criticizes us or disagrees with us. In such cases our personality usually feels hurt, demeaned and in danger.

When we feel this way, we destroy our own happiness, clarity and health and often behave in ways which we later regret.

## A simple technique for gaining clarity is to:

**1.** Remember that concerning criticism, there are two possibilities:

   **a.** The **other person might be correct** in his or her observations and criticism. In this case we would benefit by admitting it and making the proper adjustment in our behavior. We have everything to gain by listening and evolving through others' comments.

What prevents us is the belief that we are not lovable if we are not perfect. Thus, we do not want to see or admit our faults. When we realize that **we are worthy of love and respect even when we are not perfect or right,** then we will be able to look at our faults.

   **b.** The other person might be incorrect, in which case it **is his or her projection**, and we need not be affected by these misconceptions or projections. We have in this case the lesson of loving ourselves and also the others even when they perceive us in subjective and negative ways.

**2.** One solution would be **simply not to react one way or the other at first**, but to **reflect** upon what has been said for some time so as to evaluate whether or not it is true. We can establish a space in our minds where we can store such questions about our personality structure or actions so as to observe objectively for ourselves if they are true. If they are not, then we simply continue on in the way we were.

We need not feel hurt, angry, defend ourselves, prove ourselves, or attack. When we feel inner security and self worth we do not need to react in these ways.

**3.** We can simply thank the other for this feedback and tell him or her that **we will think about this observation** and will gradually come to our conclusions, and if necessary, make changes.

## Note:

A "thank you" is enough.

*Life Story no. 10*

# THE INTERROGATOR

Katherine plays the role of the interrogator. She would have made a good lawyer. She controls others by playing with their need for her approval. She does this by criticizing, doubting, giving advice and, in general, creating doubt about the others' ability or correctness in what they are doing. She is always ready to criticize how they have done something, or question why they have done it in a particular way. She gets their attention and can control them by making them answer to her questions about what they are doing.

She tends to give advice even when unsolicited and needs to express her opinion concerning whatever may be being discussed. She feels that she needs to be more knowledgeable than others are.

She is seldom able to see herself or her own faults. This would be too painful for her. Her over critical nature would make it unbearable for her to perceive her own faults. She learned as a child that mistakes are unacceptable.

Her questions are penetrating and often accusations in disguise. She binds people into long discussions in which they attempt to defend their position or actions, to no avail.

In reality, Katherine has many doubts about herself and needs to discover others' mistakes in order to feel her own self worth. For her, someone must be right and someone else wrong. There is no possibility of both being right or both being wrong. She needs to prove that she is right and the other is wrong. When she manages to do this, she feels energized, and feels her self worth.

This is, of course, very frustrating for those who live and work with her. Her constant criticism and accusation hurt them. They would like to be accepted, loved and approved of.

What can Katherine and those around her do?

**Some beliefs that might cause Katherine to behave in this way are:**

**1.** Whoever knows more is more worthy and more respected.

**2.** Whoever is right is worthier than the other is.

**3.** I know better than the others do.

**4.** I am not sure about my self worth and need to prove it in relationship to others.

**5.** The only way in which I can protect myself and my self worth is by finding faults in others.

**6.** Everyone is required to function according to my beliefs.

**7.** There can be only one right answer to a question and only one right way to do something.

**8.** Either I am right or they are. I must prove that I am.

**9.** I am the judge and I decide who is correct and who is not.

**Some beliefs that might help Katherine free herself from this role are:**

**1.** I accept and love myself exactly as I am.

**2.** I accept and love others exactly as they are.

**3.** Our self worth is not a matter of who knows more, or who is right. All deserve to be loved and respected as they are.

**4.** I respect other peoples' need to grow and function in their own unique ways.

**5.** I respect each being's inner wisdom.

**6.** I would rather be loved than be right.

**7.** I would not like others to criticize and correct me continuously.

**8.** Being right does not attract love, but love does.

**Those near to her could benefit from the following beliefs:**

**1.** My self worth is independent of what others think.

**2.** My self worth is independent of the results of my efforts.

**3.** She doubts herself and is simply trying to find her self worth or get my attention.

**4.** I give her attention in positive ways so that she does not need to resort to interrogating.

**5.** We can love each other even when we do not agree.

**6.** I deserve love and acceptance exactly as I am.

**7.** I am safe and secure even when others do not agree with me.

**8.** I am safe and secure even when I make a mistake.

**9.** I am not perfect but I deserve to be loved and respected exactly as I am.

**10.** Being right does not attract love, but love does.

**11.** Life gives me exactly what I need at every moment so that I can learn my next lesson in my growth process.

## One of those near to her might try
## the following communication.

**"Dear, I would like to discuss with you a problem which I have with our communication.** I feel myself continuously to be in the position of answering your questions and doubts about what I am doing. I feel that you are frequently correcting and accusing me. This puts me on the defensive and sometimes I get into the role of the victim and at other times I become an intimidator, or do the same to you and become your interrogator.

"This way of communicating saddens me. I believe that we can communicate much more honestly and harmoniously. For this reason, I am going to try to accept myself even when you have doubts and criticize. I am going to stop answering your questions and apologizing to your accusations. I am going to try to be happy even when you are not satisfied with me and when you criticize or accuse me.

"Please do not misunderstand this. I love you and want you to be happy and want us to be happy together, but we cannot be happy this way, with your playing the lawyer and my playing the guilty one. I cannot lose my self-respect any more in this game.

"I want you to know that I love you even when I do not try to get you to agree with what I do.

"I am very interested in knowing how do you feel about this?"

# CHAPTER 10

# THE TWELVE PATHWAYS
# TO HIGHER CONSCIOUSNESS

## Part 1

### ADDICTIONS - THE CAUSE OF SUFFERING

In previous chapters, we have identified the attachments, addictions, fears and beliefs that prevent us from creating health, happiness and peace of mind. Here we shall examine twelve affirmations, truths or beliefs that will help us liberate ourselves from those obstacles.

Happiness and peace are the birth right of every human being. We can learn how to be happy just as we can learn to succeed at any task in life. Whether we find happiness or peace of mind depends on **how we react** to life situations. How we react depends on our conditioning and programming, on the way we have learned to respond subconsciously to various life situations.

The concepts put forth in this chapter are closely aligned with those expressed by Ken Keyes Jr. in his book **Handbook to Higher Consciousness.** Mr. Keyes has brilliantly combined the wisdom of the ancient universal truths with modern psychological thought, creating a system of human development and spiritual growth from which all can benefit. It is worth mentioning that Mr. Keyes has both arms and feet paralyzed and yet has written many books and given numerous lectures throughout the world on **how to be happy**.

### PREPARING TO WORK WITH
### THE TWELVE PATHWAYS.

The 12 pathways are concepts that will help us transform our addictions into preferences and manifest the peace, love and happiness that we are seeking. These pathways are based on three basic premises, which we have mentioned in an earlier chapter, but are worth repeating.

**1. I create my reality through the way I think, act, feel and believe.** No one else is to blame for how I feel.

**2. I have the power and the right to change my conditioning**, to feel and act differently than I do now, if I wish to.

**3. I am a spiritual being in the process of evolution who is temporarily occupying this body and mind**. I exist beyond the limitations of this body and personality.

On the surface, we may feel we can accept such concepts. Upon a deeper study of our motives and emotions, however, we will realize that our emotional life is seldom in alignment with these truths. We may comprehend them intellectually, but our actions and thoughts are seldom based on them.

In this system of growth, the emphasis is **not** on changing external factors. There is no need to run away from family, profession or responsibilities, or relinquish any wealth or possessions. We need simply **to become internally free from addictions.**
Neither is it necessary to have a teacher, because **life** itself becomes our teacher by showing us, through various pleasant and unpleasant situations, where we are addicted and how we continue to cling.
In the beginning, it may not be easy to see the truth concerning which addictions are causing our suffering. A growth-group dedicated to mutual self-discovery can be very helpful. For most, this process of psychological discovery becomes one of spiritual seeking in which we expand our consciousness, love, and energy.

## THE FIVE STAGES

There are basically five stages through which we pass during the transformation from addictions into preferences.

**1.** In the first stage, we are **unaware** that we are controlled by these subconscious conditionings that cause us to suffer. Until now, we have blamed loved ones, God and society for our problems.
**2.** In the second stage, we begin to **notice the addictions** that cause us to suffer. This is sometimes difficult because we begin to see the immensity of the problem and the intricate network of addictions that are woven into the fabric of the mind. The task of removing these threads of desire one by one seems immense and impossible. There is no longer the comfort of blaming others for our problems. Now **we** must take responsibility.

**3.** The third stage finds us **working with addictions** one by one, and discovering the **core beliefs** that create them. Steadily we begin to unravel the web of our beliefs. It is important at this stage that we choose to work with our simpler addictions, those which can be more easily transformed. (Just as a weight lifter would begin with smaller weights to develop strength for the heavy ones; or as one practices with simple lessons in order to prepare for more difficult ones.)

**4.** In the fourth stage, we begin to **succeed and free ourselves from some of the addictions.** We experience greater openness, love and happiness. We discover alternative, more harmonious and freer ways of acting and reacting.

**5.** In the last stage, we are **free from most addictions, which have now been transformed into preferences**. Now we are almost always happy.

Remember that success in such an effort of self-transformation can be achieved only through the three P's.

### PRACTICE     PERSEVERANCE     PATIENCE

Additional help will be obtained by:

**1.** Frequently **reading** Ken **Keyes' The Handbook To Higher Consciousness** (or the following condensation that we are presenting you here).
**2.** Keeping a daily **diary** of all intense emotional experiences.
**3.** Attending a growth oriented **group** dedicated to this goal.
**4.** Answering the **questionnaires** presented in this book and on our web site www.HolisticHarmony.com.

### THE 12 PATHWAYS

Developing any one of these twelve concepts will bring us to the realization of the remaining eleven. They are not separate concepts but rather like 12 spokes emanating from the center of the same wheel. They each originate from a common central truth. In each case, I will first present Ken Keyes' **original statement** of the pathway and then a **simplified version**, which we have found easier to remember and have used in group sessions over the years. A few **key words** are also given for each pathway to be remembered more easily. Finally, there is a commentary based on our personal experience through our work over the last years. The pathways are broken into four groups of three for convenience in remembering. These groups are presented in four separate chapters

### FREEING MYSELF

**Pathway 1.** "I am freeing myself from security, sensation, and power addictions that make me try forcefully to control situations in my life, and thus destroy my serenity and keep me from loving myself and others."

*P.W. 1 Simplified* - **I am freeing myself from addictions, which cause me to suffer and keep me from loving.**

*Key Words* - **FREEING MYSELF** (I choose to be free.)

This pathway summarizes the method and goal of the twelve-pathway system by affirming our determination to **free ourselves** from those addictions that are preventing us from experiencing the love, peace and happiness that we have the potential to enjoy. We choose to focus on those addictions and beliefs that are causing unhappiness or conflict, at this **present time** so that we may transform them into preferences.

 We need to be honest with ourselves and dig deeply within our personality structure and habit patterns to uncover the beliefs that cause our suffering. This assumes, of course, that we are **tired of suffering.**

Let us briefly examine the relationship between an addiction and a belief. Our **beliefs create our addictions**. We are addicted to someone, something or some situation because we **believe** we must "have" **that** in order to feel secure, happy, affirmed or free.

Most of us have had the experience of believing that our happiness, security and self-worth were totally dependent on **something or someone**, only to eventually discover, after losing "that which we could not live without" and perhaps suffering for some time, that we could actually be **fine without that** which was so important.

When we change our beliefs, our addictions disappear. An addiction is a belief which says, **"I must have...... in order to feel......."** We fill in the blanks.

The first pathway is also an expression of the confidence of success in this endeavor. It is a positive statement affirming that we are determined to do it, no matter what uncomfortable situations we may encounter. In other words, we have **suffered enough** at the mercy of these old, recorded programs and are now ready to change our lives.

We might encounter resistance from those around us who are used to playing certain roles and games with us. As we try to free ourselves from those roles, they may become fearful and try to interfere or drag us backward. They may accuse us of becoming insensitive and uncaring because we no longer get upset and argue in the way we used to. They may try to revive those familiar games.

We will need to have patience and understand their position, fears and motives. They may not be ready for this change. We need not try to force them, but at the same time, we have every right to make that change within ourselves.

In the long run, everyone will be happier. We can perceive their fear and overlook their accusations and aggressions using even those negative behaviors as tests of our strength and love.

The **worst mistake we can make is to try to change others** and make them go through the changes we are now trying to make within ourselves. We make this very common mistake when we are excited about some new path or technique that we believe is helpful. Before we even prove it to ourselves, we want everyone else to try it. This creates a great deal of negativity among those whom we pressure and can even cause them to resist and delay any possible benefit they could reap if we simply allowed them to become interested on their own.

We can be much more effective by concentrating on our own transformation and simply letting **our example be an inspiration** for others to do the same. The **less we say** and the **more we do; the better**.

## DISCOVERING

**Pathway 2** «I am discovering how my consciousness - dominating addictions create my illusory version of the changing world of people and situations around me.»

*P.W. 2 Simplified* - **I am discovering how my addictions are distorting my perception of people and situations around me.**

*Key Word*: **DISCOVERING**

When dominated by addictions, we misperceive others' motives as well as situations. When we are under the influence of feelings of mistrust, we experience even the most purely motivated intentions as harmful to our security or happiness.

Each of us has experienced being misunderstood by someone who was preoccupied with some negative state. They completely mistook what we intended and interpreted it from a negative point of view.

When we fear, everyone becomes a threat. In such cases, we will act in an unloving way so as to «protect» ourselves from this imagined threat.

When we are preoccupied with politics or religion, we will see the world through politically or religiously colored glasses, unable to see any individual for what he is, concentrating only on the party or religion to which he or she belongs to.

When we are controlled by an addiction for sexual enjoyment, every relationship and encounter becomes distorted by the thoughts of the other as an object of pleasure, as a threat to that pleasure, or perhaps as uninteresting. We do not see others for who they really are, i.e. evolving spiritual beings.

When we do not feel secure within ourselves, we are not able to be open and loving with those around us. We might either withdraw, or else, create a false self-confidence "mask" in order to protect ourselves. This kind of manipulation and falsity creates suffering for all involved, and keeps us caged in our illusory view of what is happening around us.

We do not perceive the world as it is, but **as we believe it to be**. We project onto others what we fear and also our own motives and character.

This tendency to project our subjective feelings onto others creates serious relationship problems.

This pathway states that we want to discover where we are distorting or projecting so we can perceive a more objective and true reality.

We can discover our projections by noticing what kinds of negative emotions we experience most frequently and with a variety of people or situations. The common factor in all of those situations is us. Thus, it is very likely that we are projecting onto others some of our own beliefs.

## LIFE'S LESSONS

**Pathway 3.** «I welcome the opportunity (even if painful) that my minute - to - minute experience offers me to become aware of the addictions I must reprogram to be liberated from my robot - like emotional patterns.»

*P.W. 3 Simplified* - **I welcome life's lessons, which make me aware of which addictions must be reprogrammed.**

*Key Word*: **LIFE'S LESSONS**

Life is our teacher and guide on this path leading to higher levels of consciousness. Here also is the key concerning how to start with the process of working on addictions. We might be confused as to which addiction we should address first. It is very simple. The best place to start is with those addictions and beliefs that are **causing us to suffer now,** at this stage in our lives.

If we are serious about this transformation process, we will welcome all such experiences, even if painful, as opportunities to discover the belief which is distorting our perception (Pathway 2), and free ourselves from that addiction (Pathway 1).

Thus, when we find ourselves in difficult situations, beginning to feel depressed or starting to blame the people and the world around us, let us remember Pathway 3, **welcome the experience as a teacher** and reaffirm our determination to discover and free ourselves from the addiction involved.

In this way, life becomes much more interesting and exciting. Finally, we have an effective method by which to transform suffering and negativity into something positive.

With the help of these pathways, we can now accept each situation and welcome it as an opportunity to practice inner peace and contentment, or at least to discover which addictions are causing us to be disturbed. From a practical point of view, our mind will be clearer, **and more capable of solving the problem at hand.** We may use the opportunity to learn skills that we had denied ourselves before.

An example might be the experience of a situation in which our loved one is paying attention to someone else. Let us take the case in which our loved one is not actually interested in other party, but is simply being friendly. As expressed in Pathway 2, our addictions may distort our perception of the reality of the situation causing us to feel fear, jealousy and anger because we believe that we are losing our source of security, pleasure or self-worth. We might feel jealousy and then anger toward both parties.

We feel anger when we **need** something from the other. It is not the result of pure unconditional love. When we love someone for their sake, we want them to do what makes them feel fulfilled and happy. We feel pain, jealousy and anger when our own addictions are in danger of not being satisfied.

By using Pathways 1, 2 and 3, we will welcome this lesson which life is offering us in order to discover which addictions are causing us to feel fear, jealousy and anger at this moment. We can reassure ourselves that we are **complete within ourselves,** and there is no real need for fear; our addictions had been controlling us until now.

In this way, the experience becomes an opportunity to grow more emotionally mature and more self-confident, reaffirming our true spiritual nature as a **complete being whether or not we have the security of a relationship.**

### What is spiritually practical is also materially practical.

Feelings of jealousy and bitterness will only alienate us from our partner, generating negative and confrontational feelings, thus bringing the feared separation more surely and quickly into reality. Even when our partner is not interested in the other or is not dissatisfied with our own relationship, the negative encounters resulting from our feelings of jealousy, fear, anxiety and anger will certainly sour the relationship.

Many of life's lessons are predetermined by past thoughts, words and actions (karma). We have, however, the ability to free ourselves from our attachments and beliefs, **making the repetition of this test unnecessary** or, at least, less painful.

In conclusion, this chapter encourages us to believe that **we can become free** from the beliefs, fears and attachments that limit our peace, happiness and love, by **observing** where we tend to distort reality, and by **welcoming** all life experiences as opportunities to learn and grow.

Technique no. 10

# YOU ARE NOT THE TARGET

(This is the name of a very wonderful and helpful book by Laura Huxley)

### Why this is so important

Laura impresses upon us the fact that we are often not the targets of people's negative emotions and actions. Many people are simply unhappy, immature and unable to control themselves. They need to shout or complain in order to release their unhappiness. They need a place to put the blame, because they are unable to take responsibility for their lives. So they take their frustration out on others. They yell about little things and put the blame where it doesn't belong. When we take their words or behavior seriously, we feel hurt or angry. We suffer and then participate in furthering this cycle of negative energy. We all suffer. We need to be able to allow the others' negativity to pass through us and transmute it into understanding. This is a great test for our self-acceptance and inner security.

### A simple technique for gaining clarity is:

**1.** We first **imagine that this person is a 5 years-old child** (He may be emotionally). If a child did the same thing, would we be hurt or attack, or would we think, "Well, he's only a child and he is upset, fearful and hurt", and show understanding? Showing understanding does not mean that we do speak with them, expressing how we feel or what we need from them. It **does** mean that we do **not** react in a violent or demeaning ways and that we do not feel hurt ourselves. We can look at them as children, and let them do their yelling and blaming, all the time remembering that they just need to get it out of their system. They are really not meaning to harm us but are using us as an **avenue to release stress.**

**2.** If, when they are finished, we **can respond with a sympathetic and compassionate heart**, we will have resolved a negativity which otherwise would have manifested within us as negative emotions, which we would then have passed on to others.

**3.** We need to remember that whatever they may say and however fearsome they may appear, what they are really saying is **"Look at how unhappy and fearful I am."** This is what we need to focus on.

### Note:

We are not the target.
We are in no danger.
Be big and let it pass!

*Life Story no. 11*

# THE ALOOF

Manfred tends to withdraw into himself and seldom communicates his feelings, thoughts or needs. His wife and children find him to be aloof. He distances himself from others, avoiding meaningful or honest emotional contact. In this way, he feels less likely to be hurt or controlled by people's negative emotions, requests or demands. He hides from direct emotional exchange, positive and negative. The truth is that although he is afraid of close emotional exchange, within he also has a need for it, just as we all do.

His childhood was a painful one with an overbearing and abusive father and a mother who was always playing the victim. He had no choice but to become emotionally numb in order to disassociate from what was going on. This habit, which he had developed just before adolescence, is still active today.

What can he and his family do about this?

**Some beliefs which might be causing Manfred to play the role of Aloof:**

**1.** I am in danger from other people.

**2.** Others do not accept me as I am.

**3.** If they knew how I feel inside they would lose their respect for me, reject me or use that to hurt me.

**4.** Others want to control me, use me or hurt me.

**5.** If I show interest in someone and they do not respond, I will be rejected and lose my self worth.

**6.** Better to be a loner than be hurt.

**7.** In this way I protect myself from losing time and energy with other people.

**8.** People may think I am silly if I express myself freely.

**9.** By being mysterious, people will pay attention to me and try to get my attention.

**Some beliefs that might free him from the role are:**

**1.** I accept and love myself exactly as I am.

**2.** I feel safe and secure in expressing my needs, feelings, beliefs and interests in every situation.

**3.** Only by communicating can I create the loving reality that I desire.

**4.** I can be really happy only by expressing my real self.

**5.** I enjoy the process of self-discovery that comes from open honest sharing.

**6.** When I do not communicate, I cut myself and others off from the flow of energy and love which nurtures and heals us.


**His family members might be helped by the following thoughts:**


**1.** Life gives me exactly what I need at every moment so that I can learn my next lesson in my growth process.

**2.** I am not responsible for the other's silence.

**3.** He loves me and cares for me even if he cannot express it.

**4.** His aloofness is a result of his fears and anxieties.

**5.** Giving him his freedom and space, is the best way to allow him to open.

**6.** He is not my only source of happiness in life.

**7.** My self worth is not linked to his ability to open to me or not.

**8.** I can be fulfilled within myself even without someone to communicate with.

**9.** I can fulfill my needs by communicating with God daily.

**10.** I have many good friends and family members with whom to communicate.

**11.** Loving him, allowing him his freedom and accepting him as he is, are the best ways to encourage him to open.

**His wife might want to try to express the following message
either verbally or in written form.**

"Dear, I have something important which I would like to express to you and if you want to answer me that would be fine. There are times when you are silent, inexpressive or even seem sad or angry. At those times, when I do not know what you are feeling or thinking, I sometimes think that perhaps I have done something which has offended or hurt you, or that perhaps you do not love me any more. I sometimes also believe that you do not have enough trust in me, or do not feel close enough to me to share with me what you are feeling. Then I begin to doubt my self worth as a spouse.

"When I see you like this and make those interpretations, then I sometimes approach you trying to find out what is happening. Sometimes you respond and sometimes you do not. That bothers me even more. I feel hurt and believe that you do not care about me and our relationship.

"I now realize that it doesn't help to pressure you to communicate with me. I am going to try to leave that to you. I just want you to know that I love you and I want and need to know more about what you are feeling and thinking, but that I am going to leave that up to you. And if, in fact, I have done something, which has offended or hurt you, I very much want to hear about it. Do not protect me by not telling me, if something I do bothers you.

"I will try to leave you all the space you need to feel from within if and when you want to communicate with me more deeply. Do not interpret this as a lack of interest or love.  I am simply giving you the space you seem to need.

"I will be happy to hear how you feel about what I have expressed whenever you feel ready."

# CHAPTER 11

# BEING HERE NOW

## THE 12 PATHWAYS - PART 2

This next group of three concepts allows us to live in the present moment, with self-acceptance and freedom from fear and attachment, thus perceiving every experience as an opportunity for growth.

### EXACTLY WHAT I NEED

**Pathway 4** «I always remember that I have everything I need to enjoy myself here and now - unless I am letting my consciousness be dominated by demands and expectations based on the dead past or imagined future.»

*P.W. 4 Simplified* - **Life gives me exactly what I need at this moment. If I am unhappy, then, I am being dominated by addictions and expectations.**

*Key words:* **EXACTLY WHAT I NEED**

For many, this pathway is sometimes very hard to believe. Naturally, we frequently doubt that life is giving us exactly what we need in each moment. In order to understand this very important truth, we need to expand our awareness and deepen our faith. It may be difficult to understand why we might need certain difficult experiences while they are occurring. But if we perceive our lives in terms of the past, future and our eventual spiritual destiny, we will understand that what we are experiencing now is a very necessary step in our growth process. We learn and thus grow stronger, more self-confident and more self-reliant through such tests and difficult situations.

**We attract to ourselves exactly the experiences we need in order to take the next step in our growth process**. If someone mistreats us in some way, that is exactly what we need at the moment in order to understand ourselves more deeply through Pathways 1, 2, and 3.

We must make it clear, however that because it is perfect for our evolution that someone treats us in a demeaning way, it **does not mean that our lesson is to accept it.** Sometimes events or situations occur so as to stimulate us to change them.

Our lesson might be to develop **more self-respect** so that others will be inspired to respect us more.

Our lesson may be to love this person more, and help him out of his negativity. Our lesson might be to forgive or ignore.

Our lessons in response to the same stimulus will be different according to the beliefs and habits we need to change in our evolutionary process. This process of **discovering the lesson** in a situation will be discussed in detail later on in this book.

There are times, even when our present experience is pleasant, or at least without any negative factors, that we are still not happy or at peace because our mind is dominated by remembrances of past unpleasant events or the imagination of future problems.

**Very few problems actually exist in the present**. If asked at this moment whether we have any problems, our minds would search into the past and future to discover any aspects of our lives, which were not until now exactly as we would have liked them to be, or which we fear will not be as we would like them to be in the future.

**But do we actually have a problem now at this moment**? Is there a tiger about to jump out from somewhere and eat us? Is there a thief in our room stealing our belongings? Are our lives in danger; are we starving or freezing? Is our house on fire?

If we are in such a secure position as to be able to read this book, then it is unlikely that we really have a **problem in the present moment**. If we answered, "Yes we have problems," then we are most likely allowing our consciousness be dominated by the memory of past problems or the fear of future outcomes.

Another aspect of understanding that the present moment gives us exactly what we need has to do with the law of cause and effect or "karma." According to this universal concept, our life experiences are determined by the way we have thought, spoken and acted in the past. **Selfless** actions bring pleasant results. **Selfish** actions and thoughts bring about the same kind of mistreatment from others. Harmful acts generate the same kind of harm to the perpetrator. We may find it difficult to see what we have done in the past that has created a present unpleasant experience. (We seldom ask the question when it is a pleasant experience.)

Two factors make understanding the past cause difficult. Firstly, we really do not want to see the truth about ourselves and our motives, and therefore do not examine our past behavior very deeply. Secondly, our memory is weak. We can hardly remember what we did last year at this time. How can we remember actions or thoughts of many years ago?

Also, it is very possible that, if the concept of reincarnation is true, we may have created "karmic responses" in past lives, while occupying other bodies and personality structures, and we are now experiencing the results of those actions.

**Some interpret this karmic return of thoughts, words and actions as a punishment.** I prefer to perceive it as an **opportunity** to understand where we can grow and change. The event is fated, but the reactions are our free will. We can react negatively and bitterly, blaming the others and / or God for our misfortune, or we can accept that life is giving us **exactly what we need** at this moment in order to free ourselves from beliefs, fears and attachments which prevent us from being more loving and happy.

For example, our loved one may depart from this physical plane: what we call death. Almost every living being on this planet today is sure to "die" within the next ninety years. Everyone we know will leave his or her body sooner or later, **including the body that is now holding this book.**

And yet, when someone leaves his or her body, we suffer as if something unjust and unexpected has happened. Did we think that body we called our parent, sibling, spouse or child was going to last forever? We might as well accept right now that our loved ones are occupying bodies that someday must return to the earth.

Now, when a loved one leaves his or her body, we have many choices concerning how to react. We can become bitter, hurt, depressed and angry against God, who we feel has let us down and let our loved one die. We can feel self-pity and helplessness. We can develop cancer or some other illness, and leave our own bodies because we no longer have a "reason" for living.

We can find someone else to fill that emptiness and insecurity created by the loss of our loved one's physical presence.

Or, preferably, we can use this experience to **increase our faith** in Divine justice, wisdom and our eternal spiritual nature. Realizing that **no one has "died",** but that a spirit has simply left its temporary embodiment in a physical body, we can use this opportunity to become emotionally stronger and more self-dependent. We can find new interests in life and devote our energies more intensely toward discovering who we really are inside.

We can then turn our energies toward the benefit of society. There are many possibilities and the choice is ours. The experience itself was **exactly what we needed at that particular moment.**

When we constantly remind ourselves of this pathway, we learn to intuitively tune into each and every new situation with a freshness and spontaneity possible only when the past and future have been excluded. When we have expectations of a given moment or experience, we will almost always feel let down. We have all experienced being told by an enthusiastic friend how wonderful and exciting a certain movie was, and then, when we went to see it, with our expectations in mind, it was spoiled and we didn't enjoy it. Our expectations killed it for us, whereas the person next to us, who saw it without expectations, thoroughly enjoyed it.

Similarly, some persons educated in the arts such as music, art or dance, can no longer appreciate simple artistic expressions because they inevitably compare them with expectations or standards which they have created in their minds, rather than simply enjoy what life is giving them at the moment.

## LIFE IS A MIRROR

**Pathway 5** «I take full responsibility here and now for everything I experience, for it is my own programming that creates my actions and also influences the re- actions of people around me.»

*P.W. 5 Simplified* - **Life is a mirror reflecting my beliefs, emotions, thoughts, words and actions back to me.**

*Key Words:* **LIFE IS A MIRROR**

If we believe the world is full of thieves, we will attract and project thievery. If we believe that people are selfish and unloving, these are the kinds of people we will experience. If we believe that people are kind and loving, we will attract those kinds of behavior from people.

**The mind is a projector that displays its subjective beliefs, emotions and needs onto the mirror of what we call "reality".** What we experience in the world around us is nothing more than the reflection of our **present** and **past** thoughts, words, expectations, actions, desires and beliefs.
According to Ken Keyes, **"A loving person lives in a loving world. A hostile person lives in a hostile world."**

**Our minds are like radio transmitters** sending out signals that are received by others. If they are vibrating (thinking, feeling) on the same frequency, they re- act toward us in the ways which reflect those thoughts and feelings we are emit- ting. As we change the signals we are sending by transforming our beliefs, thoughts, words and actions, then others' responses and our life events will also change.

We have been creating, until now, the reality we experience and we **now** have the **power to change it**. That transformation can be actualized only in the **pre- sent moment** through consciously observing and transforming our beliefs and habits.
Reminding ourselves of this pathway helps us avoid the habit of wasting time and energy blaming others, such as the government, our spouse, our children, our society, the weather, or even God.
When we blame others, not only are we wrong in our understanding of the sit- uation but we are also helpless to change the situation, because we believe others

are the cause of our reality. If that were true, the only way to change our reality would be to change others.

That, of course, is impossible. We can change only ourselves.

Working with the questionnaires supplied in this book and on the web site will help us understand which beliefs, motivations, addictions and aversions we need to transform in order to create our desired reality.

## I ACCEPT MYSELF COMPLETELY

**Pathway 6** «I accept myself completely here and now, and consciously experience everything I feel, think, say or do (including my emotion backed addictions) as a necessary part of my growth into higher consciousness.»

*P.W. 6 Simplified* - **I accept myself exactly as I am, including my addictions and weaknesses, which I transform into preferences and strengths.**

*Key Words:* I **ACCEPT MYSELF COMPLETELY**

This is an extremely important aspect of the process of self-improvement. Many of us fall into the trap of self-rejection when we become aware of how fearful, weak and insecure we have been. We are not at all pleased when we see more clearly why we have behaved in the manner in which we have. We are not happy with the reality we have created.

If these feelings of unworthiness or other negative self-feelings arise, we need to connect with faith and sincerity to the fact that **we are worthy of love and acceptance exactly as we are; including our weaknesses and addictions,** which we are observing and transforming.

We experience ourselves as three selves. One is **conscious** mind or personality. The second is the **subconscious** that often creates emotions, states and reactions for which we can at times see no logical reason. The third is the **witness** of all these mental and emotional phenomena.

This witness aspect of our being observes the state of our body and mind, our thoughts and feelings. There is a philosophical concept that says **we cannot be that which we observe**. We have to be separate from what we are observing in order to fully perceive it. Our eye cannot observe itself. Our mind, however, can observe the changes in our sight. Thus, we are not our eyes. We exist without our eyes. In the same way, since we can observe our mind, we cannot be our mind. We must be a consciousness, which is beyond the mind in order to be able to observe it from an objective position.

We need to identify more and more with this aspect of our being that we can call our witness or Self, which, as far as we can observe, does not change and is in no way affected or influenced by the weaknesses of the body and mind. From this level of our being, we observe the changes that take place in our body and mind.

When we identify with this witness, we can accept the various mental and emotional changes because we are not them. When we view our body and mind as instruments or machines through which we live this life, we can accept their imperfections, while at the same time, work on improving them.

Many of us feel that if we could just obtain some object or title, or manage to overcome some persistent bad habit, we would be "okay". **If we do not feel okay with ourselves, as we are, whatever we manage to accomplish, obtain, or stop doing will not make us feel okay for long.** We will find some other aspect of our lives, which does not satisfy us. We are divine energy and worth being loved and respected exactly as we are with no additions or subtractions.

## PATIENCE AND UNDERSTANDING

We often become disillusioned when we don't see quick growth or when it seems as if we have taken a step backward. As we have mentioned, there are three basic steps in any growth process. We may, at any time, find ourselves in one of these three cyclical stages.

First, there is the stage of feeling **dissatisfaction** with some aspect of our lives. This does not mean we must be dissatisfied with ourselves in order to change, but that is often the case. It is, however, possible to see a flaw in the body or mind and correct that flaw, while all the time accepting ourselves as we are.

Secondly, there is a period of **effort** toward change and growth. There is often a struggle and a tendency to go to extremes in order to get out of a routine or break a habit.

Finally, there comes the success and the feeling of **satisfaction**. This satisfaction, however, is often **temporary,** and soon turns into dissatisfaction, so the next effort can be made and a new stage obtained.

These states alternate continuously and we would do well to accept them and ourselves as we pass through them. This way, we will avoid becoming discouraged or depressed when in the dissatisfied stage, or worried in the effort stage, or elated in the satisfied stage. We will accept ourselves in each stage.

As we develop patience with ourselves, we will also develop the ability to accept others as they are. By accepting and feeling more positive about ourselves and others, we will all grow much more quickly because **growth can take place only when there is security.**

When we or others feel insecure, we tend to retreat to what is familiar, even though we may suffer there. This is a major obstacle to growth. We need to accept ourselves before we can change.

For many, familiar suffering is preferable to unfamiliar happiness.

## HALF-FINISHED PAINTINGS

We will be able accept others and ourselves more easily if we think of all as **"half-finished paintings."** As half-finished paintings we are obviously and logically not complete, but we are **perfect** for that particular **stage** of completion. We could not be anything other than what we are, at this stage of our evolution toward completion and perfection. It would be illogical to expect perfection from a being that is still in the process of evolving.

Thus, when we perceive weaknesses and imperfections in ourselves and others, let us remember that we are **all** half-finished paintings, which are logically imperfect, but on the other hand, perfect for our particular stage of completion.

Another aid toward accepting others as they are is to think of them as personalities with **"broken legs."** This is especially useful when others are lazy or not conscientious about their responsibilities. We will, of course, communicate with them concerning our need for them to be more conscientious, but at the same time, as we have suggested, we can think of their personality as having two "broken legs." One is the leg of **self-confidence** while the other is the leg of **self-acceptance**. Most people's negative behavior is the result of having these two legs "broken" during childhood by well meaning, but ill informed, parents and teachers.

The essence of this pathway can be summed up in Ken Keyes' maxim:

### Love everyone unconditionally, including yourself

By inwardly strengthening these beliefs and attitudes we can greatly improve our emotional, mental and spiritual life.

They are:

**1. Life gives me in every moment exactly what I need in order to grow into the beautiful being I potentially am.**

**2. Life is a mirror that reflects to me my past and present thoughts, words and behaviors, as well as the lessons that I have come to learn.**

**3. I love and accept myself and others exactly as we are at this stage of our evolutionary process.**

Some may want to make signs of these concepts and place them in areas where they can be seen and thus remembered regularly.

**Technique no. 11**

# POSITIVE PROJECTION

### Why this is so beneficial

As we regularly think, believe and predict life will be, so will it be.
We can learn to think positively.
Much of our negative conditioning, however, has seeped down into the deeper levels of our subconscious mind. Years of feeding on these mental toxins has distorted our view of reality.
For this reason we will have to bring our positive thoughts down to a deeper, more subconscious and concentrated level of consciousness, in order to reprogram ourselves. This is something like self-hypnosis where we give ourselves suggestions, reconditioning our attitudes and beliefs. This is not difficult. Many people all over the world have successfully used this process.

### A simple technique for positive projection is:

Very briefly, the steps involved fall into the following categories:

**1.** We **relax** our conscious mind through breathing, counting, concentration or meditation.

**2.** We **give ourselves positive suggestions** and creative positive mental images concerning any specific or general problems or situations. We can do this by:

**a. Repeating** a phrase, belief or truth that strengthens our inner security. This phrase can be repeated **mentally** to our parents and teachers so that we declare this truth to those who have programmed us. The more lovingly and peacefully we can declare this truth the stronger it is. We tend to be aggressive when we are not sure.

**b. Imagining images** which show us dealing with life with self-confidence, inner security, and love for our selves and others.

 **c.** Focusing on **feeling** inner security, love, peace, freedom etc.

**3.** We need to **have faith in this process**, and when we find ourselves thinking negatively, we need to put a stop to this trend of thinking and bring back our positive mental image.

**4. Let our actions and words become consistent** with our new mental projections.

### Note:

We cannot even begin to imagine the harm we do ourselves and others by worrying and negative thinking. (This also applies to hatred, anger, bitterness, jealousy, envy, resentment, fear etc.).

**We do not help loved ones by worrying about them.** We only make their condition worse. We do help them by loving them, serving them and visualizing them as happy and healthy.

**We help people most by believing in them**, by believing in their ability to see clearly what they must do and to find the inner power to do it.

**When we worry about others**, we give them the conscious and subconscious message that we do not have faith in them, in God or in life. Otherwise we would not fear or worry. Our lack of faith in them, and in God, causes them to doubt themselves even more and lose, to an even greater degree, their contact with their inner guidance and inner power.

### The greatest help we can offer to others is
### faith in their ability to overcome their problems.

This, of course, does not mean that we do not help them practically.

But that we do not worry and fear while we are helping.

*Life Story no. 12*

# *THE VICTIM*

Martha, 65 years old, has identified with the role of the victim since she got married fifty years ago. She plays on the others' pity and guilt. When they are angry with her, she protects herself from their rage and aggression by playing the weak abused person, usually crying. When she wants something from them, she makes them feel responsible for her unhappiness or her problems.

In general, she gets what she wants from others, by making them feel responsible for her reality, and by making herself seem weak, incapable and in need of help.

She is limited to being unhappy. She needs daily to find reasons not to be happy. Those reasons frequently imply that others around her are to blame. She finds it difficult to say, "what a wonderful day it is", or "how happy I am", or "thank you for being such a nice person to me". When she meets someone new, she is often excited because she has "finally met a good and sensitive person" - but eventually she manages to find a way to **mentally transform** that person into an insensitive uncaring person, once again proving to herself that she is the victim.

Since her husband left his body, some years ago, she has been living with her daughter Jane who is married with one child. Both Jane and her husband have difficulty dealing with Martha's role-playing.

What can they do to improve this situation?

**Some beliefs that might cause Martha to play the role of Victim are:**

**1.** I am the victim. I am weak.
**2.** Others create my reality. Others are to blame for my situation.
**3.** I cannot create the reality I want. I need others to help me.
**4.** If I am the victim, then I am a good person and the others are bad.
**5.** No one knows how much I suffer.
**6.** People will pay attention to me only if I have problems.
**7.** If I am fine, no one will care about me.
**8.** Since I am the victim and weak they must not pressure me, shout at me or ask much of me.
**9.** Since I am the victim, the others must change.

**10.** Since I am weak, others must serve me.

**11.** Others are required to satisfy my needs.

**12.** If others do not satisfy my needs, that means that they do not love me and do not care for me.

**13.** I do not have the right to express my needs. They will never be paid attention to. Better not to express them and then complain later.

### The following beliefs might help Martha get free from this role:

**1.** I accept and love myself exactly as I am.

**2.** I accept and love others exactly as they are.

**3.** Life gives me exactly what I need at each moment in order to keep learning and growing.

**4.** I am 100% responsible for my reality.

**5.** I am 100% responsible for solving my problems.

**6.** I am 100% responsible for my health, happiness, economic situation and satisfaction in life.

**7.** I am interesting to others as I am, without my problems.

**8.** I would prefer to have people's pure love rather than to force them to pay attention to me or do what I want by blackmailing them, by playing with their guilt.

**9.** I would not like anyone to play with my guilt or blame me for his or her unhappiness.

**10.** I express my needs in a clear way and expect that they will be recognized and respected.

**11.** My needs and beliefs deserve to be respected.

**12.** I deserve happiness, health and success.

### Some beliefs that might make Jane susceptible to her mother's behavior are:

**1.** I am responsible for her reality.

**2.** I am worthy only if my mother is satisfied with me and with what I offer her.

**3.** I am to blame when she is not happy or satisfied.

**4.** I must have her approval and recognition for what I have done and am doing for her.

**5.** She is weak and needs my help.

**6.** I am the savior. I know better and can help others.

**7.** The more people I save, the greater my self worth.

**8.** I am being done injustice to, as I have offered so much and she is still not satisfied.

**9.** She is using me. I am the victim's victim.

**Some beliefs that will help Jane free herself from being so vulnerable to her mother's behavior:**

**1.** We each create our own reality.

**2.** I cannot create anyone else's reality.

**3.** I am not responsible for what others experience in their evolutionary process.

**4.** Others are not to blame for what I feel or create.

**5.** I can love someone without being sad when they are not happy, since each of us has what we need to be happy, if we could only see it.

**6.** It is okay to be well and happy when our loved ones are not.

**7.** I love, serve and help my love ones create the reality they want, without getting into the role of the savior.

**8.** No one can use me, if I choose to give. What I give freely cannot be taken from me since I am giving it.

**9.** If I feel used, then I am not giving from my heart but I am seeking something in return.

**10.** There are times when the greatest help we can offer is to allow the other to stand on his or her own two feet.

**11.** Others will continue to love me even if I cannot, at times, respond to their requests.

**12.** Life gives me exactly what I need at every moment so that I can learn my next lesson in my growth process.

### A possible honest communication from Jane to her mother might go something like this.

"Mother, I want you to know that I love and care for you and want very much for you to be happy and healthy and satisfied in your life. I want that very much but I am beginning to realize **that I cannot create that for you**. I realize now that I have been feeling responsible for your reality and sometimes guilty because you are not as happy and satisfied as we would both like you to be.

"I now realize that I do not help you by feeling responsible or guilty. These feelings just make me angry with you when you do not do what you could be doing to create a happier life for yourself, or do not see how wonderful your life really is, when you focus on what you do not have, rather than all the wonderful things you do have.

"Thus I am no longer going to try to create your happiness or get your approval through your expression of satisfaction. I am going to love you and offer you whatever I can, without doing more than I believe I should or getting angry with you because you are not satisfied.

Do not misunderstand or believe that I do not love you. I do love you but I cannot make you be happy. Your happiness is your own creation.

"I would very much like to know how you feel about what I have explained to you. Is there something you would like to share with me concerning this?"

# CHAPTER 12

# INTERACTING WITH OTHERS

## THE 12 PATHWAYS - PART 3

In this section, we are introduced to those concepts that have to do with our interpersonal relationships, which, of course, significantly increase or decrease our happiness. Our relationships are perhaps the main source of our security, happiness and fulfillment and also of our disillusionment, pain and suffering.

### HONEST COMMUNICATION

**Pathway 7** «I open myself genuinely to all people by being willing to fully communicate my deepest feelings, since hiding in any degree keeps me stuck in my illusion of separateness from other people.»

*P.W. 7 Simplified -* **I communicate openly and honestly with all people in order to dissolve my feelings of separateness.**

*Key Words:* **HONEST COMMUNICATION**

What are some of the reasons why we hide our feelings from others?
**1.** One may be that we are ashamed of them. We may have been programmed to believe it is wrong and weak to have certain feelings.
**2.** Perhaps we feel others will stop loving us if we tell them the truth about how we feel.
We do not, however, suppress only our negative feelings. We also withhold our love, affection, admiration, gratitude and well wishes. We might do so because:
**3.** We fear how the other will respond.
**4.** We have learned that this is sign of weakness.
**5.** We believe the other will use this against us later.
**6.** We are in competition with the other.
**7.** We have simply not yet learned to express positive feelings.

In most cases, we feel vulnerable.

The more we suppress and hide our own feelings, the less capable we are of accepting others' feelings. When we build a wall, we stop the flow in both directions. This hiding is often the result of self-doubt, alienation and feelings of vulnerability.

Consequently, we spend much energy hiding our real selves and trying project an ego front to "protect" ourselves from the "others." When this withholding of feelings and negative energy becomes intense enough, it causes imbalances in the endocrine, nervous and immune systems, which can lead to many physical and mental «dis-eases», including cancer.

If, in fact, we believe others may not love us if we are truthful, we might ask ourselves, "what kind of love is it that they have for us?" **Is such a fragile and conditional love worth protecting at the expense of our health and happiness?** Where there is true love, everything can be said, if it is said properly.

**Learning to express our positive feelings** to others is a basic part of creating a happy relationship. We all need to hear positive feedback. We can make a separate list of the following for each of our significant persons:

**1.** What are his / her **positive traits** which we admire?

**2.** What are her / his **abilities or talents** which we admire?

**3.** Why do we feel **gratitude** for this person?

**4.** What do we **wish for** this person (health, success, happiness, growth, etc.)?

**5. Why do we love this person?**

Then we can share our answers with them.

On the other hand, when we need to communicate unfulfilled needs, or the negative feelings created by those needs, we need to learn to do so with I- messages, without blaming the other. Also the truth is that **our addictions** are the cause of our suffering, not the other person. The other person's actions and attitudes are simply triggering our addictions, which then cause us to suffer.

It is important that we express our feelings in this non-accusative way. We do not need to reject or threaten the other. We can explain that their behavior is stimulating one or more of our addictions, which is causing us to feel hurt, injustice or anger. We can assertively ask them to please cease that behavior.

If we prefer being spoken to with love and respect, then we will likely want to develop the ability to do the same with others. It is entirely possible to explain to the other that his or her behavior is not satisfying our need for love and respect, that our ego feels hurt. We can suggest that this conversation should be continued in another way, or at another time, when he or she can communicate with the respect that we deserve. Thus we have simultaneously maintained respect for ourselves and the other.

**If, on the other hand, we hold back and do not communicate** these feelings at all, they will create a bitterness which will eventually harm us and others toward whom we feel them.

Some chose the possibility of screaming back at them, blaming, threatening and demeaning them. From our own experience, we know this leads nowhere, except to continual conflict and unhappiness.

**The key here is** not to blame**, but to take responsibility** for our feelings. We express how we feel and what we need, assertively, without imposing blame on the other.

Some of us are conditioned to avoid expressing our needs when choices are being made. We let the others make decisions and then feel hurt and rejected that what we wanted, but didn't express, didn't occur. We expect the others to be mind readers, and then at the first opportunity, we lash out and complain about their selfishness because they did not do what we wanted, but have never asked for.

**When we feel strongly about something, we must express our feelings to the others.** This is our right and duty. We need to be ourselves and communicate how we really feel, what we really need, and what we believe.

(The subject of how to express our feelings and needs more clearly is discussed in more detail in *Conscious Love Relationships*, a book by the same author. Chapters of this book can be found at our web site.)

As we begin to express ourselves more openly and honestly, we will experience greater love flowing to and from us in all our relationships.

## LOVING COMPASSION

**Pathway 8** «I feel, with loving compassion, the problems of others without getting caught up emotionally in their predicaments that are offering them messages they need for their growth.»

*P.W. 8 Simplified:* **I offer loving compassionate help to others while remembering that they are learning from their problems.**

*Key Words:* **LOVING COMPASSION**

We have expressed in Pathways 3 and 4 that life always gives us exactly what is necessary for us to learn the lessons we need. This is also true for **all** other beings. According to Pathway 8, we offer whatever kind of loving compassionate help we can to our family, friends, relatives or anyone in need, while at the same time remembering that **their problems exist for the purpose of helping them grow.**

Of course, we may not be able to tell them that because they may not be ready to accept it. Most often, the best help we can offer is to simply **be there, to listen** and **be loving** and **peaceful.** Our calmness, cheerfulness and acceptance can offer more help than quantities of advice.

There is no need to take on the role of the savior or martyr. Everyone must ultimately work out his or her own problems. We do not have the right to take away their opportunities to grow more self-confident by succeeding through their **own** efforts. **We can help, we can serve, but we cannot save.** We can help others, but we cannot change them.

Also, we might want to avoid helping when we do not feel the energy and love to do so. It is often preferable to be honest and explain that we are tired or have our own problems rather than to help while feeling resentment.

Neither do we help when we get lost in the other's problems and lose sight of the truth. That would be like jumping into the sea to save a drowning man and drowning along with him. This is of no benefit to anyone.

While we **feel with our heart,** we must also **understand with our minds** that all these problems are opportunities for growth and a stronger contact with the truth of our higher nature.

When others are ill, we do not help them with pity, tears and panic. They need cheerful, smiling, energetic, peaceful persons to give them hope, energy and peace of mind. If we are going to bring all kinds of sad feelings and hopeless conversation to the ill people we visit, they will become even more ill; better not to go at all.

**We do not help others by suffering for them**. Our suffering does not cancel their need to learn through their difficulties. We just add one more miserable thought to the world. We would be much more effective if we would visualize the person as permeated with and surrounded by white healing light.

Often, when people are unable to listen, as in the case of those addicted to alcohol or drugs, there is not much we can say or do except love and accept them, and daily envision them surrounded by white light. When we visualize light around the other, we can also visualize light in the center of his or her chest and head. Praying is also helpful. When we find ourselves worrying about others, we can send them light and carry on with our daily activities, living in the present moment. In this way, we will not be adding to their negative energy.

Also, a great gift we can give to others is **to express our trust and confidence in their power, ability and inner guidance** to deal with their life lessons. We seldom do this in relationship to our children. Others thrive and **connect with their inner power** when we give them the message that we have confidence in their ability to succeed.

Let us also remember, however, that this pathway encourages us to **feel compassion for all others,** otherwise we tend to close ourselves into small circles of interest and become indifferent to the problems of those living outside that circle.

We will all benefit if we can expand our circle of identification. We need to embrace all beings as our family; even those living in other parts of the earth and those from other races, religions and political systems; even the animals and the plants, and, of course, our suffering planet itself.

We experience joy and meaning in our lives when we **serve** others and in some way make their lives healthier, happier and more harmonious. We need not have special abilities (although we can develop them if we choose) we need only to care enough and be able to listen intently to others. This is enough, but as we listen, however, we need to remember that whatever is happening is not taking place by chance, and it is perfect for our mutual evolution.

## CENTERED ACTION

**Pathway 9** «I act freely when I am tuned in, centered, and loving, but if possible, I avoid acting when I am emotionally upset and depriving myself of the wisdom that flows from love and expanded consciousness».

*P.W. 9 Simplified*: **I center myself before acting. I avoid acting when emotionally upset.**

*Key Words:* **CENTERED ACTION**

This may at times appear to be in contradiction to Pathway 7, but it really isn't. We must communicate what we are feeling, but it is much better if we **communicate those feelings after we have found our center of peace**. In this way, we do not add to the conflict in the world. When we react while emotionally upset, we simply perpetuate the flow of negative energy. This frequently happens, as we have previously described, when we absorb negative energy from one person and then pass it to the next.

In most cases, we are not the targets of people's negative energy. They have problems; they are not happy. They are frustrated and have no way of centering themselves or dealing with their tension, so they seek release from their tension, or pain by blaming or threatening others.

If we understand this, we realize there is no need to take their words and actions personally. The person expressing them does not actually intend to hurt us, but simply has to get rid of these negative feelings in this unfortunate emotionally immature manner.

If we remember that most of us have the emotional maturity of children, we will have much more patience and understanding, and will be more easily able to remain in our center in such situations. Then we can act from a centered and loving state of mind, which may mean being flexible and / or perhaps firm and assertive.

Although we may still have certain negative emotions, when we act from our center, they are not controlling us. There is nothing wrong with letting people know when we are angry or disappointed. There is a great difference between explaining to someone that we are angry and why and what we need from them in order to feel better, than on the other hand, allowing our anger to cause us to reject, threaten or demean them.

When we have lost our center we can do one or more of the following in order to regain it:

**1.** Do some slow deep **breathing**.

**2.** Take a **shower**, perhaps finishing with cold water.

**3.** Take a **walk,** preferably in nature.

**4.** Retreat to a place where we can be alone and **release** our tension by crying or hitting a pillow.

**5.** Put on some **music** and **dance** out our feelings.

**6. Talk** with an experienced listener - a psychologist, psychotherapist, group facilitator, clergy person or good friend - who can listen without taking sides and help us see what we need to learn here.

**7.** Bring one or more of the **pathways** to mind.

**8.** Do a deep **relaxation**.

**9.** Get a **massage** or take a **bath**.

**10. Play** some sport.

**11.** Engage in some **creative** or **recreational activity**

**12. Analyze** what exactly is the stimulus that is making us fearful or angry and discover the beliefs that are causing us to feel that way. Some questions would be:

**a.** What do I need here which I am not getting? What is my attachment?

**b.** What do I believe which makes me believe that I cannot be well if I do not get what I want?

**c.** If life, in fact, gives me exactly what I need in each moment to learn my next lesson, what is my lesson here?

In some cases, the lesson might be to simply accept what is happening and realize that our security, self-worth and freedom are not in danger.

In other cases, we may need to learn to manifest what we need more assertively but always lovingly.

One final point concerning centered action: Life is a mirror that reflects all of our emotions and actions back to us. When we act in an emotionally upset state, we often **say and do things which we really do, not mean,** and would not ordinarily say or do to others.

When we behave unpleasantly to others, we are creating future situations that will be very difficult to correct when necessary. We will likely regret our past lack of control, but it may then be **too late** to reach this person and create the relationship we want and "need" with him. It will be a shame to lose such sources of joy in our lives simply because we have not learned to return to our center before communicating.

## The message of this chapter is balance.

**1.** We need to **speak the truth,** but only when we **are in our center.**

**2.** We need to **help others without worrying** about **them or taking responsibility** for their reality.

**3.** We need to **be in our center** before making decisions, acting or responding.

These thoughts can be **placed in written form** where they can be seen and also programmed into the subconscious with **positive projection**.

### Technique no. 12

# CONTEMPLATING
# THE OPPOSITE EMOTION

### Why this is so beneficial

Our emotional reactions are a function of our conditioning and inner temperament. These can be changed. When we feel anger starting to arise, we can bring its opposite into our mind. We can cultivate feelings of forgiveness and love or peace rather than anger. We may not succeed at first but, with practice, we will be able to catch ourselves and change the feeling before it becomes too strong. This can be true of any emotion. If we feel jealousy, we can focus on self-acceptance, self-confidence or love for others. If we feel depressed, we can contemplate happiness, gratitude and love of life. We can think **of how small our problems really are in relationship to the universe** in which we live, and in comparison with people who have problems perhaps much more serious than ours. We can remember that 40,000 children die daily on this planet, because their parents do not have the means to keep them alive.

We can focus on how much we have to be grateful for. We can also realize that **every problem that comes to us is a gift** from life and an **opportunity** for us to grow stronger, more aware and freer from our illusions of weakness and danger.

**Love is the opposite of all negative emotions**. Where there is enough love, there is no room for other feelings. Love is the medicine for all negative feelings.

We can eventually gain the inner strength to forgive others no matter what they do. As the Christ has said, judge not so that you will not be judged. **Forgiveness and love create a sure and safe path towards overcoming negative emotions.**

Bringing the opposite positive emotion to mind is an ancient technique that allows us to cultivate alternative ways of feeling and reacting to situations. We **do not ignore or suppress** our negative emotions, but **simply direct our attention to their positive opposites**, allowing the new positive "thought forms" to grow within us. It is like having a garden in which we have weeds and flowers. We do not imagine that there are no weeds, but rather focus on the flowers, give them water, and manure.

This technique may at times for certain people be in contradiction with the catharsis techniques also suggested. When we do catharsis, we purposely focus on the negative and express it, while here we focus on the positive opposite. Each will have to decide for his or her own self which is most appropriate in each situation. There will be situations in which we cannot easily or practically tune into and express these negative emotions. Also, we pass through various stages in our lives, in which we have greater need for the one or the other way of handling our emotions.

Each will have to find his or her own opposite to the unpleasant emotion. This also may change from time to time. The opposite to fear at one time may seem to be "courage" and at another, "faith" and at still another, "love". The opposite of anger may be peace, love, understanding, forgiveness, faith etc. We can allow ourselves the freedom to flow each time with the particular opposite which presents itself in response to this exercise.

### A simple technique for
### connecting to positive emotions is:

When we realize that we are becoming overcome by negative emotions, it is possible to think, «This is the way I have been mechanically programmed to feel. **I would like the freedom to feel and to experience this situation differently**».

The exercise goes like this.
  **a.** We ask ourselves, **"what exactly am I feeling"** and we search for a name for that emotion.

  **b.** Once we have named it, we ask, **"what is the positive opposite** of this?"

  **c.** We then begin to **repeat the name of the positive opposite emotion**, allowing the mind to dwell on it, as we not only mentally repeat it, but also bring to mind the memory of that feeling as we have felt it in the past.

  **d.** We allow that **new positive energy to flow** through our body and mind. We might use our imagination and **visualize** ourselves feeling this new emotion and acting upon it.

  **e.** Then, we would do well to **act on this new positive emotion.**

### Note:
We have the right to choose how we want to feel.
Real freedom is to be able to be positive and happy,
regardless of external situations.

*Life Story no. 13*

# CANNOT BE HAPPY
# WHEN OTHERS ARE NOT

Tatiana is very sensitive and identifies emotionally with those close to her. She finds it very difficult to be happy when anyone near her is not well, either physically or emotionally. She feels responsible. She also believes that it is not proper to be happy when someone she loves is not well. She considers this to be a lack of love or interest.

Her youngest child, Amalia who is 5 years old, is frequently ill and loses days at school. Tatiana's mother Margarita has arthritic pains and cancer and is in bed most of the time.

Her husband Arnold would like to live in a happier home. Tatiana would like to accommodate him but just cannot allow herself to be happy and enjoy herself when her child or mother is not well.

**What could Tatiana's lessons be?**

**1.** To understand that her loved ones are independent, eternal souls who create their own reality in order to learn the lessons they have come to learn at this phase of their lives. It is not by chance that they are not well.

**2.** To give love and assistance without feeling responsible for the others' health, happiness or success.

**3.** To believe in a wise and divine justice for her loved ones.

**4.** To perceive them as eternal souls rather than as "my" child, parent, spouse, etc.

**5.** To realize that her happiness could lift her loved ones more than her sadness.

**6.** To ask herself, "Would I want others to be unhappy when I am not well or would this add to my burden?"

**Some beliefs that might help her are:**

**1.** Each of us is an eternal, evolving soul.

**2.** My loved ones are creating the situations they need in order to grow.

**3.** I can help others, but I cannot create their reality.

**4.** I can help others much more with my happiness.

**5.** There is a wise and just power controlling the universe.

# CHAPTER 13

# DISCOVERING MY CONSCIOUS AWARENESS

## THE TWELVE PATHWAYS - Part 4

These last three concepts of the Twelve Pathways have to do with being aware of our thoughts and energy, and bringing them to higher and finer levels of awareness, as well as remembering that we are all spiritual beings in the process of awakening.

### CALMING DISTURBANCES

**Pathway 10** «I am calming the restless disturbances of my mind in order to more clearly experience and merge with the world around me."

*PW. 10 Simplified:* **I am constantly calming my mind so as to clearly experience and merge with the world around me.**

*Key Words:* **CALMING DISTURBANCES**

An observation of how our minds function will expose the simple fact that they are not very organized, that they quickly shift from one subject to another. Our minds are at the mercy of a web of addictions that pull it here and there, into the past and future, away from the present.

Our happiness is continuously undermined by these thoughts of the past and future which prevent us from enjoying the present moment. Only when these disturbances are removed will there be peace. One way to lessen them is to transform our attachments to preferences. No attachments; no disturbances.

At the same time, however, we can also practice calming the disturbances through the practice of yoga, relaxation, **meditation** and other concentration techniques. Such techniques help us gain control over the mind and increase our freedom from the bondage of the addictions. In this way, we become **more aware**

**and united with the present and our environment.**

As the mind is freed from the debris created by these addictions, our reality is perceived more objectively and clearly. We experience the same events from a more peaceful and loving point of view. We are less stressed and less threatened by new experiences. We are more at peace with ourselves.

Techniques such as relaxation and meditation for calming the mind are most effective when performed daily with at specific times for 15 to 30 minutes. In addition, we can observe the mind throughout the day and **remind it to remain calm and quiet while in activity**.

In this way, we develop our **inner witness**. Our behavior becomes less robotic as we see each situation as new in itself.

Some might choose a special word or phrase for this work. Those of us who are religiously oriented can focus on any **name of God** that suits us and our belief systems. We might also focus on a **word** like "peace" or "love" or a **color** like green or blue.

The idea is that whenever we sense that the mind is becoming restless and losing its center, we introduce our **special word**, sound, color or idea, which removes the disturbances and brings us peace.

We can also bring to mind any of the concepts expressed in the **twelve pathways** or in this or any other book.

**Philosophy, wisdom and faith help quiet the mind.**

Some philosophical or spiritual perceptions that could help us rediscover our peace are:

**1.** Life gives me **exactly what I need** at every moment (at this moment) in order to learn my next lesson in this evolutionary growth process. (Learning our lessons in most cases simply means remembering the truth within.)

**2.** We are all **brother and sister souls brought into this world by the same creator** with the same fears, needs and emotions.

**3. I am capable of dealing** with whatever challenges life presents me.

**4.** I am an immortal divine soul.

**5. I am divine creation, energy** in the process of expressing myself in matter.

**6. I accept and love all unconditionally**, including myself.

**7.** My **self worth and security** have nothing to do with others' beliefs, behaviors or actions.

**8.** As long as I am in **harmony with my conscience**, surrounding circumstances and the actions of others do not concern me.

We do not, however, need to wait until the mind starts to wander to cultivate these truths. We can make a habit of daily focusing on a special word, phrase or concept whenever the mind is not occupied with reading, talking or listening. We can repeat this concept while walking, driving, waiting or while taking part in any type of activity in which we do not need to think.

Most religions use this technique for purifying the mind and making it suitable for higher states of consciousness. It calms the mind and allows us to **perceive the one reality behind all of these various forms and events.** We then experience more love and unity with all beings.

## AWARE OF MOTIVES

**Pathway 11** «I am constantly aware of which of the Seven Centers of Consciousness I am using, and feel my energy, perceptiveness, love and inner peace growing as I open all of the Centers of Consciousness.»

*P.W. 11 Simplified*: **I am constantly aware of my motives, and feel my energy, perceptiveness, love and inner peace growing as my centers open.**

*Key Words:* **AWARE OF MOTIVES**

The concept of the seven levels of consciousness is ancient and found in many systems of religion, mysticism and spiritual growth. Ken Keyes has formulated a modern explanation of this traditional concept. Each of us is motivated by different needs. These needs will depend upon and also affect our level of awareness, as well as our goals and behaviors.

As we evolve into higher levels of consciousness, we begin to function increasingly from the higher centers of consciousness, which are beyond the first three that are primarily concerned with fulfilling our security, pleasure and affirmation needs.

According to this pathway, we attempt to be conscious of what level we are operating from in a given situation. What is our **motive** at this moment? What are we seeking? How do we feel about ourselves and the world? Do we feel alienated or intimidated? Or, do we feel open and loving?

Our mind may move quickly from one center to another. We may be feeling love and happiness at one moment, and then find ourselves trapped in one of our addictions, closed up, and feeling hurt and anger the next.

In the process of evolution into higher consciousness, our higher centers of increased love and awareness are awakened, and the lower centers are satisfied from within and thus requiring less time and energy. At the present, most of us are controlled by our lower centers. Now we seek to free our thoughts, emotions and behavior from their control. It is like the difference between our car taking us where it wants to go and **our** taking **it** where **we** want **it** to go.

When we observe that we are functioning with motives or from states that we would not **prefer,** we can:

**1. Focus on a higher motive** or mode of functioning.

**2. Discuss** this with someone close to us.

**3.** Bring our **awareness to our heart center** or forehead, and allow our awareness to remain there for a few minutes.

**4. Remember any truths** that will liberate our energy from that level of relating to the world.

**5. Meditate, pray, dance** or do anything which makes our energy move.

**6. Offer** what we are doing to the **Divine.**

**7. Focus on love** toward others and what we are doing.

You may want to have this list with you so as to refer to it when there is need.

## EVOLVING BEING

**Pathway 12** «I am perceiving everyone, including myself, as an awakening being who is here to claim his or her birthright to the higher consciousness planes of unconditional love and oneness.»
*P.W. 12 Simplified:* **Everyone, myself included, is an awakening being evolving into higher planes of consciousness and love.**

*Key Words:* **EVOLVING BEING**

Each and every human being, **including** the one holding this book**,** is an **immortal soul** occupying a temporary body and mind for the purpose of evolution into higher levels of consciousness. This evolution of form started with tiny one-celled organisms on the earth millions of years ago. The consciousness, which occupies our bodies, has evolved through the animal kingdom and is now able to "operate" a human body and mind.

There is no reason why we should believe this process of evolution has stopped. We are continuing to evolve. We have no choice. We can either proceed unconsciously through experience and suffering, or consciously through the various systems that are available.

Thus, our children are not **our children,** but **awakening souls** who have their own destiny to fulfill. Our spouse is not **our** spouse, but a fellow soul, an **evolving being.** We need to see beyond the superficial clothing of nationality, political party, religion, color, sex, age, appearance and social class, and perceive all as evolving beings on their way to higher consciousness.

We will benefit also from seeing ourselves as souls and not as bodies and allowing ourselves to ascend into the higher levels of consciousness that are our right and our destiny.

We can frequently remember, **"I am not this body and personality. I am an eternal soul."**

There is a great difference between the meanings of the verbs **to have** and **to be.** We **have a body,** but we are not the body. We **have a personality,** but we are not the personality. We are the consciousness, which is observing the mind and thus, must be separate from it in order to observe it.

Who is this I who says "I" when we are two years old, ten years old, twenty five years old and fifty years old, even though the body and personality structure and beliefs are so different? Who is this being who is constant throughout those changing bodies and personalities throughout the years? The soul is the I who observes the mind and who is constant throughout the various changes.

Thus, we are **souls who have bodies.** We are not bodies who have a soul. As we do not yet experience our soul nature, we may benefit from **imagining how it feels to be a soul,** an immortal and perfect being in union with all other beings. In this way we will feel greater security and oneness.

Repeating this pathway often will help us find the peace and happiness we seek. This is perhaps the key to all of the other pathways.

The **essence** of these three pathways is:

**1.** To be continually aware of the mind and to **relax it** in ways which suit us.

**2.** To be aware of and **refine our motives** as much as possible.

**3.** To perceive all, including ourselves, as **souls in the process of evolution.**

## HOW TO EFFICIENTLY USE
## THE TWELVE PATHS FOR BECOMING FREE

Let us conclude with some suggestions regarding the most efficient means by which we can use the twelve paths to higher consciousness.

**1.** Those who have not yet **read** Ken Keyes' **Handbook to Higher Consciousness**, might chose to do so now so as to increase their understanding of the pathways and the best ways to work with them.

**2.** We can **memorize the pathways** so they are always ready to come to our aid and so we can become more and more convinced of their truth. Some find it helpful to use self-hypnosis or mind control techniques in order to implant these concepts more deeply into the subconscious mind.

**3.** We can realize that happiness can be found only by making **internal adjustments**, not by trying to change the outside world. We can seek to change the world simultaneously.

**4.** We can study the centers of consciousness and **become aware** of the centers from which we are primarily thinking and acting.

**5.** We can become more **clearly conscious of which addictions** are causing us to suffer, and in which ways. Then we will need to discover the beliefs that cause those addictions and begin to liberate ourselves from them.

**6.** We can **keep a diary** in the third person using the pronoun «he» or «she» or our name, noticing the patterns of behavior and the cause and result relationship between addictions and suffering.

**7.** We can use **questionnaires** to more objectively to observe our personality and motives.

**8.** We can join **growth groups** dedicated to acquiring freedom from addictions and evolution through the levels of consciousness.

**9.** We would do well to **keep company** with people who are less controlled by addictions. Addictions are contagious.

**10.** We can cultivate **practice, patience and perseverance.**
Here again are Twelve Pathways in simplified form for our convenience. You may want to photocopy it and carry it with you so you can refer to it when necessary.

# THE TWELVE PATHWAYS - SIMPLIFIED

P.W. 1 - I am **freeing myself** from addictions that cause me to suffer and prevent me from loving.

P.W. 2 - I am **discovering** how my addictions are **distorting** my perception of people and situations around me.

P.W. 3 - I **welcome life's lessons** that make me aware of which addictions must be reprogrammed.

P.W. 4 - Life gives me **exactly what I need** at this moment. If I am unhappy, then I am being dominated by attachments and expectations.

P.W. 5 - **Life is a mirror** reflecting my beliefs, emotions, thoughts, words and actions back to me.

P.W. 6 - **I accept myself exactly as I am,** including my addictions and weaknesses, which I transform into preferences and strengths.

P.W. 7 - I **communicate openly** and honestly with all people in order to dissolve my feelings of separateness.

P.W. 8 - I offer **loving compassionate help** to others while remembering that **they are learning** from their problems.

P.W. 9 - I **center myself** before acting. I avoid acting when emotionally upset.

P.W. 10 - I am constantly **calming my mind** so I may clearly experience and merge with the world around me.

P.W. 11 - I am constantly **aware of my motives** and feel my energy, perceptiveness, love and inner peace growing as my **centers open**.

P.W. 12 - Everyone, including myself, is an **awakening being evolving** into higher planes of consciousness and love.

Technique no. 13

# PUTTING OUR SELVES
# IN THE OTHER'S POSITION

### Why this is so beneficial

When we are in conflict with others, or are feeling hurt or angry, we can often gain insight and peace of mind by putting ourselves in the their position. When we imagine how the others must be feeling in order to act in the ways they do, we gain understanding, which simultaneously reduces our feelings of hurt, anger and rejection towards them. **Both our pain and anger are diminished through understanding.**
Our understanding allows us to help others move through their negativity.
The virtue of understanding is a basic prerequisite for love and conscious love relationships.

### A simple technique for gaining understanding is to:

We bring the other to mind and mentally seek to answer the following questions:
**1.** What might he or she be **feeling** in order to act in this way?

**2.** Is there anything that she or he is **not be getting** from me that is causing him or her to feel this way?

**3.** What does he or she **need from life** which might be causing this behavior?

**4.** What is she or he **trying to protect** with this behavior? (Perhaps security, self worth, freedom, certain pleasures?)

**5. What would I have to feel** in order to act this way?

**6.** If I were the other, **how would I like to be healed** in this situation?

We may need to realize that behind his or her behavior is a small fearful child who is trying to survive emotionally. Most of the time the problem is fear and self-doubt.
### Note:
Basic to this process is the understanding that all negative human behavior is a result of ignorance of our true nature, which leads to fear and then to all forms of self-centeredness and selfishness.

*Life Story no. 14*

# DO NOT CHANGE MY PROGRAM

Albert is a very organized person. He likes everything to be in its place and to be in control in all situations. In order to feel safe, he needs to be functioning within a program. He needs for this program to be airtight and not change. If for some reason beyond his control what he has programmed should change, he loses his serenity and can become very negative and even threatening. He immediately needs to find someone who is "responsible" for this unacceptable event and release his anger or frustration on the "guilty one". He has difficulty in flowing with changes as they develop.

His wife Candice on the other hand finds it very difficult to program anything. She feels limited by routines and time itself. She feels suppressed when she knows she has something specific to do the next day. She is usually late for her appointments and cannot understand why the others are upset with her.

Her tardiness in all matters is a constant source of conflict between her and Albert. Also, she is not very interested in keeping up the house. This infuriates Albert who is extremely attached to cleanliness and order. He cannot relax unless everything is in its "place". He also believes that the house is his wife's responsibility, and feels cheated when she does not take care of it to the degree that he would like.

The more he pressures her, the more she rebels and does less. The less she does, the more he becomes angry and aggressive. They live in a vicious circle of negativity.

How can they get free from this situation?

**Albert may need to strengthen the following beliefs:**

**1.** I feel safe and secure in every situation.

**2.** I trust in the wisdom of anything that might happen.

**3.** I feel secure and safe in dealing with anything that might occur.

**4.** Life gives, has given and always will give me exactly what I need for my evolution.

**5.** I feel safe flowing with life's changes.

**6.** I feel safe and secure regardless in all environments.

**7.** I understand and respect that my wife has different needs.

**8.** I express my needs assertively but lovingly.

**9.** I seek a balance between my needs and those of my loved ones.

**10.** I feel totally safe in an imperfect world.

### Candice may need to strengthen the following beliefs:

**1.** I would not like to wait for others, and thus do not keep them waiting.

**2.** I am free to be on time.

**3.** I am free to direct my energy in ways that create harmony with my family and others.

**4.** I understand and respect that my husband has different needs.

**5.** I communicate my needs assertively and lovingly.

**6.** Freedom is an internal state that I can experience in any situation.

**7.** I seek a balance between my needs and those of my loved ones.

**8.** I am free to direct my energy in ways that manifest my life goals.

# CHAPTER 14

# CHANGING OUR REALITY THROUGH POSITIVE THINKING

## THE NATURE OF MAN

Any explanation offered by man concerning his relationship to the universe will be subject to criticism, doubt, change, additions or subtractions. Here, I will only try to create a «working model» which will be simple enough and yet inclusive enough to communicate what I would like to express. For this purpose, we will borrow information from many systems of philosophy, religion, psychology and science.

As you read, try to remain open and avoid judging or rejecting any statements as right or wrong; just hold it all in the back of your mind as possibly true, then make your final judgment after a few months or years.

A look at the history of science and knowledge will show us a steady process of changing and adopting more all encompassing belief systems, without which we would still be living in the Dark Ages.

We have resisted every major scientist and thinker of their own time, only to have our children and grandchildren put them on a pedestal. Our great-grand-children will likely tear down those monuments and erect their own new ones. So, it is simply unscientific, unwise and futile to remain rigid in our beliefs and resist the evolutionary flow of our mental and spiritual development.

We are multidimensional beings. We contain many levels of being within ourselves. We have a body, a mind, and a soul. We might say that we have a physical body, an emotional body, a mental body and a spiritual body. These bodies are listed in their increasing subtly from more physical and dense to less physical, more energy-like.

It doesn't take much stretching of the mind or imagination to see that strong emotions can effect a person's thoughts and actions. Medical research has discovered the devastating effect strong emotions have on the body, sometimes leaving it completely exhausted and vulnerable to many disorders and aliments.

## WE CREATE OUR REALITY

We have already mentioned this fact a number of times, but it bears repeating because it is very slow to pass into our subconscious mind. Yes, we create all of the situations around us through our beliefs, thoughts, emotions, imagination, values and actions.

Very simply stated:

**As we believe we are**, so will we be.

As we believe **others** to be, so will they be.

As we believe **reality** to be, **so will it be.**

As we do unto others, so will they do unto us.

We can see this very clearly in the story of the little girl (Chapter 1) who thought she was a failure and thus created failure to suit her beliefs. Once she changed her attitude, beliefs, and corresponding behavior, she became a success and then created a new belief system, which created a new reality: success.

## THE PERSONALITY FILTER

Let us refer to diagram presented. In the top center, we find a circle from which runs a long tube labeled Ego Structure. The circle itself represents the soul, our source of life and thought.

Here in the center we find pure spiritual consciousness. As this pure consciousness begins its path down the tube, that is, through the Ego Structure, toward the external reality, it passes through the many "filters" of our Personality Conditioning. By the time this pure, unmodified, thought-energy reaches the external reality, it has been distorted and altered many times and finally emerges quite different from its original pure nature.

A common example of this is a man who feels affection for his friend and the impulse to express that love begins from the soul, but by the time it reaches the surface, it has gone through such filters as:

"Men don't show affection,"

"If I show this affection, will he misinterpret it?"

"What if he rejects my friendship?"

"I don't want to be rejected."

So, instead of a warm, loving embrace, the impulse comes out as a slap on the back and a, "How the hell are you?"

Such conditionings enter into every action, thought and perception that creates our reality. We see people in terms of our beliefs and values, not in terms of what they are.

We see them as Americans, Russians, Arabs, Europeans, Iraqis, Greeks, rich,

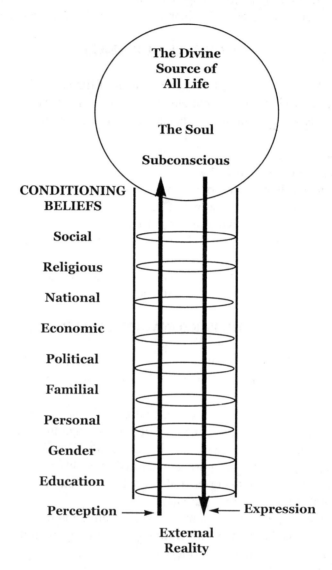

poor, beautiful, ugly, men, women, old, young, Christians, Jews, Moslems, Buddhists, spiritual, unspiritual, important, unimportant, intelligent, unintelligent, etc. All these judgments are based on our individual conditioning. We seldom see ourselves or another in a true and undistorted way.

Our conditioning begins at a very young age with our parents. From the moment our consciousness is focused in the womb, we begin to perceive the vibrations, attitudes, and emotions within and surrounding our mother.

This conditioning continues through our early years with our family, where our basic values and attitudes are formed by observing and copying or otherwise reacting to our parents' thoughts and actions.

At school, through the interactions with our teachers and pressure from our peer group, we begin to accept certain social values. We form our beliefs concerning male-female relationships by watching our parents, and later in life, we will almost surely recreate those same mechanisms and games we observed in their relationship or our relationship with them.

If our parents were frequently fighting, we may establish subsequent beliefs about the nature of a "normal relationship," which will include possessiveness, jealousy, competition, and general disharmony. We may set ourselves up for such similar situations that we believe must be so. This will occur until we can transform such a situation through personal growth and honest communication.

If we were mistreated as children and considered ourselves victims, we might believe we are bad, unworthy, and deserving of punishment and suffering. We will seek out, directly or indirectly, friends, relationships or marriage partners who will help us recreate this reality by mistreating us, thus fulfilling our inner belief that we are victims.

If we were surrounded by illness and beliefs about our "helplessness" in the face of "savage germs that will attack us for no reason at all," we will likely become psychologically and physiologically more susceptible to illness.

If we believe we can get attention and love only by being ill, we may subconsciously create illness so as to demand the attention of our loved ones, who we believe would otherwise ignore us.

If while in school, our teachers told us we were stupid and incompetent, and punished us for our mistakes, we may grow increasingly afraid of trying new things, due to the fear of failure.

## OUR CYCLE OF BELIEFS

This circular mechanism is:
   **1.** Our **beliefs** create our **emotions**.

   **2.** Our **emotions** create our **reactions** or **behaviors**.

   **3.** Our **behaviors** then provoke **reactions from our environment**.

   **4.** The **results** that are created by our reactions and behaviors **now confirm our original beliefs.**

Our beliefs create our reality and our reality then reconfirms our beliefs. We are confined within a prison in which the bars and walls are our beliefs.

These results and reactions are perceived by our senses. This information must then pass through the filtering process of our mind, which tends to accept only those facts that are in harmony with the present belief system. Depending on the facts accepted by this filtering process, the belief system is either confirmed or modified in some way. On the one hand, this process helps us maintain a stable personality structure, but on the other, we become prisoners of our own limited belief structure.

For example, if we believe that we cannot succeed at a certain task, we will create thoughts and emotions that will undermine our energies and thoughts in a way that will lead to failure. We will then perceive our failure, which will be accepted by our filtering system, which recognizes this as a verification of our original belief and will say, "See, I was right; I am a failure".

This example is true of every positive and negative belief system. There is a cyclical reconfirming action between the belief structure and the external reality. This holds true for beliefs about health, money, relationships, personal capabilities, the nature of life and death, and every other human idea.

The cyclical self-imprisoning activity usually continues until there is some type of crisis that forces us to break away from a particular belief. These life crises may occur in many ways: through illness, separation from a loved one, or loss of something important to us such as money, fame, success or perhaps a depression, when we become disillusioned with our life.

These "self-created" catastrophes, originating from within, must be distinguished from those negative circular traps, which are a habitual functioning of the personality conditioning. The former is created to break down the activity of the second.

## LACK OF SELF CONFIDENCE

A common example of this mechanism is what often happens to people who lack inner security and believe they must have someone upon whom to depend. This is most often expressed in terms of a husband-wife relationship. Our social conditioning (especially in the Middle East and Orient) causes many women to feel inadequate without a man because they are conditioned to believe that:

**1.** A woman must be married to be happy.

**2.** She is not successful or acceptable unless she is married.

**3.** She is the weaker sex and must become dependent upon her husband and succumb to his will.

In many cases, this conditioning is also accompanied by more destructive beliefs like:

**1.** Women must be ignored and mistreated by their husbands.

**2.** Men are insensitive and lacking in affection.

**3.** Men are unfaithful.

**4.** Men are unloving.

These are very common beliefs, especially in countries, where sex roles are more rigidly defined. Not all succumb to these beliefs, but they are common and have a hold to varying degrees on both sexes.

A woman who believes these programmed concepts will set herself up with a man at all costs because to remain unmarried will simply be intolerable. She will likely fear that some day her husband will stop loving her, leave her or cheat on her.

Furthermore, if she has the second set of beliefs, her relationship will be one of the victim, suffering mistreatment from her husband. She will complain about it and reconfirm it daily, thereby affirming her beliefs that she is a victim. In addition, her husband may find a lover to correspond with her inner belief of the unfaithfulness of men, and she will now live the reality that she believed would come to exist. Although it is actually a projection of her beliefs, she experiences it as something separate from her and out of her control.

Then, perhaps a "catastrophe" of some type may occur, such as a separation through a parting of ways, or perhaps her husband's departure from his physical body.

If such a situation should arise, this woman is placed at a crisis point at which if she continues with her present belief system, she will fall into complete despair based upon the fact that, "she must be married to be happy, safe and accepted."

If she also believes that the body is all that there is, she will be even more devastated by the finality of the event of her loved one's death. Whereas a woman with a faith in the existence of the soul will experience the same less painfully. (The same could be true for a man who loses his loved one.)

She now has the opportunity to change her beliefs and realize that she has the same potential for happiness without a husband as she had with one, and that happiness is an inner state, independent of external factors. Then this crisis will have served as a growth experience and she will become stronger and more dynamic, functioning now more from her previously ignored inner strengths.

Some of the above beliefs might create conflict within her when she begins to find her own strength. She might be living with two conflicting belief systems until she proves one or the other to herself.

## THE BELIEF THAT "I CANNOT"

We set ourselves up for many failures when we are convinced that what we are about to attempt won't work out even before we try. We convince ourselves with statements like, "I can't draw; I'm not artistic; I don't have talent." What we mean is that in the past we hadn't been able to draw, and hadn't taken the time to develop our artistic talents, perhaps because when we were younger someone laughed at our attempts or played down the importance of this activity for us.

We all have abilities within us that we can cultivate, if we so desire, with discipline and a positive attitude. We also have some specific talents which we may develop more easily or quickly than others.

Some people say, "I can't relax; I am too nervous; I can't stop thinking and worrying." What they really mean is that they haven't really tried with an open mind to learn how to relax. They haven't given it the time and energy, for example, that they have given to watching television, reading books, working or recreation.

They have come to believe they are nervous and helpless, and that since they have no control over it, they are trapped in this state. They might not believe they could be, or deserve to be, relaxed and happy.

Almost all persons who have systematically applied the techniques of breathing, exercise, relaxation and meditation have achieved some degree of success in learning to relax.

## CRYSTALLIZED BELIEFS ABOUT OTHERS

Some say, "There is no way I can talk to my husband," or "There is no way my wife will ever change; she will always be that way."

These types of beliefs and expressions do nothing but prevent the situation from improving. If we have precluded the possibility of change in our minds, we have helped to preclude it in reality, and have constantly contributed to the circular negative reality about which we are complaining.

If we cannot see our spouses as communicative or accepting, we are forcing them to remain as they are by our thoughts, words and actions.

If we believe people are closed and selfish, we will project those qualities onto them, and thus be surrounded by people of that type. Even if they are not normally that way, we will, by subconscious communication, draw those qualities out of ordinarily open and generous people, or we will perceive motives that are not there and misinterpret neutral comments as offensive and negative. We will perceive reality, as we believe it to be.

If we believe taxi drivers to be ill mannered and inconsiderate, then we will invariably experience exactly those qualities in the cabs we enter.

There are times when we don't even give people a chance to respond because we have a preconceived idea of how they will act before they even do.

This reminds me of a joke I once heard.

"A man was traveling on the highway between Athens and Thessalonika when he unfortunately ran out of gas. Thoroughly disgusted and annoyed by his predicament, he began walking up the road with the empty gas can he had in his trunk, looking for a house from which he might borrow some gasoline to get him to the next gas station.

"As he was walking along, he began thinking of his terrible situation and how very great his problem was because no one really cared anymore. No one was going to help him anyway. He began to curse the modern Greeks because they had lost the openness and hospitality of the ancient Greeks, and everyone was out for himself.

"Finally, he arrived at a house and banged angrily on the door. When the unsuspecting owner of the house answered the door, the disgusted man threw the can at him and turned away shouting, 'Take the can and go to hell'."

None of us are innocent of this tendency to play and replay out in our minds the upcoming events and interactions, creating completely preconceived expectations as to how things will work out. (Not to mention the wasted hours we spend thinking over past encounters, mulling over what we could have said in our defense.)

Still, this tendency to create future events in our minds before they happen can be used to our advantage if positively applied.

## THE NEED FOR CHANGE

There exists within us a natural impulse toward evolutionary growth leading us towards the development of our human potential and creative power. This can be witnessed in the continual evolution of our knowledge and creative expression, from our days as cave dwelling beings to our present technological society. This, however, shows only one aspect of our growth: the intellectual, rational development.

We could compare ourselves to a diamond in the rough whose beauty is hidden by coarse and irregular surfaces. Slowly, as we learn through life's lessons, overcoming obstacles and developing inner strength, our outer roughness is polished off and our inner beauty begins to shine through.

For most of us, this growth takes place unconsciously. Just as there are ways to learn physics, music or cooking, there are methods by which to consciously and more effectively learn about our self.

Doctors look at persons as bodies and treat them accordingly, paying little or no attention to the mind, emotions or soul. The psychologist emphasizes the mind and emotions, ignoring the body and the soul. The religious leader speaks of the soul, but cares little for the needs of the body, mind, or emotions.

If we are to help ourselves, we will have to become our own "doctor-psychologist-priest" and work simultaneously on our "body-mind-soul". These three aspects of our being are inextricably bound together and require equal attention on the evolutionary path.

It is true that each will have his or her own emphasis. Some of us will need to pay more attention to getting our body together, while others will need to emphasize the mind, and yet others will need to dedicate themselves to their spiritual development. Each one of us will find his/her own balance and our individual emphasis will also vary with time as our needs shift.

## HOW WE CHANGE OUR BELIEFS

The central premises of our work until now are:

**1.** That our reality is created through the filters of our changing belief systems.

**2.** That we have an essential inner nature that is beyond the conditioning of those beliefs.

**3.** That we can change our reality by changing our belief system.

In such a case, we will be interested in discovering and transforming the beliefs that limit and obstruct our peace, love and happiness.

Identifying our beliefs will be the first step. We can do this by observing our lives and writing down what it is that we believe. We can make a list of beliefs and values. This will require careful and objective observation of our perceptions and actions. The questionnaires in this book and on our web site will help.

We may want to set up some main categories under which we will itemize our beliefs. For example, we might find some of the following self- limiting beliefs:

### A. I CANNOT...
**1.** Protect myself from: (Microbes, people, animals, life, etc.)
**2.** Cope with life alone.
**3.** Relax or meditate.
**4.** Sing, dance, draw, play a musical instrument.
**5.** Feel comfortable with unfamiliar people.
**6.** Lose weight, quit smoking or stop drinking.
**7.** Become well physically (emotionally).
**8.** Cope with aggressive people.
**9.** Overcome my fears.
**10.** Feel safe and secure.
**11.** Succeed professionally.
**12.** Receive the respect and love I need from others.
**13.** Cope with the death of loved ones.
**14.** Operate machines of various types.
**15.** Be happy without _____
**16.** Feel safe without_____
**17.** Feel worthy unless _____
**18. Other**_____

### I AM NOT WORTHY:
(Of what? love, health, happiness, happiness, success, satisfaction?)
**1.** When others criticize me, accuse me or reject me.
**2.** When others are angry with me.
**3.** When my children (or spouse or parents) are not happy, successful, satisfied loving.
**4.** When I do not know as much as others.
**5.** Unless I have a love partner.
**6.** If my house is not clean and in order.
**7.** If my spouse loves or pays attention to someone else.
**8.** If I am not professionally successful.
**9.** If I do not have enough money.
**10.** If I am not physically attractive.
**11.** If I do not make an impression on others, or if they do not pay attention to

me.

12. If I do not have many sexual successes.

13. If others do not respect me.

14. If my child is not healthy.

15. If I do not have what others have.

16. If I am not perfect.

17. If I do not do many things.

18. If the others laugh at me or tell me lies.

19. If I do not have _____

20. If I do not _____

21. Other_____

## C. I MUST HAVE
(in order to feel secure, worthy, satisfied, free, happy, etc.)

1. Others' love and acceptance.

2. Others' help and support.

3. Others' attention and admiration.

4. Coffee, cigarettes, or alcohol.

5. Various specific foods

6. Sex

7. Tranquilizers

8. A specific spouse or love partner

9. Money

10. I must have / do _____in order to feel safe.

11. I must have / do _____in order to feel happy.

12. I must have / do _____in order to feel my self worth.

13. I must have / do _____in order to feel free.

14. I must have / do _____in order to feel meaning in life.

15. I must have / do _____in order to feel satisfaction.

16. Other _____

## D. GENERAL BELIEFS

1. Life is difficult and dangerous.

2. People are egoists and not trustworthy.

3. I am weak, a victim of the powers around me.

4. There is no love in this world.

5. My self worth depends on others' opinions.

6. My self worth depends on the results of my efforts.

7. My self worth is dependent on how I am compared with others.

8. I need others in order to feel safe.

## E. OTHER SELF LIMITING BELIEFS

1. I must be like others in order for them to accept me.

**2.** If they do not love and accept me, I am not safe.

**3.** If others do not accept me, I am not worthy.

**4.** I must be "right" in order to be worthy and for them to love me.

**5.** I must be perfect in order for others to accept me and love me.

**6.** I must be better than others in order to be worthy.

**7.** I must be loved and accepted by those close to me in order to be happy.

**8.** In order to feel worthy I must be capable and successful.

**9.** My happiness is not in my own hands. I am the victim of external factors.

**10.** My past experiences have created my present life and will limit my future. I am not free to change.

**11.** There is only one possible "right" solution for my problems. If that does not happen, it will be a catastrophe.

**12.** I am in danger and must be afraid. I must continuously be prepared for on-coming dangerous situations.

**13.** I must be dependent upon others and have someone stronger than myself to rely on.

**14.** If my life does not unfold in the way I imagine it should, my existence will be unbearable.

**15.** It is easier to avoid difficulties and responsibilities than to face them.

**16.** Some people are evil and sinful and should be judged and punished.

**17.** We must be anxious and upset about our problems.

**18.** Those around us will never change.

**19.** Others are to blame for my unhappiness.

**20.** I cannot accept my problems.

**21.** If others learn about my weaknesses or faults, they will reject me.

**22.** I cannot feel peace if my loved ones are not well, happy and satisfied.

**23.** I cannot love myself when others reject me.

**24.** If I do not suppress my feelings, they will overwhelm me and I will be in pain.

**25.** I am this body and this personality.

**26.** I must control everything that happens in my life, especially the health and actions of my loved ones. Otherwise something will go wrong.

**27.** Others do not care about me.

**28.** I am unlucky.

We can see that the above beliefs will distort our perception of ourselves, others and life.

## A TECHNIQUE IN SELF OBSERVATION

A useful practice which will help us with this is to sit for a few moments, let our minds become empty and relaxed (concentration on our breathing is also helpful here) and then begin to remember the day's activities from an objective point of view. Be a witness to everything that has happened; do not make any judgments as to whether any of the actions were the right or wrong.

Do this for about fifteen minutes and then write down the beliefs that instigated and affected your behavior and perceptions during that time. You can do this for your early childhood experiences as well.

This practice should be done often; at least once a week (if not daily). After a year or two, it can be done less frequently.

At first, it may be difficult to uncover our most deeply rooted conditionings, because we may not want to face them. It may mean a more rapid change of reality than we are ready for in the beginning. But regular practice of this system will slowly dislodge these hidden core beliefs from their adamant position and we will be able to identify them clearly.

This, of course, will not always be a pleasant process for we will be forced to face many inconsistencies and imperfections within our personality. There may occasionally be a period of feeling that there is no ground to stand on, that we are hovering in the air between two opposing cliffs of belief structures.

There is, however, no other solution. This is similar to suddenly becoming aware that we are less happy than we would like to be because we are actually in prison. We never knew why were not as happy as we would like to be and are just now realizing that it is because we are actually living in a prison created by the bars which we call our beliefs. This may not be a pleasant realization, but it is the first step towards getting free. We can dissolve and replace them with beliefs that will create a much happier reality.

Eventually, we will need to dissolve all beliefs and experience the truth without concepts, but this is for most like walking on water before we have learned to walk firmly on land.

## VISUALIZING POSITIVE REALITIES

Imagining alternative realities will be the next step in this process of change. At this stage we can begin to work with specific problems and imagine alternative realities in which those problems don't exist.

Some example would be:

**1.** If we frequently have a cold during the winter, we can close our eyes and visualize that we are **completely healthy** throughout the year. A part of our problem was a result of our belief that we will "have a cold" in the winter.

**2.** If we frequently argue with our spouse, we can visualize ourselves enjoying a **harmonious relationship** with him or her.

**3.** If we fear speaking to large groups, we imagine ourselves feeling **comfortable and full of love** as we stand before them.

**4.** If we fear traveling in airplanes, we take an imaginary trip with take off, flight, and landing all **being safe and enjoyable**.

**5.** If we are ill, we imagine ourselves as **well and happy**.

**6.** If we are frequently tired, we imagine ourselves with **vitality and stamina**.

**7.** If we are worried about a loved one, we perceive him or her immersed in **white healing light**.

**8.** If we lack confidence in ourselves, we visualize ourselves as **confident and comfortable** in every situation.

**9.** If we doubt our self worth, we visualize ourselves with **self-acceptance and self-respect** in every situation.

**10.** If we fear dancing in front of others, we visualize ourselves **dancing freely and gracefully**, sharing our creativity and inner beauty with others.

**11.** If we fear a certain person, we visualize ourselves in **loving contact** with that person, feeling equality, inner power and compassion for him or her.

**12.** If we are unable to tell the truth, we visualize ourselves **sharing the truth** with others.

**13.** If we are afraid to "be ourselves," we visualize ourselves **"being ourselves"** in all situations and with all people.

**14.** If we fear some types of persons or animals, we visualize ourselves in contact with them **feeling very comfortable and loving**.

## A VOTE FOR OUR PREFERRED REALITY

We are not seeking to ignore reality. We are casting a "vote" of conscious mental energy, affirming the reality in which we would prefer to live.

The positive projection of an alternative, more positive, life-fulfilling reality is most effective when it is done in a deeply relaxed state of mind, in which the conscious mind is calm enough to concentrate on one image, concept or idea more profoundly and completely. In this way, the subconscious mind is more effectively programmed. This is a type of self-hypnotism, positive projection or "Mind Control". There are many ways to reach this relaxed state of mind and body for making projections.

At the end of this chapter, we have placed an outline for a possible projection technique.

We may also sit with the spine straight, and while breathing deeply and counting backward from 20 to 1, arrive at a relaxed and concentrated state of mind. With each backward- counting step, we feel the mind sinking deeper into relaxation. Once the body and mind are relaxed, we can project our preferred positive reality. This can be very effective in changing our actual physical reality, if practiced for ten minutes, two or three times each day.

## A WORD OF CAUTION

We can save ourselves a great many problems by using this technique for unselfish purposes only. It would be unwise to waste such a technique on material objects or for causing harm to others. Whatever we project outwards will come back to us. Our positive thoughts will come back to us as pleasant experiences, our selfish thoughts as unpleasant experiences.

This is very subtle. I knew a woman who used this technique to supposedly "send happiness" and love to a man she loved, but she limited that love and happiness as coming only from herself. In other words, what she was really sending out was that she wanted that man to be with her and marry her. I have no doubt that she loved him and wanted him to be happy, but she was placing conditions on how he was to acquire that happiness, that he could only be happy if he was with her. We simply don't have the right to place such conditions on our love and projections because we will be projecting our will on another person.

It is best to see the person we love surrounded by light and healing love, without any attachment or desire for recognition on our own part. This brings us to the next step of this process.

## FORGET THE PROBLEM

Then we forget about the problem. Once we have projected the reality we would like to see, it is necessary to completely disregard it. We should not wait around, worrying and wondering if something will happen. "A watched pot never boils." Our anxiety will obstruct our success. This shows a lack of faith in what we have just done.

We need to have faith that if we have set the proper forces in motion, although there might be a certain amount of delay involved, all will turn out perfectly for the best possible evolution for all involved. Patience is essential.

This also means that we should avoid talking about our problems. Words, like thoughts and actions, feed reality. We just perpetuate the condition in that way. Of course, if we are sharing our problems with a person who can help us see it more objectively, then such discussion is useful. This is different from complaining about our problems to family and friends.

## LIVE IN THE PRESENT

We need to live in the present moment. Let our eyes and ears be open and experience the here and now. The present is actually our only reality. The future and past are illusions. They do not exist except in our minds. All our limitations are based on the past and our anxieties are of the future. Our freedom lies in the present moment, which can be completely unconditioned if we let go of the past and future.

A technique would be to sit for a few minutes each day and repeat:
**"The point of power is in the present."**
We should forget everything else, open our eyes, and look around us and become absorbed in the present. This will have a very powerful, energizing and harmonizing effect if practiced regularly.

## ENERGY EMBRYOS

An example of how our thoughts become reality can be seen in a scientific discovery through Kirlian photography in which photographs were taken of a fertile chicken's egg. The energy field that appeared on the photograph was in the exact form of the chicken embryo, although there was no physical embryo formed at this stage of development. We could hypothesize that the consciousness of the chicken-to-be gave a form to the energy field, which began to condense along the meridians of the embryonic chicken. Then, the physical elements began to form around these energy lines, which might be correlated to the energy centers of the body and the acupuncture meridians with which Oriental doctors work.

We can hypothesize that our thoughts are gathering energy and creating our physical reality, including our body and material conditions.

## DISCOVERING AND RELEASING THE CAUSE

We might also need to discover the origin of the negative and limiting beliefs we would like to transform. We will find that they are based on past experiences. This work usually requires an experienced guide whom we trust and feel safe with. It usually requires some type of inner search through regressions, EMDR or other similar techniques in which we bring to the surface the experiences of the past and allow them to be discharged through some type of catharsis, such as yawning, crying, shouting, hitting (a pillow), moving, etc.

This obviously cannot be done through a book, but the reader can get a clearer picture of what this entails in the chapter on **Healing Our Inner Child**.

## BEHAVIORAL THERAPY

Now we need to let our actions follow our new beliefs. As much as possible we allow our actions to be based on the reality of the new alternative beliefs we are working to manifest. These actions will bring into physical reality the vibrations we have been working with in our imagination.

All this is based on the fact that consciousness directs energy, which controls matter. In other words, the thoughts we send out are followed by a flow of energy, which will slowly take the form of that consciousness, and that energy will precipitate the actual physical form or reality.

There comes a point where analyzing and searching for reasons must to lead to action. We can analyze why we fear something for years, or we can simply, as already discussed, gradually approach it. Each individual will need find his or her own process and timing for this. We might want to answer the following questions:

**1. If I had already changed my old limiting belief** to a positive one, **what**

**would I be doing** that I am not doing now because I am still obstructed by the old limiting one? We can make a list of activities.

### Some sample answers might be:

**a.** If I were free from my belief that they would laugh at me if I took dance classes, I would start today.

**b.** If I believed I was worthy enough, I would take a vacation or do something just for my pleasure.

**c.** If I were free from my fear of what my mother thinks, I would start this _____ activity.

**d.** If I were sure I would succeed, I would start a business.

**e.** If I were free from what others think, I would go back to school.

**f.** If I had more inner security. I would change jobs.

**g.** If I accepted myself more, I would be myself in more situations.

**h.** If I believed I was a soul in evolution, I would spend much more time on my spiritual evolution.

**i.** If I were free from the idea that others are trying to limit me, I would exercise and meditate daily.

When we have made a list of activities or behaviors we would increase or initiate if we had already changed our belief system, we can choose which action we will start with, even though we have not yet actually changed the belief.

Acting as we would if we already believe something positive allows our subconscious to gradually adapt to that new positive belief.

We can change behavior by transforming beliefs or change beliefs by altering our behavior.

**2.** A second question would be, **"What would I cease doing** if I had already freed myself from a particular limiting belief because I am doing so now only because I am forced to by that belief?"

We can make a list and then choose the activity that we will begin to limit or cease altogether as a step toward freeing ourselves from a situation that causes pain for ourselves and others.

### Some sample answers might be:

**a.** If I were free from the idea that others evaluate me by my appearance, I would spend less time and energy worrying about how I look.

**b.** If I believed that I am an immortal soul, I would spend less time trying to make on making more money than I need, and give time to my spiritual growth.

**c.** If I were sure that I am worthy as I am and that I am not responsible for others' realities, I would say "no" more often.

**d.** If I knew for a fact that I was divine energy, divine creation, I would cease spending time trying to prove my self worth.

**e.** If, in fact, I experienced that we are all one spiritual family, I would spend less time on my superficial needs and more time helping those with more basic needs.

**f.** If I knew I would be safe and secure, I would leave my job for more satisfying one even if it is a lower paying one.

## CONNECTING TO SPIRITUAL
## AND LOGICAL TRUTHS

Ultimately, we must perceive reality from a more logical or spiritual point of view. This is the essence of philosophy, where we seek to discover the truth. This means we either seek to see what is happening more objectively or to connect to the spiritual truth behind what we are observing. There is a slight difference between a logical and spiritual truth.

For example, let us say we believe that our self worth is dependent upon what others think of us. The **logical truth** would be that this cannot be true as each person has a different subjective opinion of us. Thus, upon whose perception is our self worth based? It makes no sense. (Our answer is usually, "The person who has the worst opinion.")

The **spiritual truth** would be that we are creations of the divine and thus worthy of love and respect at all times, despite our weaknesses and mistakes, just as all aspects of nature.

Spiritual and logical truths can free us from much emotional pain without making us insensitive.

Many of the spiritual and logical truths that will free us from our mistaken self-limiting programming are mentioned in the chapters on the Twelve Pathways to Higher Consciousness. Others are mentioned in the chapters on Written Affirmations and Self-Acceptance.

## A FIVE PRONGED APPROACH

Working on transforming our belief system is a five pronged approach
   **1. Create a vital body and mind** with proper diet, exercises, breathing techniques, relaxation, meditation, etc.
   **2. Analyze** and **transform** our belief system.
   **3.** Daily **visualize** ourselves having already made that change in our belief system.
   **4. Act** as if we have already changed our beliefs.
   **5. Strengthen** within those **spiritual and logical truths** that will free us.

**"The truth will set you free."**

Jesus Christ

Technique no. 14

# GUIDELINES FOR
# POSITIVE THOUGHT PROJECTION
(Similar to the Silva Mind Control Technique)

**A. The body position** is with the spine straight and the muscles comfortable and relaxed

**A. The surroundings** should be protected from disturbances. If alone, disconnect the telephone. Better to be alone unless others are also participating with you.

**c. The technique**

1. Take 5 to 10 slow deep breaths

2. Now take a deep inhalation, hold your breath while focusing on the forehead, and then while exhaling, imagine the number three **flash** in your mind **three times**. Then, on a second breath, do the same with the number **two** three times and then the number **one** three times.

3. Now check your body and **relax** the parts that are not completely relaxed.

4. **Count backward** from **10 to 1**. With each number feel your body and mind falling inward into a deeper and deeper state of relaxation.

5. Imagine that you are in a **place in nature** (real or imaginary) where you feel even more peaceful and relaxed.

6. If this is the **first time** you are performing this technique for changing a **specific** negative thought form, then create a mirror in your mind with **blue** light around it. In this blue rimmed mirror imagine your negative thought form - your negative belief - or your self as you were but would not like to be anymore.

7. Now **smash** this mirror into pieces and see the old thought form totally **destroyed**, never to be created again.
When doing this after the first time with each specific issue that you want to change or work on, you will **never** recreate the blue rimmed mirror but will bypass parts 6 and 7 and go **directly** from no. 5 to no. 8.

**8.** Now bring to mind your positive affirmation that you would like to program into your subconscious mind.

**a.** Repeat it **three** times, feeling it and letting it pass deeply within you.

**b.** Now repeat it three more times imaging that you are declaring this truth to your **family** and that they accept and affirm it.

**c.** Now repeat it mentally three more times imagining that you are **shouting** it with such power that it is heard throughout the **universe**. Imagine your mental shout reaching the far reaches of the universe.

**9.** Now imagine your **new positive thought form** of your self, as you would like you to be. As you will be when you have changed your beliefs system. Imagine however that **you are that way** now already. This can be done in a **white rimmed mirror.**

**10.** Visualize yourself with inner **security** and **self-confidence** in all situations. Imagine yourself feeling **peaceful**, comfortable and **loving** with all persons, including your self.

**11.** Create **positive images** concerning any other issues that are important to you.

**12.** Slowly count from **1 to 5 returning** to waking consciousness.

### Some Guidelines:

**1.** Work on your own **character transformation** rather on changing the world around you.

**2.** Send **light and love to others** without specifying **what** should actually happen in their lives.

**3.** Be **regular** practicing at least once a day, but twice or thrice would be even better.

# *PERFECT, STRONG AND CONSCIENTIOUS*

Janet is a superwoman. She is extremely capable, efficient and conscientious. When she has something to do, she will not rest until it is accomplished. She can not live with "matters pending". She can rest only when they have been completed. She is strong and does not ask help from others. She is always volunteering her services and taking on more and more work at home, at the office and in the community.

At work, she prefers to execute projects herself rather than allocate them. She does not have much trust in how others will perform. Basically, she trusts only herself.

In addition to an eight-hour day at the office, she does all the cooking and housework as well as taking care of any car repairs and driving the children back and forth to their various extracurricular activities. She has plenty of energy, sleeps only about four hours and is usually very positive, except in relationship to her husband Louie whom she rejects for his "laziness, lack of responsibility and indifference to the fact that she does so much and he so little".

A year ago she and her family learned that she has cancer. No one in the family seems to have digested this. They can not conceive that she might not be well or that she might need help. They have all become so used to and dependent on the idea that she is strong and without needs, that they cannot perceive her as needing. No one can hear her needs, because she herself has not yet accepted that she is allowed to have them. She has identified with the role of the strong and conscientious person and has never allowed herself to feel or express weakness.

Louie was not always so inactive. He has become much more so since he has been with Janet. Her speed and stamina, have given him an inferiority complex and he reacts by simply withdrawing and letting her do everything. Even if he did something, she would find some reason why it was not good or fast enough. He has lost his self-esteem. He has lost his inner sense of self-worth and is not interested in doing things at her pace, and thus, does nothing in addition to his workday except watch television.

The children too have become used to being taken care of and have not learned to help out in the home. Louie and the children simply cannot perceive her as weak or needy. Neither can she.

But now her cancer demands changes from all of them.

How can they approach these changes more harmoniously?

### Janet might have to learn some of the following:

1. To accept others as they are.
2. To learn to express her needs and what she expects more clearly assertively and lovingly.
3. To explain more clearly to others how she feels when their agreements are not kept.
4. To detach her sense of self-worth from the results of her actions. Not to be attached to the results of her actions.
5. To allow others the time and space to be motivated to do their work.
6. To have more faith in others and their abilities.
7. To listen to others so as to understand what their problems are.
8. To love and accept others even when they are unable to be conscientious.
9. To accept need and weakness in herself and others.
10. To feel worthy of love and respect even when she is in need of help.
11. To understand how a person's needs or fears can obstruct his or her effectiveness.

### Some beliefs which might help her:

1. I love and accept others as they are, along with their faults and weaknesses.
2. I accept and love myself regardless of the results of my efforts.
3. I have faith in the divine being in each, and allow all to execute their own responsibilities.
4. The world can function without me.
5. I offer whatever I can, but allow others to maintain responsibility for their realty.
6. I care for myself creating a healthy body and a peaceful mind.
7. I feel safe and worthy even when I am not able to complete what I have to do.
8. My self worth is based on my being and not on what I achieve.

### Some beliefs that might help Louie are:

1. I love Janet and I want to help her, regardless of her attitude.
2. I am capable and enjoy being useful and helpful.
3. I accept and love myself exactly as I am.
4. I understand my wife's needs and wish to help her.
5. My wife needs me at this time and I want to be there for her.
6. I am capable of handling any responsibility.

# CHAPTER 15

# WHY SOME OF US
# DO NOT REALLY WANT
# TO IMPROVE OUR LIVES

When we have decided to make an effort toward self-transformation or self-improvement, we might encounter various types of subconscious resistances. Understanding them might help us free ourselves from them and proceed more smoothly and effectively.

## RESISTANCE TO DEVELOPMENT.

What are some of those resistances?

**1.** Some of us may be caught up in **resistance toward what others would like from us**. We might have developed rebellious or antagonistic relationships with others, and become determined not to let them have their way or get what they want. Perhaps we do not want to allow them to believe they might be right about something they are asking us to do. Thus, even though we want to make a positive change in our lives, we subconsciously refuse to do so in order to make sure we don't give this satisfaction to someone who is trying to pressure us, change us, or who does not accept us as we are.

In such cases, we might function in self-destructive ways. Many adolescents go through this stage, occasionally resorting to narcotics or other self-destructive lifestyles. I have seen persons refuse to finish one last course which they need in order to complete their university diploma simply because they do not want to give that satisfaction to their parents who have "suppressed them or rejected them", or as means of making a statement against the "system".

Some of us carry this obstacle of rebelliousness with us all the way to the grave.

In such a case, we must distinguish between **freedom** and **rebelliousness or reacting**. Rebelling or reacting is a form of programming in which we are forced to do the opposite of what others or sometimes even we ourselves want. **We are not free in such cases to do what is truly in our best interest,** but rather are forced by our programming to do the opposite of what is asked.

**2.** A second obstacle is the **inertia of habit.** We get locked into habits that then become our familiar reality. We become accustomed to this reality and feel safe in it even when it is painful or self-destructive. For many people, **familiar suffering and limitation** are **preferable to unfamiliar happiness and freedom.** Many of us prefer to stay in the narrow confines of the familiar and known, rather than risk the freedom of the unknown. Improvement and change mean moving beyond the known.

Also, these habits can engage our energy patterns in ways that control our minds without our conscious awareness. For example, we reach for food, a drink or a cigarette, turn on the TV, zap through the channels, pick up the phone and call someone, all mechanically without being conscious of what we are doing. We do not consider whether what we are doing is **actually beneficial for us** or even if it **is what we really want to do.** When the mind loses its ability to control these unconscious movements, we suffer from compulsive acts and thoughts.

Such problems are seldom solved through analysis alone. They require a strong decision and a willingness to endure the pain of withdrawal symptoms by placing ourselves in a situation in which we simply **cannot get to what we mechanically desire.** Centers for detoxification offer such opportunities.

**Twelve step groups** consisting of people with similar addictions can also be very helpful. Being in the presence of those who have actually freed themselves from that particular habit, and also with those who still have the habit but have vowed to get free, is a very powerful support mechanism. Perhaps the first and most important step in this process is our ability to recognize that we are stuck and to admit that we have, until now, been incapable at overcoming it.

The third main door to freedom in such situations is **faith in God.** Developing a relationship with the Divine (each according to his own beliefs and perceptions) is a very powerful solution for transcending habits. This relationship offers us feelings of protection, support and love. We also sense a deep inner caring coming to us from this Universal Being, who will never betray us. This love relationship is our only lasting and invulnerable one. The security and self worth which we receive from this relationship will allow us to go beyond the needs that are at the root of our addictions.

Thus, if we are held back in our process by strong self-defeating habits, we would do well to complement our analysis with the following actions:

**a.** Find a place where we can live for a time without having access to our habits.

**b.** Seek membership in a group of people who are working on the same problem.

**c.** Develop our relationship with the Divine.

**3. Conflicting desires and needs** can be obstacles to change. We may have needs which conflict with our original goal of self-improvement.

For example, we may want to experience our own creative expression, but we might also fear that others would not accept us if we do so.

We might feel a need to have a relationship, and on the other hand, have a need to be free to do whatever we want whenever we want.

We may have the need to lose weight or create health, but also desire sweets and chocolates.

These are conflicting needs that will have to be worked out through analysis and inner dialogue.

In such cases, we will need to analyze our conflicting "sub-personalities" and see what each part of ourselves actually needs and which beliefs create those needs.

We have the right to choose security and social recognition over our freedom and growth, if that is our choice.

**4.** We may have **fears** that may cause us to avoid change. Although we may desire to something better for ourselves, we might also fear we would lose something important if we change. The following chart points out a number of those reasons.

### WHY IT MIGHT NOT PAY FOR ME TO GET WELL OR TO SUCCEED, OR TO BE WITHOUT A PROBLEM

**1. If I get well:**

**a)** They might not pay attention to me anymore. I might lose their attention and love.

**b)** I will be expected to assume responsibility for my life (work, survival, etc.). I am incapable of doing that.

**c)** It will be necessary to tire myself and I will lose my comforts.

**2. I can control others though my illness:**

**a)** They must serve me.

**b)** They must not make me worry.

**3. Others are responsible for what happened to me.**

**a)** I have been treated unjustly, so others are unjust whereas I am justified, correct and good.

**b)** This way I punish them with my illness. I make them feel guilty.

**4. I am guilty and I don't deserve to be well. I must be punished; I must suffer.**

**5. Without my illness, I am not important or interesting enough.**

**6. If I admit to being happy or well, my contentment could be followed by something horrible.**

Just a few words about each of these, as they are most likely self-explanatory to most readers.

**a.** Some of us have come to believe that **others will pay attention to us only if we have problems.** This may have actually been our experience until now. We may believe we have nothing else interesting about us, and thus fear we will not hold others' attention if we no longer have a problem. Thus, although we suffer from our problem, we are subconsciously afraid to let go of it. Do we really want others to be this person who others pity or want to save?

**b.** Some of us have come **to believe we are incapable of coping with life**, responsibilities or the rat race of survival. In such a case we can use our "problem" as a subconscious excuse for not facing up to all this. In this way, others must protect and help us. If our problem is solved, we will then be forced to face life by ourselves, something we fear. This then will act as a subconscious obstacle to solving the problem.

**c. When we are lazy,** we might find that having a problem is a good excuse not to exhaust ourselves. Thus, although we may suffer and ask for help, we subconsciously prefer to have this problem which prevents others from asking much from us.

**d.** Some of us discover that **we can control others** when we have problems. Since we have a problem, others must treat us in a special way. They must not ask much of us. They must serve us and help us, try to solve our problems. In such a case, the only thing we need to do is hook up to someone who is playing the role of the savior or who feels responsible for others, and get them to try to solve our problems. We are then able to control them and consume their attention.

**e.** In the same situation, they also **must not worry us**. They must not ask much of us, or speak harshly to us, or ask us to carry our load. They must do what we ask and not cause us to feel hurt. They must never ask us to see ourselves because that might upset us. In such a case, why should we let go of our problem? It is our greatest "asset and protection."

**f.** Those of us who have come to identify with **the role of the abused, the martyr and the victim** need to keep our problem because our self worth is based on being wronged by someone, at least by life, if not by specific persons. Being wronged by others serves as verification that others who do us harm are wrong and evil, and that we ourselves are right and good.

**As victims, we create a false sense of self-worth by being abused.** If we have no other source of self-worth, then, although we may complain about the problem and how others are mistreating us, we subconsciously need this abuse in order to feel our self worth. Thus, we undermine any solutions. If asked to imagine that the problem has disappeared completely and that that others treat us, exactly as we desire, we will most likely feel an emptiness, depression or even panic.

**g.** Some of us **may use our own self-destruction to punish those whom we consider responsible for our pain**. For example, some children go into a mode of self-destruction as a form of blackmail, control and revenge towards their parents. As long as we are locked into this game of blaming others for our reality, we will feel the need to cling to our problems because they make others feel guilty. Solving our problems allows them to let go of their guilt, something we are not ready to allow.

**h.** Negative childhood experiences can create **the false belief that we are not worthy** and thus do not deserve a happy problem- free life. Although we want to create a happy reality, we fear we are not worthy of one, and thus subconsciously undermine our own attempts to create happiness because we do not believe we deserve it.

**i.** Our illness or problem may **become our life focus**, our connection with others. We have become that problem. If we do not have it, we do not know who we will be, what we will do, or how we will interact with others. We have no other frame of reference. Life without our problem is unfamiliar and scary.

In such a position, we frequently play the **"yes – but" game**, in which we present our problem to others, so they can get hooked into trying to find the solution. For every solution they suggest, we will have a very good answer as to why it will not work. They keep seeking the solution as we drain all their energy by monopolizing all their attention and effort. This is the way we energize ourselves.

This is why it is essential when others play this role that we leave the responsibility for the solution to them by simply asking questions which might help them decide what they want to do.

**j.** Those of us trapped in a belief system of clear cut opposites, such as good and evil, happiness and pain, success and failure, may **fear that allowing ourselves to accept that we are happy might attract evil**. Those who believe in the "evil eye" will be more prone to such a problem of not being able to accept that everything is wonderful.

## SETTING REASONABLE GOALS

We proceed more effectively when we can define specific goals in small reachable increments. One of the obstacles we encounter in our growth process, or in any endeavor, is that we perceive the problem or the goal as very large, complex or almost unattainable, and thus we discourage ourselves for getting started. We look to the top of the mountain and say, "It is too high. I will never be able to do it", and make no effort.

An alternative would be to look at the **next step** up that mountain and say, "I can do that", and take it". Then we are confronted with the next step and again we realize that " Yes, I can do that." With perseverance and patience, we arrive at the top.

Of course, in order to specify what exactly the next step is, we will need to see the top of the mountain or at least know its direction. Thus, we occasionally re-evaluate to determine in which direction we want to go, and then take the next step.

We can regularly redefine our goal or life purpose and take the next step toward fulfilling it. Then we watch for signs, such as coincidences or messages from within or without, concerning the next step. We continue moving forward until we come to the next crossroad, and the next question or choice comes to mind.

Having established our present goal, which might be material, physical, emotional, mental, social, economic, spiritual, etc., we then continue to determine as specifically as possible the steps we want to make **this week**, or at least this month, toward realization of that goal.

**Some questions which might help us with this are:**

**1.** "How would I express my goal at this point? What is it that I want to change, create, attain or transform first? What do I want to act on first?"

**2.** "Why have I chosen this? Why is it important for me? How do I hope to benefit from this change or effort? How is my life less pleasant by not making this effort?"

Establishing why we want to make these changes produces the awareness, motivation and momentum to develop the necessary discipline.

**3.** "How do I plan to start? What will be my first step?"

Here we want to reach as specific an answer as possible.

"I will begin to love myself more," is not a specific answer. More specific is, " I will offer myself a massage once a week."

" I will work on my relationship with my spouse (or child)," is not specific. More specific is, "I will arrange to have a deep discussion with my spouse (or child) this week in order to explain what I have discovered."

**4.** "When exactly will I do this and where? Can I be more specific about days or dates?"

Now we are being asked to commit ourselves to a more specific plan like, " I am free on Saturday morning. I will get my massage then, or I will arrange to have a discussion with my spouse (child) on Sunday morning."

Once we have clearly defined what we are going to do, it is much easier for us to proceed forward. We still may, however, be under the influences of various resistances that may undermine these decisions.

After a week or two, we will want to evaluate how our decisions went. If we discover we have not acted on them as of yet, we should avoid getting into the role of the teacher or parent and rejecting ourselves. We need only to seek to objectively answer these questions again.

**1.** Do I **want** to do it?

**2. Why** do I want to do it?

**3.** What are its **benefits** for me?

**4.** What is the **step** I want to take this week? Was the previous step perhaps too difficult? Would I like to start with something else and build up to that one, or will I work again on the same goal?

**5. When** and **where** will I take these actions?

This goes on week after week until we have accomplished our goal.

Then we ask these same questions about the next step. When we have not accomplished what we set out to do, we must simply work through it again with self-acceptance, patience, perseverance and determination.

If we see that the resistance perseveres, we may want to work with the following questionnaire, which will aid in revealing possible thought-forms that might be obstructing our process of growth.

## DISCOVERING OUR RESISTANCE TO CHANGE

As you answer these questions, have in mind a particular positive change you want to make in your life, but have noticed that you actually are not doing what you could or would like to do in relationship to that change.

**1.** Is there a **part** of you which:

**a)** Doubts whether you have the ability to succeed in this effort? What does this part of yourself actually believe?

**b)** Doubts whether you have the right to create something better?

Perhaps you believe that you do not deserve something better.

Perhaps you have feelings of guilt, and believe you should not be happy.

Perhaps you believe someone else will feel badly if you make this change in your life?   ·

What does this part of yourself actually believe?

**2.** Is there a **part** of you that **fears** if you make this change, something might be lost or put in danger?

   **a)** Perhaps you fear that you will lose:
   your freedom,
   others' attention,
   their love,
   their protection,
   perhaps some rights,
   some pleasures or comforts, or
   some external form of support?

   **b)** Is there a part of you which fears that, with such an improvement or success, you will then need to take responsibility for your life, and perhaps you may be unable to cope?

   **3.** Is there a **part** of you which **prefers** not to change or for this problem not to be solved because in this way because:

   **a)** You can keep others feeling responsible for you?

   **b)** You can make them feel guilty?

   **c)** You can punish them or have your revenge?

   **4.** Is there a **part** of you that does not want this change because:

   **a)** Others also want it and you do not want to give them the satisfaction?

   **b)** It comes into conflict with other needs that you have. For example, the need to lose weight conflicts with the need to enjoy food or the need for a relationship conflicts with the need for freedom?

   **5. In relationship with the change you want to make:**

   **a)** What messages or examples did you have concerning that subject when you were young?

   **b)** Did you, in general, receive what you wanted from your parents?

   **c)** Did your parents have what you are now trying to create in your life with this change?

   **d)** Do you believe you deserve this change?

   **e)** Do you believe it is easy and natural for you to have what you want at this time, or is it difficult?

   **6.** Based on your above analysis, what would you say are your inner obstacles towards making this particular positive change in your life?

   **7.** What would you like to do in order to overcome these obstacles?

   **8.** If at this moment, you had total self-confidence and self-acceptance:

   **a)** What would you do that you have avoided doing until now?

   **b)** What would you stop doing that you have been doing only because you do not have self-acceptance?

   **9.** Finally, what are you going to do?

If you have discovered you have avoided employing the various exercises and techniques, or have avoided answering the questionnaires in this book or on the web site, you may want to benefit from them now.

Technique no. 15

# TRANSFERRING ATTENTION
# TO THE PHYSICAL BODY

### Why this is so useful

Relaxing our muscles, nerves and mind create health and inner peace. Allowing tension to build causes psychosomatic illness and negative emotions.

### A simple technique for relaxing is to:

When we begin to feel an unpleasant emotion arising from within, we can focus on the parts of the body that are being affected. We can feel which groups of muscles are tense or experiencing any other phenomena such as pain, numbness etc. We can check the neck, throat, head, abdominal muscles, hands, thighs, etc. Each stores his or her tension in different places.
This will be easier if we take a position in which we can relax such as:
Sitting straight in a chair
Lying on our backs
Lying on our backs close to a wall, so that our legs can be raised and rested on the wall allowing the blood and extra oxygen to rejuvenate the brain.

Once comfortable in our chosen position:

**1.** We **locate which muscles are tense**, and we begin to transfer our attention to those muscles.

**2.** We then **breathe deeply and slowly**, and as we do we allow the muscles to relax.

**3.** We can imagine that, as we inhale, **we draw in peace into that area** and that, with the **exhalation we release any tension or tightness** that might be there. As we relax the muscles with slow deep breathing we will feel the emotions subsiding, and our body and mind being filled with peace.

### Note:
This is obviously not to be performed
while operating any vehicle or machinery.

# *FEAR CONCERNING THE CHILDREN*

Nora has intense fears concerning her children's welfare. She is afraid that they might become ill and has nightmares about the possibility of their departing from their bodies. She also fears that they might become involved in drugs, be kidnapped, have an accident or in some way be harmed. She simply cannot handle the possibility of her children suffering or being harmed in any way.

Because of this, she has become extremely protective and controlling. She needs to know where they are at every moment and considerably restricts their movements. This is tiring for her and very unpleasant for the children. The older they get, the more they rebel against this suppression.

Her extreme stance causes her husband Michael to balance her by going to the opposite extreme and allowing the children more freedom than he would if he were alone with them. This creates frequent conflicts between Nora and Michael concerning how much the children need to be controlled in order to protect them and how much freedom they need in order to mature and gain inner strength.

This situation is unpleasant for all of them.

**Some of Nora's lessons might be:**

**1.** To have more faith in her children, their intelligence and ability to protect themselves and succeed in life.

**2.** To have more faith in God and the Divine plan for her children; that each is being cared for by the one Universal Consciousness and that nothing "accidental" can happen.

**3.** To see her children as immortal spirits in a process of evolution, temporarily incarnated in these bodies for the process of learning, and that nothing could ever happen to them which is not a part of their learning process.

**4.** To free herself from the role of parent and to realize that her self-worth does not depend on what happens to her children.

**5.** To free herself from anxiety about what other people will say about her if something happens to her children.

**6.** To find other interests in life so that she does not need them so much and focus on them excessively.

**7.** To free herself from any feelings of guilt which make her feel that she might be punished through her children.

**8.** To love them without needing to receive from them or being attached to affirmation through their success.

**9.** To realize that we learn through our experiences and that we develop strength by confronting difficulties.

**10.** To realize that she is undermining their own self-confidence by worrying about them.

**11.** To understand that her negative thoughts pass on to them whether she expresses them or not.

**12.** To realize that worrying and fear can solve no problems.

**Some beliefs which might help Nora to deal with this situation:**

**1.** My children are immortal souls in the process of evolution. Within them lies all the knowledge and power to protect themselves and continue their evolution.

**2.** Life gives them in each moment exactly what they need for their inner development.

**3.** My self worth is in me and cannot be measured by how my children do.

**4.** My children are God's children and they are only temporarily given to me for their first years in this world. As they grow older they becomes God's responsibility not mine.

**5.** I trust in the wisdom of the Divine Consciousness that controls the universe.

**6.** I do whatever I can for my children and leave the rest up to God.

**7.** I would not like to be suppressed in this way because of someone else's fears for me.

**Some beliefs which might help Michael to deal with this situation:**

**1.** I love Nora and want to understand and help her.

**2.** I desire to find a balance between protection and freedom.

**3.** Through open communication we can all find a solution for this problem.

**4.** I understand and accept Nora as she is.

**5.** I understand her fears and needs and comply with them as much as possible, while simultaneously helping her to confront them.

**Some beliefs which might help the children to deal with this situation:**

**1.** We love our mother and perceive her love behind those fears.

**2.** We understand her fears and needs and comply with them as much as possible, while simultaneously helping her to confront them.

**3.** If we were in her position, we would want help and understanding from others.

# CHAPTER 16

# WRITTEN AFFIRMATIONS

Just as our minds have been programmed through repetition, they can be cleared and **reprogrammed** by the same power of reiteration. Written positive affirmations are an excellent way to reprogram the mind.

They serve a dual function. On the one hand, they are a **diagnostic tool,** while on the other, they serve as an effective **therapeutic technique.**

As a diagnostic tool, they allow us to **discover our specific resistance** toward accepting positive thoughts or truths.

As a therapeutic technique, they allow us **to implant a new perception or thought-form into our mind.**

Let us see how we can apply these positive affirmation techniques. We take a sheet of paper and divide it in the center with a vertical line. At the top of the left column, we write **AFFIRMATION**, and at the top of the right, **RESPONSE**.

Then on the left, we begin to write the affirmation we are interested in strengthening in our conscious and subconscious mind. Some examples are:
**1.** I love and accept myself in every situation.
**2.** I love and accept myself exactly as I am.
**3.** I feel safe and secure in every situation.
**4.** I feel sure and confident in every environment and situation.
**5.** I accept and love others as they are.
**6.** I feel free to be myself in every situation.

These are some «**general affirmations**» which should be used at first to discover our various inner obstacles toward feeling self-confidence, security, love and self-acceptance or freedom. Without the previously mentioned inner qualities, it is difficult to experience happiness, peace or love. Thus, we work first with these basic affirmations which focus on our common weak points: security and self-worth, love and freedom.

## WE PROCEED IN THE FOLLOWING WAY

**1.** We select the affirmation that seems most important for us to cultivate at the present time and **write it** in the left column once.

**2.** Then **we reflect** we think about and try to feel what we have written. We mentally imagine ourselves in various situations, and examples come to our mind concerning when we actually **do** feel secure or self-accepting, free or loving, and when we do **not**.

**3.** We **write** all of the **responses** to what we have written that come to mind, in the **right column**.

Some of them will be positive and some will be negative (see the example given). At some point, our mind will cease to think of other situations in which we do, or do not, feel these feelings (security, acceptance, love, freedom) which we are trying to program into our subconscious.

**4.** Then we **write the same affirmation** in the left column, and again try to feel and accept into ourselves what we are writing.

**5.** Again, we wait for **and write our responses in the right column**.

**6.** In this way, we **write the affirmation in full**, without ditto marks or abbreviations, a total of **twenty times**, stopping each time to write our responses in the right column.

## SOME HINTS

Some guidelines that come to mind after years of experience with this invaluable technique are:

**1.** We should **not hesitate to write** the **same response more than once** if it keeps coming up over and over. This will be an important clue in our self-diagnosis process.

**2.** If no answers come to us as we write the affirmation, we should not terminate the exercise until we **write the affirmation in full twenty times.** We may have no answer after four or five repetitions and then suddenly experience a free flow of responses from the subconscious.

**3.** We need to be as **honest as we can with ourselves.** We have everything to gain and nothing to lose, except our illusions and suffering.

| AFFIRMATION | RESPONSE |
|---|---|
| 1. I love and accept myself in every situation. | 1. Not when I make a mistake. |
| | 2. Not when others criticse me. |
| 2. I love and accept myself in every situation. | 3. Yes, when I succeed at something. |
| | 4. Not when others are more intelligent. |
| | 5. Yes, when I am clear minded and productive |
| 3. I love and accept myself in every situation. | **6. Not when I harm others.** |
| | 7. Yes, when I receive love and attention from others. |
| | 8. Not when I do not live up to my expectations. |
| 4. I love and accept myself in every situation. | **9. Not when I tell lies.** |
| | 10. Yes, when I wake up early. |
| | 11. Not when I succumb to my weakness. |
| 5. I love and accept myself n every situation. | 12. Not  when I am selfish. |
| | 13. Yes, when I serve others. |
| | 14. Yes, when I am focused on the present moment. |
| 6. I love and accept myself in every situation. | 15. Yes, when I love others. |
| | 16. Not  when others reject me. |
| | 17. Not  when others ignore me. |
| 7. I love and accept myself in every situation. | 18. Not  when others do not repect me. |
| | 19. Not  when I do not have a mate. |
| | 20. Not  when I am ill. |
| | 21. Not  when I am weak or show weakness. |
| | 22. Not when I fear things there  is no reason to fear. |
| …20. I love and accept myself in every situation. | 23. Not  when I think that God sees me. |
| | 24. Yes, when I feel close to nature. |

---

### FIVE REASONS WHY I ACCEPT AND LOVE MYSELF

1. Because I care for others
2. Because I try my best.
3. Because I learn easily.
4. Because I am faithful in my relationships.
5. Because I love nature.

**4.** There is **no specific number of responses** we should have after writing each affirmation. We could have none and we could have more than fifty.

## THE DIAGNOSIS

Once we have written one of these general affirmations twenty times at each session for a number of days, we will then want to analyze and discover the "root" or "core" beliefs which obstruct a more continuous and permanent feeling of inner security and self worth. As this process proceeds, we will see that behind this variety of external stimuli and situations that intimidate our happiness and inner peace, the **same root beliefs keep cropping up**. This is because we depend almost exclusively on others, and on various external factors, for our feelings of inner security and self-worth. Thus, we remain vulnerable and continuously lose our emotional center.

(Before reading the next paragraph study the sample affirmations on the opposite page.)

## THE ANALYSIS OF THE RESULTS

As we can see, there are two basic types of answers to the affirmation concerning our feelings of self-acceptance.

**1.** One category has to do with **how we appear** to others and **how we compare to others**. The following responses fall into that category: 1,2,3,4,5,7,16,17,18,19,20, and 21. In these cases we want to analyze **why we cannot accept ourselves just as we are,** regardless of what others think or how we compare to others.

**2.** The second category has to do with situations in which we **do not behave in accordance with our conscience.** In such cases, we are interested in three processes:

**a.** We need to **discover and understand** the beliefs, needs and feelings which cause us to behave in ways that are not in harmony with our conscience. (We do to others what we would not like them to do to us.)

**b.** Once we discover these beliefs, needs and emotions, we want to **free** ourselves from them so that our behavior can align with our conscience.

**c.** Simultaneously, however, we would like to **accept ourselves** and avoid rejecting ourselves and thus getting into a vicious circle of guilt, self-rejection and then imprisonment in the very behavior that causes our self-rejection. We tend to prolong our subjugation to weaknesses and self-destructive behaviors when we reject ourselves for them. This is true because our poor self-image is usually what causes our original inability to live up to our conscience.

Some examples will help us understand this:

**1.** We usually tell lies or hide the truth when we are afraid of what others will think about us. We are afraid of losing their love, acceptance or support.

**2.** We are unjust in our professional exchanges because we feel economically insecure or need success in order to feel our self worth or security.

**3.** We threaten and hurt others with aggressive and violent behavior because we are afraid we will lose control and thus our security, self worth or freedom.

**4.** We criticize and gossip about others because doing so makes us feel we are worthier than they are.

We can see that our social programming, which creates fear concerning our security, self worth and freedom, is the basic cause of our unethical behavior.

## THE PSYCHOLOGY OF PURITY

Most of **our negative behavior is the result of our own self-doubt.** When we reject ourselves or others for this negative behavior, we simply increase the original cause of it.

When we are dirty, we do not care about getting dirtier. When we have just taken a shower and have put on clean white clothing, we seek to avoid anything that will soil us. Consequently, when we feel impure and "soiled", it is easier for us to participate in actions which "soil" us. When we believe in and feel our inherent purity, we are much more able to avoid becoming "soiled".

A healthier solution would be to accept our weaknesses as a natural **phase** in our evolutionary process with the understanding that we will be **moving on from that stage as we grow in inner strength and clarity.**

Some ask the question, "If I accept myself with these weaknesses and faults, what motive will I have to change them?"

The answer is that **self-improvement is a natural human instinct,** which when unobstructed, motivates a continuous process of change and improvement. Remember the example of the child in grade school. If we ask him if he accepts himself at his present level of relative understanding and ability, he will most likely answer, "yes". He is satisfied with himself as he is. He perceives it as natural to be limited in his understanding and abilities since he is only in grade school. However, if we ask him whether he would like to remain there next year, or for a number of years or permanently, he will answer with an emphatic, "NO".

Thus, **we can recognize ourselves as first graders in the school of life** and accept our weaknesses and faults, but simultaneously attend to transcending them, so we can move on to the upper grades in this cosmic school of life.

Regarding the second category of responses (for example 6,8,9,10,12 and 15), we must recognize and **accept** that we have these weaknesses, but can simultaneously search for the beliefs which prevent us from behaving in ways which are more in harmony with our conscience. When we can discover the beliefs, which force us to become egotistical, to tell lies, or to harm people, we will gradually become free from the cause of our weaknesses and move forward in our spiritual maturity process.

## PERSONAL AFFIRMATIONS

Once we discover the **root beliefs,** which grow into the tree of our illusionary perceptions of ourselves and the world, we can then begin the process of uprooting this tree and cultivating another one based on a more positive belief system. We do this by adapting our original general affirmation to the specific situations we have found to be our particular weaknesses.

These are called "**personal affirmations.**" For example:

**1.** I feel safe and secure even when I cannot control those around me.
**2.** I accept and love myself even when I make a mistake.
**3.** I accept and love myself even when I am not perfect.
**4.** I love and accept myself independent of what others think of me.
**5.** I feel safe and secure regardless of my economic situation.
**6.** I feel safe and secure regardless of the condition of my health.
**7.** I feel safe and secure even when I am alone.
**8.** I feel safe and secure in the dark.
**9.** I accept and love myself regardless of the results of my efforts.

We can also use affirmations to strengthen our positive feelings toward others:
**1.** I love and accept others independent of their behavior.
**2.** I love and accept others regardless of their weaknesses of imperfections.
**3.** I love and accept others even when they are unable to fulfil my expectations.

All of these **personalized affirmations,** whether directed toward ourselves or others, are applied in exactly the same way as the general affirmations we mentioned earlier. We write them twenty times in the left column, pausing each time and writing all of our responses in the right column, before proceeding to write the affirmation again in the left column.

Continuing in this manner, we can narrow in more and more specifically on the basic belief that prevents a more continuous feeling of peace and unity with ourselves and others. By writing these affirmations on a daily basis, we can reprogram our false beliefs about ourselves and the world with these new positive truths.

Let us now look at a similar example concerning the general affirmation, **"I feel**

**safe and secure in every situation"** and the personal affirmations which might be generated from our results.

Some of the possible responses which might come up in response to the affirmation «I feel safe and secure in every situation» are listed below. After each response, we have listed some personal affirmations that can reprogram these objections. Let us look at a few examples.

*1. Not when others do not show me love or approval.*
Some affirmations to counter this would be:
**a.** I feel safe and secure even when others do not show me love and approval.
**b.** I always feel loved and approved of.
**c.** I experience my self worth and inner security regardless of others' attitudes.

*2. Not during earthquakes.*
**a.** I feel safe and secure even during earthquakes.
**b.** I will be guided from within through every danger.
**c.** I am an immortal, indestructible spirit.
*3. Not when others know more than I do about some subject.*
**a.** I feel safe and secure regardless of how much others know.
**b.** I love and accept myself regardless of what I know or do not know.

*4. Not when I am ill.*
**a.** I feel safe and secure regardless of the condition of my body.
**b.** I am resistant to all illness.
**c.** I am a spirit beyond all illness.

*5. Not when I think of money.*
**a.** I feel safe and secure regardless of my economic situation.
**b.** My power to earn grows each and every day.
**c.** Live gives me exactly what I need to be happy and fulfilled.

*6. Not when my husband drives wildly.*
**a.** I feel safe and secure regardless of how my husband drives.
**b.** Life gives me exactly what I need.
**c.** I have the right to express how I feel without getting angry or losing the love of others.

*7. Not when I make a mistake.*
**a.** I feel safe and secure regardless of the results of my efforts.
**b.** I use my mistakes to learn to grow.

*8. Yes, I actually feel more secure everyday in every way.*

We can see that the affirmation "I feel safe and secure in every situation" will bring to the surface of the mind both those situations in which we have felt secure and those in which we have not felt secure in the past.

We can use this to our advantage to uncover those negative **memories** that undermine our feeling of security in the present and future. By understanding that we are letting our past control our present and future, we can **realize that our insecurity is not rational** and is based on a few negative past experiences rather than on our present reality.

We are free to create any affirmations we feel may help us to reprogram negative feelings or habits. The affirmations should be in our own words, as short and to the point as possible. This should be done daily for about 10 days for the best results.

Some more affirmations we could use are:

**1.** I accept and love myself regardless of how others behave.
**2.** I can deal with whatever life presents me.
**3.** I forgive myself for my ignorance-based reactions to people.
**4.** I forgive others for their ignorance-based behavior towards me.
**5.** I perceive myself and others as evolving spiritual beings.
**6.** Others love me even when I say "no."
**7.** I love and accept others even when they do not respond to my needs.
**8.** I am responsible for the reality I experience.
**9.** I have everything I need at every moment to be happy.
**10.** Life's experiences are exactly what I need in order to grow more aware.
**11.** I can succeed in any endeavor that is important enough to me.
**12.** I am lovable, and therefore, love others.
**13.** I love others and myself regardless of their feelings.
**14.** We are all expressions of the Divine.
**15.** We are all creations of the Divine.

## WASHING OUR MINDS

Some of us may feel we are brainwashing ourselves or we are trying to convince ourselves of something that is not true. What we must realize is that our brain needs "washing" because it is deeply soiled by false truths and misconceptions we have inherited from our parents, teachers, siblings, friends, and society in general.

It is **not true** that we are weak, incapable or unable or unsafe. This is an illusion. It is **not true** that we are unworthy of love and respect. These are misconceptions made by a child who did not receive unconditional love from those around him.

We misconceive and misinterpret many events in our childhood. I have seen adults who have come to the conclusion that they do not deserve love, respect or affection because:

**1.** Their parents abandoned them as children.

**2.** Their parents worked many hours and did not have time for them.

**3.** Their parents had emotional problems and released their negativity on the children.

**4.** The parents separated and the child felt responsible or unloved.

**5.** The parents were unable to express affection.

**6.** The parents became ill or died and the child felt responsible.

**7.** The parents died and the child interpreted this as a voluntary abandonment.

**8.** The parents were always fighting and the child did not experience love.

**9.** A teacher ridiculed the child in front of others.

**10.** The child was told he/she was evil.

**11.** The child was called demeaning names.

**12.** The child did not do well at school.

**13.** The child felt rejected because of physical or mental characteristics which made him or her different from others.

**14.** The parents punished the child frequently.

**15.** There was no dialogue with the parents.

In most of these cases, as children, we formed the conclusion that we are not worthy, lovable, or capable of succeeding. We rejected ourselves, and these feelings and beliefs became deeply rooted in the subconscious.

When we mature, even though we receive many forms of affirmation concerning our worthiness, acceptability and capabilities, our subconscious remains programmed by our mistaken conclusions, formed in response to earlier experiences. Although we consciously recognize that people around us love and accept us and that we are actually safe and secure, we remain plagued by feelings of self-doubt and fear.

## FIVE REASONS WHY

These written affirmations are essential for rooting out these false perceptions and replacing them with these objectively positive truths.

In order to strengthen and deepen this new positive attitude, we can employ another technique that is quite related. We complete our written affirmations by writing **five reasons why** we accept and love ourselves or why we feel safe and secure. Thus, each day we write five reasons why we should accept and love ourselves or feel safe and secure.

The written affirmations focus on **when** we feel or do not feel these positive emotions, and this last exercise focuses on **why** we could or should be feeling more positive.

We may or may not find new reasons each day concerning why we should feel more positive. If we do not find new reasons, we can **rewrite some of those** we have already written.

Some examples of what we might write as reasons why we should feel our security or self worth:

**1.** I am a good person.

**2.** I am trying to improve myself.

3. I have various abilities and talents. (Specify each separately)

**4.** I care about people.

**5.** I try to be as helpful as possible.

**6.** I am an eternal consciousness in a process of evolution.

**7.** I am a divine creation.

**8.**  I am worthy of love and respect regardless of others' opinions or behavior.

**9.** My self worth is totally independent of how I compare to others.

**10.** My self worth is totally independent of any external factors, such as intelligence, wealth, my home, appearance, talents, professional success, my children's success, my being attractive to the opposite sex, my ability to make friends, disciplines or spiritual activities.

**11.**  I am worthy of love and respect regardless of the results of my efforts.

**12.** I am worthy and will be loved even when others are being given more attention.  I am happy for others when they receive love and attention.

**13.** My self worth is within me and totally independent of whether I am loved exclusively by someone or not.

**14.** I am worthy of love and respect even when I am not perfect in what I do and even when I make mistakes.

**15.** My self worth is totally independent of how much I accomplish.

**16.** My self worth is a reflection of my divine nature and not my gender, religion, social class etc.

**17.** I am intelligent and capable enough to succeed at any endeavor which is important to me.

**18.** I deserve to be loved and respected exactly as I am (at this stage of my evolutionary process).

**19.** I have the inner power and strength to deal with whatever life brings me.

**20.** I am capable of handling any possible difficulties that might occur.

**21.** I am beautiful exactly as I am - just as all aspects of nature are.

**23.** I am a good person, a worthy person.

**24.** I respect and love all persons (especially my parents and family) without feeling any need whatsoever to live my life according to their beliefs or values.

**25.** I live my life in harmony with my inner values and beliefs.

**26.** My self worth is based on my inner being, my existence itself, and my inner divine nature, not on external factors.

**27.** My self worth is a simple function of the fact that I, as all others creatures, am a unique aspect of divine creation. My self worth cannot be increased nor decreased. I can never be more or less worthy of love and respect than another.

**28.** Although I am not perfect and have various faults, I deserve to be loved and respected as I am, just I as I love and respect others with their faults.

**29.** When I do not love myself, I do not love an aspect of divine creation.

**30.** All beings deserve my love and respect, including myself.

### Technique no. 16

# AFFIRMATIONS

### Why this is important

Our thoughts create our reality. We create our health or illness, success or failure, harmonious or disharmonious relationships and, in general, the totality of our reality with **how we think.**

We can use written, mental or verbal positive affirmations to reprogram our negative, health-and-happiness-destroying beliefs with positive life-building ones.

### A simple technique for thinking positively is:

We may choose any of the beliefs, concepts or truths expressed in this book or any affirmation which suits us in order to reprogram our subconscious mind in a more positive way.

Whenever we feel weak,
we can imagine ourselves as **strong**.

Whenever we feel fear,
we can reprogram ourselves with **courage and faith.**

Whenever we feel that we are a failure,
we program ourselves with **success**.

Whenever we feel negative, separating emotions,
we can  focus on **love**.

### Note:

Affirmations are also explained in other chapters.

*Life Story no. 17*

# PARENTAL PRESSURE

Steven is a student at a well-known university. He is not happy. He has lost interest in his major and does not want to continue. His parents will not even discuss the possibility of his not completing his degree. He is fast approaching a depressive state, as he sees no solution. He is not interested in what he is studying and does not want to pursue this occupation, and yet he feels very much responsible for his parents' happiness and cannot bear the idea of their disappointment and pain.

They have given him so much in life. Yet, now, responding to their needs is a painful experience. He feels obliged and also fears their rejection.

They, on the other hand, cannot think of any reason why he would not want to continue. They believe that such a degree will be a great asset in establishing himself professionally, economically and socially. "What else could he want?"

Stevens wants to do something that gives meaning to his life. For him, professional, economic and social success without meaning have no value.

What can they all learn from this?

**Some lessons that Steven might have to learn are:**

**1.** To love others without believing that he is responsible for their happiness or reality.

**2.** To realize that love does not require that we sacrifice our values and interests in life.

**3.** To overcome any blockages which prevent him from being interested in and completing his major.

**4.** To clarify his life goals.

**5.** To get free from the role of the child (emotionally, materially and financially).

**6.** To love others even when they make demands on him.

**7.** To love himself even when he cannot satisfy their expectations.

**8.** To discover what he might be doing which might make others continue to perceive him as a child.

**9.** To make a more serious effort at learning and overcoming any possible laziness or fear of failure.

**10.** To express more clearly, assertively and lovingly his needs, beliefs, values and goals.

**11.** To overcome any fears of facing life alone.

**12.** To accept that his parents may need to grow and learn through this pain and not feel responsible for that. (But also to help them with his love through this period.)

### Some beliefs that might help Steven find a solution:

**1.** I love and accept my parents without feeling the need to fulfill their expectations.

**2.** I am lovable and acceptable even when I cannot fulfill the others' expectations.

**3.** I am an immortal soul with equal rights and powers with all other beings.

**4.** My life is my own creation and I have the right to make my own mistakes and live with and grow through their consequences.

**5.** I am able to study and get this degree which will always be useful in some way.

**6.** I have the right to live a life with meaning.

**7.** I can find meaning in these studies.

**8.** It is only a short period of time before this period of study is over and then I can move on to something else if I feel the need to.

**9.** I understand my parent's beliefs and needs and accept them as they are.

### Some beliefs that might help his parents relax:

**1.** Our child's happiness is more important than any diploma.

**2.** We trust in our child's inner guidance. There must be a reason he is being guided in another direction.

**3.** Social, economic and professional success are not always equivalent with health, harmony and happiness.

**4.** He can always return to these studies later if he chooses to.

**5.** We trust our child to God's Divine wisdom.

**6.** We express our beliefs clearly and loving and allow him to make his own decisions and live with those consequences. Our responsibility for his economic and social survival is ending.

**7.** We love and accept him as he is, no matter what he chooses to do.

**8.** Many have gone through such crises and eventually made much of their lives.

**9.** Having completed our responsibility to give this soul a start in life, we now release him to his own powers and to God's guidance.

# CHAPTER 17

# LEARNING TO LOVE OURSELVES

Our doubt concerning our self-worth is the main obstacle to our emotional and inter-relational harmony. This doubt is the cause of our greatest fears such as being rejected, laughed at, ignored, unloved, and most of all, of being alone.

## LONELINESS AND DOUBT

Loneliness is the disease of our age, and its cause is self-doubt. Fear of being alone is perhaps our most ancient one. It comes from the fact that in the past, he who was not accepted was ostracized from the group. In those days, that did not mean simply feeling lonely, but also being unable to survive. That safety and survival have become so directly associated with being with others is clearly evident in the illogical phenomena that, an individual who fears being alone in a house at night might feel safer even with the presence of a small infant or even a cat, both of which are totally incapable of protecting him from any danger.

Another factor that makes us fear rejection or not being accepted by others is the fear of being punished by them or by God. We have been brought up to believe in a God, whose love is conditional, depending upon whether we are perfect in His eyes or not. We have learned that God's love and protection are also conditional, and that punishment results when we displease Him. We have also learned that our self-worth is to be measured by what others think of us and whether they accept and respect us.

## CHILDHOOD PROGRAMMING

As children, we learn from adults that we must measure our self-worth by what others think of us, the results of our actions, our appearance, how much money we have, etc. We receive messages from our parents and other important persons throughout our childhood years concerning whether and under what conditions we are good or worthy.

Our doubt of our self-worth then becomes our greatest obstacle to inner peace, harmonious communication and loving relationships. These doubts are the foundation of most of our negative emotions and relationship conflicts.

**If we had more self-acceptance, we would have less need to prove ourselves to others**, and we would feel offended much less frequently. Then we could to overlook others' negativity and be at peace with them regardless of their behavior.

Let us now look at how we can increase and stabilize our self-acceptance.

The first step is to discover the situations in which we lose our sense of self-worth or self-acceptance. This can be very clearly seen in our answers to the written affirmations (previous chapter) "I love and accept myself in every situation." In our responses to this affirmation, we can see the basic conditions we place on our self-acceptance. What we discover in the answers to the written affirmations can be summed up into categories listed in this next questionnaire.

## OBSTACLES TO LOVING OURSELVES

In which situations do you lose your sense of self-love, self-worth, self- esteem or self-acceptance? You might feel negative feelings such as alienation (from self and others,) fear, insecurity, negativity, discomfort, aversion, repulsion, anxiety, bitterness, anger, hate, guilt, shame, worry, disillusionment (with self or others), frustration, jealousy, envy or any other unpleasant emotion.

Note some of the feelings you might have in the following situations.

**1.** When others ask for your help and you **do not say "yes"**, or do not respond.

**2.** When you have **made a mistake** or have **failed** at some effort.

**3.** When **others are more capable** than you are at certain tasks or concerning certain qualities (i.e. intelligence, artistic ability, speech, sports, cooking, professional success, their children's success, economically, making friends, employing disciplines).

**4.** When **others attract more attention**, esteem and respect in a group situation.

**5.** When others **have offered more to you** than you have offered them.
**6.** When you are **not perfect**.

**7.** When **others criticize or reject you**.

**8.** When **others do not agree with you**.

**9.** When others **are able to manipulate you**.

**10.** When **you have "created" pain** for others.

**11.** When you are **not in harmony with your conscience**.

In each of the above cases
**a.** How do you feel about yourself?
**b.** How do you feel toward the others?

## SOCIAL PROGRAMMING OR CONSCIENCE

Once we have established the particular situations or stimuli that obstruct our feelings of self-worth or self-acceptance, we will need to separate our answers into two groups.

**1.** Those which have to do with **social programming** and not with our conscience. We then need to analyze each one separately as we attempt to discover the beliefs that cause us to lose our self-acceptance in those situations.
**2.** Situations in which we reject ourselves because our **actions are not in alignment with our inner conscience**. We behave toward others, as we would not like them to behave toward us. Our answers to 10 and 11 above might indicate such situations.
Here we are interested in how we could react differently in those situations.

The accompanying more detailed questionnaire will help us determine more clearly when we lose our feelings of self-worth. We suggest that as you read through it, you mark those items that might relate to you.

## I TEND TO LOSE MY FEELINGS OF SELF-WORTH:

(Worth what; love, happiness, health, success, satisfaction?)
**1.** When others criticize me, blame me, or do not approve of me.
**2.** When others are angry with me.
**3.** When my children, spouse or parents are not happy, healthy, successful, or satisfied.
**4.** When I do not know as much as others around me.
**5.** When I do not have an intimate relationship partner.
**6.** When my house is not clean and in order.
**7.** When my partner shows interest in others.
**8.** If I am not successful professionally.
**9.** If I do not have enough money.
**10.** If I am not attractive to the opposite sex.
**11.** If I do not make an impression on others.
**12.** If I do not have many sexual successes.

**13.** If others do not respect me.
**14.** If my child is ill.
**15.** If I do not have what others have.
**16.** If I am not perfect.
**17.** If I do not achieve many things.
**18.** If others are able to cheat or mislead me.
**19.** If I do not have _____
**20.** If I do not _____
**21.** Other reasons _____

These beliefs may have come from some of the experiences as a child listed below. With the help of this list, try to remember when you might have felt guilt, shame or rejection as a child.

## WHEN HAVE I FELT
## GUILT, SHAME OR SELF-REJECTION?

### I. IN THE PAST

### A. When did you feel guilt, shame or self rejection as a child?

**1.** When they shouted at you or beat you?
**2.** When you did not do what they asked you to do?
**3.** When you made mistakes?
**4.** When you hurt someone?
**5.** For sexual feelings or acts?
**6.** For the others' problems?
**7.** For negative feelings which you had?
**8.** For desires which you had?
**9.** For the others' illnesses?
**10.** For the others' unhappiness?
**11.** When you did not do well in school?
**12.** When you were criticized or blamed?
**13.** When you felt fear?
**14.** When you told lies or stole?
**15.** When they declared you were a sinner or that you were no good?
**16.** When they talked to you about God and the devil?
**17.** When you did something forbidden? What? _____
**18.** When you came into contact with the opposite sex?
**19.** When they told you in some way that you were a bad child?
**20.** When others were not happy?
**21.** When others were not pleased with you?
**22.** When you were not as good at something as others were?

**23.** When others did not pay attention to you?
**24.** When you did not speak out about something that was important to you?
**25.** When you didn't help someone when you could have?
**26.** When you did not succeed at something?
**27.** When others were disappointed in you?
**28.** When your siblings had problems?
**29.** When others around you were done injustice?
**30.** When they used you or took advantage of you?
**31.** When you did not receive the attention, affection and love you needed?
**32.** When they compared you with others?
**33.** Your parents, or other members of your family, did not behave properly?
**34.** When you were blamed for something?
**35.** When you did not get good grades at school?
**36.** When you were not able to be like someone else?
**37.** When you were not able to live up to others' expectations?
**Other**_____

**B. Did you ever feel shame or self rejection concerning any of the following?**
**1.** Your body? Which part?
**2.** Your appearance?
**3.** Your gender?
**4.** Your family?
**5.** Your speech?
**6.** Your friends?
**7.** Various characteristics (which)?
**8.** Your behavior? Which?
**9.** Your mistakes?
**10.** Your country?
**11.** Your parents?
**12.** The attention you received from others?
**13.** Your sexuality?
**14.** Something else? _____

**C. What messages did you receive through others' words and actions about the following?**
**1.** God?
**2.** The devil?
**3.** Money?
**4.** Sex?
**5.** Who is worthy?
**6.** Who is not worthy?

### II. THE PRESENT

**A.** Complete the following phrases with at least thhree different answers keeping in mind even small parts of yourself.

**1.** There is a part of myself that feels shame, guilt or self-rejection when I partake in the **following actions**:

**2.** There is a part of myself that feels shame, guilt or self-rejection when I have the **following thoughts**:

**3.** There is a part of myself that feels shame, guilt or self-rejection when I **express myself in the following ways**:

**4.** There is a part of myself that feels shame, guilt or self-rejection **when I do not**:

**5.** There is a part of myself that feels shame, guilt or self-rejection when **I neglect or forget to**:

**B.** In addition to the above, I occasionally feel shame, guilt or self rejection when:

Concerning those obstacles toward self-acceptance and self-love based on false social programming, see the questionnaires for that purpose on our web site.

### OUR CONSCIENCE

The second category of obstacles towards self-acceptance consists of those situations in which our actions are in conflict with our moral values or conscience. For example, "I do not accept myself when I beat my child or wife, or when I tell lies or steal."

In this case, we are not interested in compromising our values but rather in discovering the emotional mechanisms that lead us to beat, lie or steal. Some fears or other emotions based on false beliefs are forcing us to act in ways that do not coincide with our morals or conscience.

Thus, our self-analysis will necessarily follow another line of questioning.

Concerning those obstacles toward self-acceptance and self-love, which are based on conflict with our conscience, see the questionnaire for that purpose on our web site.

### TRANSFORMING BELIEFS WHICH OBSTRUCT SELF -ACCEPTANCE WHEN IN CONFLICT WITH OUR CONSCIENCE

In the case that we are in conflict with our conscience, we would do well to remember some thoughts.

**1.** It is well that **we realize** that we are not functioning in harmony with the laws of nature that are imprinted in our conscience or higher intellect. This allows us to see where we are in our evolutionary process and help us decide where we want to proceed. We each have an archetype of perfect love, peace, nonviolence, truth and right action encoded into our subconscious mind, thus we naturally feel disappointed when we are unable to live up to that standard.

**2.** It is important that we see those weaknesses, faults and mistakes that need to be corrected, and we **would do well to decide the most effective means by which to correct them.**

**3. Rejecting ourselves**, however or believing that God rejects us and that we are not worthy of being loved and respected by others, **because of those weaknesses is a big mistake for a number of reasons.**
   **a.** As we are souls in the process of evolution, it is not possible for us to be perfect as long as we are in that process, and thus it is illogical to reject ourselves for not being perfect.
   **b.** It is also illogical for the divine being, God, to reject the very beings He has created with exactly all those weaknesses and faults.
   **c.** If we analyze those parts of ourselves that function in ways, which we ourselves do not accept, we will realize that those parts of ourselves live in self-doubt and self-rejection. By rejecting them, we are simply augmenting the reason why they act in this way.
   **d.** By rejecting ourselves, we create an inner war which can only undermine our actual escape from the prison of this vicious circle of self-rejection and the repetition of this same act for which we reject ourselves. A common example of that would be to reject ourselves because we have overeaten, and then since we are a "lost cause", just go right on eating more.
   **e.** The **psychology of purity** is an important factor in any process of self-improvement. If we have been working in the garden or basement and our body and clothing are dirty, we have no aversion toward handling soiled materials. If, however, we have just taken a shower and are wearing clean white clothing, we will likely feel a strong aversion toward coming into contact with dirt.
   In the same way, when we consider ourselves to be dirty, sinful or bad, we have no problem with partaking in unethical activities. Whereas if we feel pure, holy, and lovable, we prefer to avoid participating in activities which might soil that purity.
   Rejecting ourselves is an obstacle toward cultivating the psychology of purity that is so necessary for tuning into a pure life in harmony with the Laws of Nature.

**4.** Some fear that self acceptance might weaken our need for self-improvement. This is seldom true. The reason is that evolution is a basic natural force in the universe and thus needs no negative force to assist it. The opposite is true. When we do not accept ourselves, we get caught up in resisting change.

Acceptance allows change to take place naturally and not out of fear or anxiety. There is a driving force that causes us to evolve, manifest and externalize our power and beauty.

**5.** We would also do well to remember that the word repentance in Greek is "metanoia", which means to "change one's mind". Repentance does not mean to reject or punish ourselves, but rather to transform our belief system so as to think differently. To repent is to change our beliefs so we are no longer out of harmony with the laws of nature, specifically the law "not to do anything to any one which we would not like done to us."

In the case that our self rejection is based on our actions being out of sync with our conscience, we definitely want to see what is motivating us to function in that way and transform it, while simultaneously accepting and loving ourselves at this level of evolution. Accepting and analyzing that part of ourselves which functions in this way will be the first step toward transforming it.

## TRANSFORMING BELIEFS WHICH OBSTRUCT SELF ACCEPTANCE WHEN UNDER THE INFLUENCE OF FALSE SOCIAL PROGRAMMING

Some of the techniques and concepts presented below will also apply to the situations of conflict of conscience.

**1.** We can use **written affirmations**, such as, "I accept and love myself in every situation (or exactly as I am at this stage of my evolution)", as described in the chapter on written affirmations as an invaluable means of reprogramming ourselves.

**2.** These general written affirmations can then be continued as **personally designed ones**, as explained in that chapter.

**3.** The **research technique** for self-acceptance can be employed. This technique requires two persons.
**a.** The one who wants to work on him or her self, sits comfortably with eyes closed. The other has a pen and paper on which to write.
**b.** Hold hands and take the oath of secrecy concerning whatever is said. Then take a second oath of truth that each will speak out whatever comes to his or her mind.
**c.** Release the hands. The person who is working on himself remains with closed eyes and places his hands on his lower abdomen. As he focuses on that part of the body, he begins to verbalize the following phrase, "I lose my feelings of self-worth or my self acceptance when..." and then allows the phrase to complete itself spontaneously.
He repeats this phrase over and over, allowing the answers to flow forth freely

without control, as the person next to him writes down the reasons and situations he verbalizes. This goes on for about ten minutes, creating a list of obstacles toward feelings of self-worth and self-acceptance.

The person should not open his eyes and should continue for the whole length of time without stopping because "he has nothing else to say". Duration is an important factor for bypassing various defense mechanisms. It is not necessary that we have an answer in our minds before we start verbalizing the phrase. Even if we have nothing in our minds as an answer, we should repeat the phrase at least once per minute and allow the subconscious to supply an answer. It is perfectly okay to repeat the same answer more than once if it keeps coming up. This is significant.

**d.** When this part of the exercise is completed, we move on to the phrase, "I feel especially good about myself when ...." or "I love and accept myself especially when...." The same guidelines apply to this phrase, and this continues for 10 minutes. The other writes all the answers to these incomplete phrases.

**e.** In the case that both individuals are interested in searching the subject, they would now change roles. In the end, each of you will have a much deeper realization of your obstacles toward self-acceptance. You will also a list of reasons and truths that enable you to love and accept yourselves.

Some might say that they could do this alone or in written form. I would encourage them to do both, but not to imagine they are getting the same benefits. Each exercise has its own benefits. We come to different realizations when working alone, when writing or when working verbally with another person. One technique is no better than the other, but they do not replace each other. Each has its own very special attributes.

This same exercise could be applied in exactly the same way with other phrases such as:

**1.** "I lose my sense of **love and union with others** when..." followed by "I feel especially open and close to others when..."

**2.** "I lose my **sense of security** when...." followed by "I feel especially secure when..."

**3.** " I lose my **feelings of being close to God** when..." followed by "I feel close to God when..."

**4.** " I find it difficult **to be myself** when..." followed by " I find it is easy to be myself when..."

**5.** "I lose my **sense of freedom** when..." followed by " I feel free when..."

There are many other possibilities depending on what we want to explore.

## GETTING IN TOUCH WITH THE SUBCONSCIOUS

In most cases, we will want to search deeper to learn the causes of the beliefs that obstruct our self-acceptance by investigating the contents of the subconscious in some of the following ways.

**1.** We can start by making **a list of "reasons" for which we were criticized as children.** This will help us understand:

   **a.** Why we illogically lose our feelings of self-worth in some cases.

   **b.** Why we are attracted to some activities which we ourselves reject. We are often attracted to that which was forbidden.

   **c.** Why might have an irrational desire to relive the rejection we experienced as children. If we do not find others to reject us, then we subconsciously reject ourselves.

   Our parents' voices work within us, creating guilt and pressures, even long after they have left their physical bodies.

   **d.** Why we get involved in internal conflicts where one part of ourselves is playing the parent, who is forbidding and rejecting the child, who also dwells within us.

**2. Regressions** to childhood years in which we focus on moments when, as a child, we felt rejection, shame, or guilt.

**3.** We can **write letters** to those persons who were present in those childhood moments, explaining to them how we felt then and how we feel now about what happened then.

**4.** We can participate in **Psychodrama** with an experienced professional, in which we play out those scenes from the past so as to release them and gradually rebuild them, transforming the way in which we perceived them and reacted.

**5.** We can apply the technique called **the Transformation of the emotion**, especially for the emotions of self-doubt and self-rejection. (Requires a trained professional.)

**6.** We can also write letters asking for forgiveness from others, as well as from God and perhaps even ourselves. This might uncover even deeper feelings of guilt or hurt festering beneath the surface. These letters need not be given to anyone unless we are inspired to do so. Their power is in our ability to express these thoughts and realizations, and most important of all, our regret for any pain we may have triggered in anyone.

   This may be a humbling experience, but it is exactly what the ego needs to release itself from these repetitive patterns of guilt.

   This is the psychology behind the sacraments of Confession, Repentance, and Holy Communion.

   **a.** First, we realize where we are in conflict with our conscience. This is self-knowledge.

   **b.** Then we gain the strength to admit this to others.

   This confession frees us from the ego through humility.

   **c.** We then change the way we think and act. This is repentance.

In this way, we recreate feelings of purity and union with the Divine. The benefit of this process can be understood theologically, psychologically and vibrationally.

The process of writing these confessional letters will help us to realize and release what weighs heavily on our conscience, thus freeing large amounts of energy and inner peace.

**7.** This **confessional expression** in which we also ask for forgiveness can be done **verbally** in the form of psychodrama with a priest, psychologist or facilitator. It can also be done alone while looking at photographs of the persons to whom we wish to speak. We can also close our eyes and speak verbally to a wall, as we imagine the persons we are addressing standing before us.

**8.** In some cases, we might seek out the persons and **speak to them directly.**

These last few techniques will be most applicable to those guilt feelings based upon actions in conflict with our conscience. In some cases, however, our problem might be a mixture of both, that is we feel guilt because we are under the influence of social programming, and also because of our conscience.

Our social programming undermines our feelings of self-worth, and thus leads us to actions about which we feel guilty. It becomes a vicious circle.

In these cases, **we must apply techniques for both types of obstacles toward self-acceptance**, some for getting free from social programming and others for aligning our behavior with our conscience.

## 9. Reevaluating how we measure our self worth

We need to realize how we have been programmed to measure our self-worth.

We generally measure our self-worth by:

**a.** The results of our efforts.

**b.** Others' opinion of us and our results.

**c.** Our subjective perception of what others think about us.

**d.** How we compare to others in some specific ability or quality.

The diagram on the next page will help us understand how we measure our self worth in relationship to the results of our efforts. We might be talking about any effort such as baking a cake, decorating a house, closing a business deal, passing a test, teaching a class, bringing up a child, enamoring someone of the opposite sex, winning a competition of some type etc.

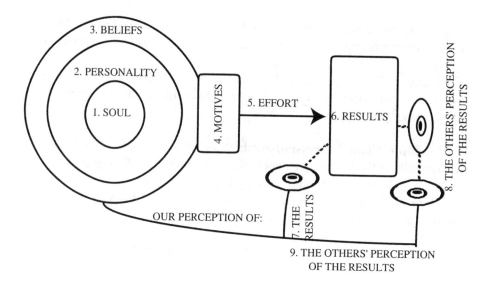

## How we measure our self-worth

**a.** In the center of the concentric circles to the left, is the **soul** (1), our true being. The soul is divine in nature and worthy of love and respect as it is. We cannot increase or decrease its eternal value. The soul is, however, evolving in its ability to express this innate divine nature.

**b.** This expression takes place through the **personality** (2) and body. This personality is in a process of evolution, and thus is not perfect.

**c.** The outer most concentric circle represents our **beliefs** (3) with which the personality has been programmed.

**d.** These beliefs limit and govern the personality's reality and dictate its **motives** (4). Our motives depend upon our values, which, in turn, depend upon our beliefs.

**e.** These motives inspire us to act, to make **efforts** (5) toward desired goals. We are motivated to seek various persons, objects and situations that we believe will secure our safety, pleasure, satisfaction, affirmation, power, love, acceptance, respect, freedom or even spiritual growth or salvation.

**f.** At each stage of these efforts, there is some type of **result** (6).

**g.** We then **judge ourselves** based on this result (7). If we have achieved what we perceive as success, we feel we are worthy. If we interpret the result as failure, or as less successful than someone else's with whom we compare ourselves, then we feel unworthy, a failure.

**h.** Often, however, we do not measure ourselves by the results, but rather by **what others think about the result** (8). We will search their facial expressions or ask them outright, "What do you think of that?" We have so identified our self-worth with how others evaluate the results of our efforts that we believe they love us and we are worthy if they like our food, drawings, house, garden, etc. If they do not like them, or do not show much enthusiasm, we feel rejection and perhaps even negative feelings toward these persons.

**i.** Even worse is that we measure our self-worth **by what we believe the others think about our results (9).** We perceive their opinion subjectively through our own programming, and often mistakenly believe they do not like our creation or they do not love us.

We need to free ourselves from this childish way of perceiving ourselves. As children, we did not have a clear self-image and looked to others to see what they thought about us, usually in response to our behavior or something we had done or created. We continue to do this with spouses, friends and coworkers.

We have been told that it does not matter whether we win, but how we play the game, yet we never truly believe it. (Neither did they who told us so.)

Our self-worth is independent of the results of our actions and of what others think about those results, or how they compare with the others' results.

**If we want to evaluate ourselves, let us evaluate our motives and efforts.** If our motives were pure and our efforts the best we could do at that stage of our evolutionary process, then let us accept ourselves regardless of the results.

If the motives were not pure, or the efforts not our best, then let us analyze how we can improve them.

We would also do well to distinguish between ability, talent and worth. A person who is uniquely capable is not more worthy of love and acceptance than another who is less so. He is worthy of being given more responsibilities, but not more love or respect. All deserve the same love and respect.

In conclusion, our being worthy of love and respect has nothing to do with our abilities or the results of our efforts. **Abilities give us the right to position and responsibilities,** but not the advantage of being loved or respected more than others.

Our self-worth as personalities depends upon the purity of our motives and the quality of our efforts.

Our self-worth as divine creation is absolute and equal to all.

## 10. Writing (letters of truth) to the source

We can write a letter to those who programmed us in this way, explaining what we now consciously and logically believe about those beliefs we were programmed with.

We do not reject these persons who have been instrumental in our programming, but **simply explain that our belief system has changed**, and that when we think logically, we see these assumptions which we made as children as false.

In some cases, the assumption we have made may not be at all what the others believed, but rather our subjective interpretations. This does not matter. **These people are in no way responsible for our reality.** We, as souls, have chosen them exactly because they would transfer to us these ancient illusions, so that we could continue our evolutionary process.

This exercise is called speaking (or writing) to the source. We write or speak to the source of our beliefs, explaining that we can no longer accept these restricting concepts and that we are determined to live our lives from here on in based on our own **conscious beliefs** which we also declare in this exercise.

This is very effective, both as a **written** exercise and as a **verbal** one, or as a **psychodrama** with someone playing the role of those persons. Or we could simply close our eyes and bring each person into our mind, as we clear up accounts and explain what we now consciously believe.

If possible, we can then have this discussion directly with those persons. If they have left their physical bodies, we must imagine them before us.

**Samples of false thoughts from which we might want to declare our freedom:**

    **a.** My self-worth depends upon:
      **1.** What others think about me.
      **2.** The results of my efforts.
      **3.** My appearance.
      **4.** How much money or how many possessions I have.
      **5.** How much I know.
      **6.** How I compare to others.
      **7.** Whether or not I am perfect.
      **8.** Whether or not I have a love partner.
      **9.** My professional position.
      Other_____
    **b.** I am safe only when:
      **1.** I have a relationship.
      **2.** I have money.
      **3.** I have specific persons around me.
      **4.** I am accepted by others.
      **Other**_____
    **c.** My freedom is in danger.
    **d.** I am responsible for others' reality (health, happiness, success, and satisfaction).
    **e.** I am not a good person.
    **f.** God does not love me or His love is with conditions.
    **g.** I am a body and not soul in evolution.
    **h.** I am not pure.

**i.** I am responsible for your unhappiness or problems.
**j.** I am a sinner.
**k.** I am weak or unable.
**l.** I should not follow my intuition.
**m.** I should not believe in myself.
**n.** I must not believe in others.
**0.** Mistakes are unforgivable.
**p.** Others are responsible for my reality.
Other _____

Again, this exercise has nothing to do with rejecting or ceasing to love the others, or holding them responsible for our problems or programming. We can very much love them and feel union with them as we also explain that we perceive reality in a different way. No problem.

If, on the other hand, we find our expression aggressive and condemning, allow that to be for the time being. We might need to pass through this stage of releasing our resentment. We should prefer to release our negative energy in ways that do not harm those around us. We can do so in psychodrama with a trained professional.

**11. We can employ daily relaxations with positive visualization** in which we focus on positive messages concerning our self-worth and self-acceptance. In such relaxations, in addition to positive images, we can cultivate feelings of inner worth, security and confidence.

**12. We can make a list of reasons why we should love, respect and accept ourselves.** This list can be added to daily as we think of more reasons why we should love and respect ourselves. Some of the reasons may have to do with our talents, values, efforts or qualities, while others may have simply to do with the fact that we are divine creation. Some examples follow.

**a.** I am God's creation, a manifestation of the Divine.
**b.** I am a soul in the process of evolution.
**c.** I am God's child.
**d.** Any negative aspects are a result of my ignorance and fear.
**e.** I try the best I can.
**f.** I love others.
**g.** I possess the following **qualities**:
**h.** I embrace the following **values**:
**i.** I have the following **talents**:
**j.** I am making the following **efforts**:

**13.** We can **write letters to that part of ourselves which feels self-doubt** or self-rejection, explaining the objective reality of things. We can explain the various logical and spiritual truths that have be discussed throughout this book.

**14.** We can also **write letters to our inner child** in which we explain the logical, objective and spiritual truth as we see it. Some of the messages, which we might want to pass on to our inner child or to that part of ourselves that experiences self doubt, might be found in the accompanying list. We are presenting this list for a second time because we consider it to be especially important.

## TRUTHS WHICH ENABLE US TO FEEL OUR TRUE SELF

**1.** I am worthy of love and respect regardless of others' opinions or behavior.

**2.** My self-worth is totally independent of how I compare to others.

**3.** My self-worth is totally independent of any external factors, such as intelligence, wealth, my home, appearance, talents, professional success, my children's success, my being attractive to the opposite sex, my ability to make friends, disciplines or spiritual activities.

**4.** I am worthy of love and respect regardless of the results of my efforts.

**5.** I am worthy even when others are given more attention. I am happy for others when they receive love and attention.

**6.** My self-worth is within me and totally independent of whether I am loved exclusively by someone or not.

**7.** I am worthy of love and respect even when I am not perfect in what I do and even when I make mistakes.

**8.** My self-worth is totally independent of how much I accomplish.

**9.** I am worthy of love and respect even when I feel weak or needy.

**10.** My self-worth is totally independent of whether others agree with me or are satisfied with me.

**11.** I deserve love and respect even when I need to say "no" or do not respond to what is asked of me.

**12.** My self-worth has nothing to do with how much I give or receive.

**13.** My self-worth is totally independent of whether or not some people trust me or open up to me.

**14.** My self-worth is totally independent of how people behave toward me.

**15.** My self-worth is totally independent of how much others work or how they work in relation to my work.

**16.** My self-worth is a reflection of my divine nature, not my gender, religion, social class, etc.

**17.** My self-worth is totally independent of whether others recognize it or how they feel toward me.

**18.** I accept and love myself as I am, with my faults and weaknesses, as I steadily and methodically evolve out of them.

**19.** I deserve to be loved and respected exactly as I am (at this stage of my evolutionary process).

**20.** I am beautiful exactly as I am - just as all aspects of nature are.

**21.** I am a good person, a worthy person.

**22.** I am worthy of love and respect regardless of how others behave toward me.

**23.** I respect and love all persons (especially my parents and family) without feeling any need whatsoever to live my life according to their beliefs or values. I live my life in harmony with my inner values and beliefs.

**24.** I am in no way responsible for others people's reality, but only for my own motives and behavior toward them.

**25.** No one else is responsible for my reality. I am totally responsible for what I feel and experience in life.

**26.** My self-worth is based on my inner being, my existence itself, and my inner divine nature, not on any external factors.

**27.** My self-worth is a simple function of the fact that I, as all other creatures, am a unique aspect of divine creation. My self-worth cannot be increased nor decreased. I can never be more or less worthy of love and respect than another.

**28.** Although I am not perfect and have various faults, I deserve to be loved and respected as I am, just I as I love and respect others with their faults.

**29.** When I do not love myself, I do not love an aspect of divine creation.

**30.** I often accept traits in others that I reject in myself. Why?

**31.** I am in a process of evolution and am attending to that process

**32.** All beings deserve my love and respect, including myself

**33.** God is unconditional love and cannot ever "not love" me.

### VERBAL EXERCISES FOR THE
### TRANSFORMATION OF SELF-DOUBT

**1. Declaring the affirmation:**
This exercise can be performed with another person wanting to work on him or her self. Look into the other's eyes and repeat the phrase, **"I love and accept myself exactly as I am."** If you want, you can add the conditional phrase, **" ...at this stage of my evolutionary process."**

This, or some similar phrase, can be repeated 15 times as we look into the other's eyes. We take three deep breaths in the interval between each verbalization of the phrase. As we breathe, we observe our inner reactions to declaring this to someone.

This exercise should be done slowly and consciously as we focus on, feel and think about what we are saying. We let the thought of total self-acceptance sink deeply into the center of our being throughout the exercise.

After fifteen times, we can write down what we felt as we said this phrase.

As we focus on this phrase, we connect to our purity, goodness and any other reasons why we actually should be accepting ourselves

If the other wants, he or she can now do the same with our assistance. If no one is interested, we can do it looking into a mirror.

**2. Experiencing opposition:**
Similar to the previous exercise we will need a partner. Sit face to face. The other says to us in a convincing way, "You have no self-worth," or " You are worthless," or " You have no value as a person."

We look into his or her eyes and answer, **"I deserve your love and acceptance exactly as I am."** If we choose, we can add the condition, "...**at this stage of my evolutionary process."**

This goes on for about five minutes as the other continues to reject us in as a convincing way as he or she can (avoid laughing), while we continue to affirm that we deserve to be accepted and loved exactly as we are.

The more calmly we can affirm our right to be accepted and loved as we are, the more sure we are of the fact. The more we feel the need to force the other to accept it, the less sure we are.

### 3. Experiencing rejection:

Continue sitting face to face. Now the other holds a list that we have created containing the three criticisms we hear from others or from ourselves which most strongly or frequently undermine our feelings of self-worth. These should be written clearly so the other can read them.

The other looks into our eyes and tells us we are no good, or that we are not worthy because of one of the reasons we have written on the paper. He is now hitting us in our weak spot, where we usually lose our clarity and self love. We look into his eyes and answer, **"the truth is that I deserve your love and acceptance exactly as I am."** We can add, **"...at this stage of my evolutionary process."**

The other repeats the same phrase to us three to five times, and each time we answer him in the above mentioned way. Then he starts on the next stimulus on the list we have written.

In this way, we come to face our weak points concerning self-acceptance. The truth is that we have many weaknesses and faults, but as souls in the process of evolution, we deserve to be loved and respected as we are. In the same way, all others deserve our love and respect just as they are.

This exercise should be done slowly and consciously, as we seek to really feel that we deserve to be loved even when confronted with those criticisms which until now triggered our self-doubt.

### 4. Declaring to the group:

This exercise can be done in a group (or if we have enough imagination we can visualize a group of persons before us). We stand before the group. If there is a microphone, we can use this to ensure we are heard loudly and clearly. As we look into their eyes, we declare to the group, **" I am worthy of your love and acceptance exactly as I am."**

We can add something to this statement, such as declaring some of the reasons why we deserve their love, or we can rest on the fact that we deserve their love and respect regardless of any attributes or achievement, simply because we are divine creation.

The microphone can then be passed around, as each stands and declares that she or he deserves our love, acceptance and / or respect exactly as she or he is.

### 5. Looking into each others' eyes:

This exercise can be done best while sitting opposite each other. Some prefer to hold hands as they are looking into the others' eyes.

One of the main reasons we cannot look into the others' eyes is that we do not feel pure. We want to hide anything we fear the others might reject, and we want to project whatever we feel might impress them. In this exercise, we simply look into the others' eyes without speaking. Speaking is the main way we hide and project. We look into the other's eyes, cultivating feelings of being at ease, without any need to hide anything or project anything.

We can simply be ourselves with this person, without trying to think of something to say to fill in the uneasiness of looking into his or her eyes. We can then develop feelings of oneness and open our hearts, feeling love energy flowing out of our heart center toward the other, filling his or her body and mind with light.

We attune ourselves to the other's beauty, inner and outer. We appreciate the other's being. This then brings us into contact with our own beauty and we feel good about ourselves. We both deserve to be loved, accepted and respected exactly as we are.

We can stay about 15 to 25 minutes as we focus on releasing all feelings of separateness, experiencing love and unity.

In this chapter, we have been presented a wide variety of questionnaires and other techniques for helping us increase our love and acceptance of ourselves, something which is a prerequisite for accepting and loving others.

If you don't feel ready to work with them at this point, you might come back to them later. Thousands have already benefited from these techniques.

Much more information can be found on this subject on our web site.

Technique no. 17

# HEALING LOVE ENERGY

### Why this is beneficial

The power of love energy can be directed as healing energy through the mind and the hands, to any being who needs help (including ourselves if necessary). This is a great way to uplift otherwise misdirected energies and concentrate them in a positive way to help others and simultaneously ourselves.
Regular employment with loved ones will transform the most difficult relationships into loving ones. This is a very powerful technique and is very successful in changing our environment

### A simple technique for focusing on
### healing love energy is:

**1.** We can close our eyes, and bring our minds to a point of relaxation and concentration through breathing, relaxation or meditation.

**2.** Then we can mentally create the image of the person who needs help and see him or her surrounded by light and love, with no sign of the problem which he or she might have had.

**3.** We visualize him or her well and in harmony.

**4.** We visualize ourselves feeling open and loving towards him or her.

**5.** If we have difficulty, then we should start off by bringing to mind five positive traits that we can respect in the other. The other might have negative aspects, but will also have a number of positive ones. Focusing on their positive traits frees us from our negativity and is healing to all of us.

### Note:

This is especially useful to employ for people whom we are having difficulty getting along with, or who are directing negative energy in our direction. By sending them love and light we are able to reach deep into ourselves and transform these potential negative energies into love and healing power.

*Life Story no. 18*

# LOUD NEIGHBORS

Beverly lives with her husband and children in an apartment building. The tenants upstairs seem to have little consideration or respect for others. They play their television and stereo quite loud until early hours of the morning and walk in such a way as to create a loud tapping noise with their every step.

It is unlikely that they are doing all this with the intention of making Beverly suffer, but this is certainly how she perceives it. Her sleep is obstructed more by her feelings that they are not respecting her than by the noise itself. As a result, she feels injustice, bitterness, anger and frustration. She would prefer not to call the police for fear of creating an even greater problem. She does not know what else to do.

Beverly has complained a number of times. The neighbors say they will solve the problem, but nothing changes. She has even thought of buying them a carpet to muffle the noise, but due do to the loss of sleep, she is becoming even more irritable, upset and angry.

The feeling that she is not respected is even more of a problem than the noise itself. Her family is bothered to a much lesser degree and no one else has a problem sleeping.

What can she do?

**Some of Beverly's lessons might be:**

**1.** To express her needs to others with greater clarity, assertiveness and love.

**2.** To free herself from the belief that there will be conflict if she becomes more assertive, that she will hurt others or that they will hurt her in the event of a confrontation.

**3.** To free herself from the importance which she places on what others think about her.

**4.** Not to take this sound personally as a rejection of her needs or person, but simply as something which the others need to do or as something which makes them happy.

**5.** To accept others and love them even when they are unable to respect her needs.

**6.** To send positive thoughts and light to these people, even when they are unable to cooperate.

**7.** To believe that others can be interested in her needs and be willing to cooperate with her.

**8.** To love herself even when others are unable to respect her needs or feelings.

**9.** To check and see if perhaps she herself is not respecting other's needs.

**10.** To request the assistance of the police without hate or anger.

### She might be helped by some of the following beliefs:

**1.** I love and accept myself even when others do not respect my needs.

**2.** I love and accept others even when they are unable to respect my needs.

**3.** Others love and care for me and want to cooperate with me.

**4.** I can confront others assertively and lovingly without there being a conflict.

**5.** I can be even more assertive in order to demonstrate how important this is to me.

# Chapter 18

# LEARNING FROM
# LIFE'S DIFFICULTIES

Illness, pain, difficulties and obstacles are usually confronted with sorrow, fear, resentment and a feeling of injustice. Generally speaking, we desire that problems disappear as quickly as possible, often relying on such superficial solutions as alcohol, pain pills, tranquilizers or sleep. We might even seek to forget our reality by bombarding our senses with an unending flow of stimuli, so that the mind will be distracted from pondering its predicament. Here we shall present a different way of approaching these unpleasant experiences.

We shall examine the possibility of perceiving illness and pain as our **guides towards health and harmony.**

We all would like to be happy, healthy and in harmony with ourselves and our environment, but very few of us actually are. One reason for this is that we do not live according to the basic laws of nature. When function in harmony with these natural laws, we will experience harmony.

Animals and plants unconsciously live in this harmonious flow. They have no choice. Man, however, has free will to flow with the laws of harmonious living or ignore them. The results of both choices are obvious. When walking in a forest, on a mountain or at a seaside, we experience the natural harmony of our surroundings flowing into us and stimulating our own inner sense of harmony. We feel it. It relaxes us and puts us at peace with ourselves. There is a sympathetic vibration between the external harmony and our inner unconscious archetype of harmony.

We do not get the same feeling, however, when we are walking on polluted city streets or when the people around us are negatively stressed and behave in indifferent or aggressive ways. We seldom feel that same sense of inner peace in our interaction with people.

## OUR EGO SEPARATES US FROM THE WORLD

Nature does not possess an ego as man does. Our ego or personality complex covers our inner natural beauty. Because we do not feel our inner beauty, we try to become superficially beautiful by "ornamenting" or manipulating our bodies and personalities in different ways.

Ignorant of our inner strength, love and beauty, we unintentionally cut ourselves off from the flow of life. In our effort to protect ourselves and our families, we often lose our interest for and connection with those outside our immediate circle. This lack of unity is one of the basic causes of disharmony on a personal and social level.

Also, because we tend to doubt our self-worth, we seek love and approval from others, often in ways that are at the expense of our health and true fulfillment.

Flowing in harmony with the natural laws means moving in two basic directions:

**1.** Toward a **discovery of our inner divine potential.**

**2.** Toward **a feeling of unity and universal love** for all beings.

## THE SCHOOL OF LIFE

Physical life is an embodied state into which we incarnate in order to learn the above two basic lessons. Life is a school, in which we walk along the path from ignorance to enlightenment and from separateness and fear to unity and love. Life has perfect feedback mechanisms that inform us with unpleasant stimuli such as illness, pain, conflict or disharmony whenever we move away from these natural laws. When we are on the path of evolution, we experience positive inner feelings, giving us the signal to keep going in the right direction. We may also experience change-provoking stimuli when we have become stagnant in our growth process or when we simply need to move on.

## THE EFFECT OF THE PAST

One natural law is the **law of sympathetic vibration** which attracts to us whatever corresponds to our inner world, which means beliefs, needs, fear and other emotions, desires, expectations, behaviors, and choices of the past and present. This law also includes but is not limited to a type of mirroring process like the "law of cause and effect" or according to Eastern philosophies, the law of karma. This law is also frequently referred to in the Bible, as in the phrase, "as you sow, so shall you reap". When the paralyzed man was brought to Christ to be cured, He said to him, "get up and walk, your sins are forgiven." This clearly affirms the fact that the man was paralyzed as the result of some past actions.

This relationship between "sin," or egotistical action, and illness and suffering is well accepted by all religions, and is clearly one of the great truths all human beings must come to understand on the way to enlightenment.

Eastern philosophies, however, include the concept of reincarnation, which adds that if we cannot find the cause of our pleasant or unpleasant experiences among our thoughts, words or actions of our present life, perhaps these experiences stem from a past life. According to this concept, the soul has a number of opportunities to return to the school of life in its quest to perfect itself. As Christ explained, one cannot enter into the Kingdom of Heaven "until he becomes perfect." Odds are that we do not know anyone who has become perfect as yet. If there is only one life, then Heaven will likely be a very sparsely populated "place."

Whether reincarnation is true or not, the fact remains that the law of cause and effect is universally accepted by all sources. Thus, this law serves as a **feedback mechanism** that facilitates our growth process. I prefer to perceive it as an educational process rather than as one of punishment of retribution. There is little use for punishment in an evolutionary process. We need to experience these events and situations because they offer us the opportunity to see ourselves, our thoughts and our behaviors more clearly and objectively for the purpose of freeing ourselves from negative programming and limiting beliefs.

## OUR PRESENT BELIEFS AND EMOTIONS

Another aspect of this law is that our **present beliefs, emotions and behaviors** are being reflected back to us from others and life. In this case, it is not simply that we have "put up with" something because it is a result of the past, but rather that we must make adjustments in the ways we perceive and react to life in the present moment. Of course, this is the solution even in the case where we are experiencing the results of our past. We still need to make the adjustment and learn the lesson in the present.

## OUR CHOSEN LESSONS

Another possibility is that as souls we have chosen to learn some specific lesson, and that which is happening now has been chosen by us on our soul level so we may be "pressured" as personalities into growing and evolving.

Happiness, contentment and inner peace are indications that we are on the right path. Unhappiness, discontentment and mental agitation are signs that we are stuck, that we have taken the wrong path, or that we simply have something new to learn.

By "happiness" we are referring to an **inner state** and **not the external circumstances** that befall us. Someone could be dying of cancer and be perfectly at peace with him or herself as well as with life and death. This cancer may very well **not** be an indication of wrong living, but simply one of life's opportunities for growth. Another person could have health and affluence, but feel miserable inside. He then needs to make some type of adjustment in the way he lives, feels or thinks.

Thus, whenever we are unhappy, discontent or in conflict with ourselves or others, we are receiving a message from life telling us **it is time for a change.**

## OPPORTUNITIES FOR SPIRITUAL GROWTH

The process of growth or evolution is always one of change. The old must die so as to give space for the new to develop. Life is a continuous process of letting go of old habits and ways of living, feeling and thinking. "Messages" from life's events may try to inform us that we need to change our eating habits, give up smoking or alcohol, rest more, care for our bodies more conscientiously or that we need, in general, to respect the needs of our body and mind.

We might attract unpleasant experiences that have the purpose of encouraging us to become less ego-centered or more understanding of the other's inner state in order to create the harmony we seek. We may need to exercise, meditate, pray or relax more regularly so as to regain our lost vitality and mental peace or in order to come into contact with higher sources of peace and energy.

Life might be asking us to reexamine our goals, values and life style, to determine if we are, in fact, living in such a way as to fulfill our **real goals,** or have simply fallen into a mechanized socially programmed means of seeking happiness.

If we find we are frequently anxious or in conflict, we may need to examine our attitudes, beliefs and self-image. We may need to develop more self-confidence, self-acceptance, and self-love, or let go of bitterness or jealousy and forgive and love. Perhaps we need to place more faith in God and in Divine Justice, or learn how to surrender to the Divine Flow of life itself.

We will likely need learn to let go of attachments and dependencies, such as codependent relationships, the need for approval from others, the use of tranquilizers, etc, which ultimately cause us to feel weak inside. Most of us need to learn to think positively and discover the great creative power that lies within us.

Basically, what is required in each case is some type of internal change. When we seek external solutions by taking tranquilizers, alcohol or cigarettes, or by changing our spouse, job or location, we often fail to see the real problem and learn what life is trying to teach us. As a result, we will most likely create the same situation under new conditions.

These and many other lessons all lead to the final lesson of life, which is the realization that we are not limited to these bodies, nor these personalities, but are immortal expressions of one divine consciousness.

## HOW TO USE LIFE'S DIFFICULTIES

Our difficulties and tests are like the weight lifter's weights that help him to build up his muscular power. By exercising our inner power against these challenges, we develop our emotional, mental and spiritual muscles. We become emotionally stronger and mentally more positive and assured of our ability to face any possible situation.

Here are some concepts that will help us to grow through our life experiences:

**1. Perceive life as a school.**

**2.** Remember that **every experience is a lesson designed** to teach us something about ourselves and the nature of reality.

**3.** Remember that **life gives us exactly the lessons we need** in every moment.

There are no accidents or injustices. Whatever happens to us is exactly what needs to happen, in order for us to learn our next lesson. If we believe this, we will cease fearing what might happen and stop complaining about the injustices of the past. We will let go of the bitterness we feel toward those who have been used by life to offer us some lesson or with whom we have made a subconscious agreement to test us. We will let go of the jealousy we feel when others appear to have more than we have.

We all receive the exact situations we need in order to learn the unique lessons that we have come to learn. These lessons come to us to promote our spiritual growth.

This does not mean there are no unjust actions. Many actions and behaviors are unjust, but they could not happen to us unless we have created or subconsciously chosen that event for our growth process. Thus, the other's action may be objectively wrong and unjust, but we are not suffering from an injustice. We have chosen as a soul to pass through this in order to learn something.

**4. Discover which lessons life is trying to teach us.**

Richard Bach, author of *Jonathan Livingston Seagull and Illusions* reminds us that a **"problem never comes to you without a gift in its hands".** Our life challenge is to fearlessly study our problems and discover the gifts therein.

**5. Determine what changes we need to make in our living or thinking habits in order to become free from this problem** or, in some cases, to realize that there actually is no problem).

We can ask ourselves these questions:

**a.** What must I let go of? (Habits, emotional tendencies, addictions, attachments, fears, expectations, attitudes, beliefs.)

**b.** What can I begin to develop? (Positive beliefs, disciplines, attitudes, abilities.)

**c. Is there actually any problem here or I am making it into a problem?** In some cases, our lesson may simply be to realize that what we consider to be a problem is not one at all. Thus, we simply need to learn to accept what is happening.

**6. Decide how we can start making these changes** so as to once again find peace, health and harmony.

**7. Accept that only we ourselves can solve this problem,** otherwise its solution is of no use to us. We can take advice from our doctor, psychiatrist, clergyman or guru, but it is up to ourselves to make the actual changes. It is our **responsibility** as well as our **opportunity.**

The difference between the pessimist and the optimist is that the pessimist sees the problem in every opportunity and the optimist sees the **opportunity** in every **problem.**

Let us now look at a few examples of some common problems and the possible lessons (gifts) we might learn from them. As the possibilities are infinite, I will mention some that come to my mind at this moment. You can supplement this text with your own experience, by reflecting on how you have grown or benefited through facing difficult life experiences.

## WHAT WE CAN LEARN FROM ILLNESS

I remember a story told by Dr. Jayadeva of the YOGA INSTITUTE OF BOMBAY.

"Once an enlightened being was asked 'Who was your guru?' He answered, 'Sinusitis.' The enlightened one went on to explain that in order to free himself of his sinusitis he had to change his diet completely. Then he started doing exercises and breathing techniques to purify and remove the stresses from his body that intensified the problem. After that, he started practicing deep relaxation and meditation in order to quiet the mind and nervous system, which seemed to be at the root of the sinusitis. Finally, he had to completely alter his understanding of himself and the world around him, so as to remove the basic causes of imbalance in his body and mind. As a result of all these efforts and changes, his body and mind became so purified and in tune with the Spirit, he became enlightened."

Some possible lessons we might learn from illness are:

**1. To improve our diet: Choose** to eat healthier foods in proper quantities, so the body and mind will be strengthened and able to function effectively and clearly, biologically, mentally and spiritually.

**2. To adopt healthier living habits:** Learn to exercise, breathe and relax regularly, so as to create a body that has the strength to protect itself from microbes and various malfunctionings.

**3. To analyze and correct any negative thought patterns** that may create emotional, mental or physical blockages.

**4. To learn to be more humble** and compassionate through this rather humbling position in which we are temporarily weak, vulnerable, and perhaps even dependent upon others.

**5. To learn to accept, love and care from others:** Some of us cannot accept affection or even simple compliments from others. We always want to be on the giving side. This can sometimes be based on egotistic motives.

**6. To think more deeply about the meaning of life:** Why are we here? What is the purpose of life?

**7. To reexamine our goals and value system:** What do we want from life? What is important to us? Are we living in such a way as to achieve our goals?

**8. To develop mental powers of positive thought projection** so as to send healing energies into the various parts of our body and heal it.

**9. To take a more active role in the creation of our health, happiness and harmony:** Only we can create our illness and health.

**10. To surrender to God's will:** Although we do everything we need to do in order to create health, we must also be able to accept whatever the results may be in order to unite our will with the Divine Flow.

**11. To concentrate more on our contact with the Divine** through prayer and meditation.

**12. To realize that we are not this body** and begin to dis-identify with it, feeling ourselves as an immortal spirit.

## WHAT WE CAN LEARN FROM A
## RELATIONSHIP BREAKDOWN

A divorce, separation or, in general, any relationship breakdown is an unpleasant experience which may provide us with various lessons. There are many lessons we need to learn before we come to the conclusion that we must separate from someone. But if the other leaves us or this separation has already happened, we might be able to benefit from the following.

**1. To examine our behavior** to see how we have contributed to the problem: It is unlikely that we are 100% innocent. The other was probably mirroring some aspect of our character that we need to study in greater detail.

**2. To learn to love the other in spite of his or her behavior,** regardless of whether we stay with that person or not: We can continue to love the other even when our personalities are not suitable for mutual habitation or work. Some may remain in a relationship while harboring bitterness and hate, which is detriment to our happiness and spiritual growth.

**3. To discover that we can live without this person:** We often believe we will never feel secure or happy again without a particular person, but life shows us differently. We discover that happiness, security and love are internal states which are always within us, if only we allow ourselves to experience them.

**4. To develop greater inner strength** so as to feel confident to face whatever may come to us in the game of life: we need to realize we are strong and capable, as opposed to weak and dependent.

**5. To change our self-image:** We may find that one of the problems in the relationship was that we did not enough self esteem, and thus, did not inspire the other's respect, acceptance and love. We need now to learn to accept, love and respect ourselves more, so that we do not create the same problem in our next relationship or in life in general.

**6. To direct our energies in a spiritual direction** and develop a relationship with God: By focusing on our relationship with the Universal Being, we are no longer vulnerable nor so dependent on others to give us the feeling of security and love we need. We receive these through our relationship with the One Being, who will never leave us, not even when we leave these physical bodies.

Once our happiness, security and love have become internalized, we can feel **real love** towards all we meet without fear. Then we can experience unconditional love.

## WHAT CAN WE LEARN THROUGH
## THE DEATH OF A LOVED ONE

The death of a loved one is considered to be the most painful life experience. Many of us would prefer to die ourselves rather than face life without someone who meant so much to us. Some mourn for years, experiencing depression, bitterness and resentment toward life and God "who has dealt us such an unfair blow."

If we accept that life is a school, and that every experience is an opportunity to move forward our evolutionary path, there will be some very useful lessons to be gained even in this most unpleasant experience. Let us look at some of them.

**1. Accept that loss is a basic part of our life cycle.** Whatever is born must die. Whatever grows must decay. These are universal laws. Did we forget that these physical bodies are mortal? Everything we see around us will one-day decay and cease to be. That includes all plants, animals, people, buildings, cities, the planet earth, the sun and even the galaxy. **Everything** in the physical universe is **temporary.** When this fact is understood and accepted, we will begin to seek another source of security and happiness which does not depend on these temporary, animate and inanimate structures.

**2. We can live and be happy again.** Some feel that we cannot go on or ever be happy again without our loved one. But time slowly heals the wounds of the heart, and we dare to laugh again (at first when no one is looking, lest it not be proper). We begin to discover that there is more strength within us than we knew.

**3. We can increase our faith in the wisdom and justice of the universe.** We might feel anger towards God when our loved one leaves his or her physical body. When we lose our faith in the **wisdom** and **justice** of the universal laws, we cannot accept that this event could have been a part of a greater plan simply because it was not a part of our own plan. Nor can we envision this event as essential to our evolutionary process. We can learn to have faith and accept that there must have been a reason for this event. There are no accidents.

**4. Develop a relationship with God:** After seeking happiness, affirmation, love and security in various relationships, we begin to realize there are two main obstacles to succeeding in that effort.

The first is that most people are not yet mature and/or strong enough to really love us as unconditionally as we want to be loved. We, in general, do not even love ourselves enough, so it is difficult, if not impossible, to find someone who is spiritually advanced enough to love us unconditionally and make us feel secure.

The second obstacle is that the bodies, which those souls we love presently occupy, are mortal. Thus, even if we find someone who is capable of giving us what we need and want, we may lose him or her at any moment. It is a certainty that some day we will be separated by our or the other's departure from the physical body, and although we may have a happy relationship, we might at times be unable to enjoy it completely because we fear losing it, especially if the other is ill.

When we develop a relationship with God, we cultivate an inner source of security and love which does not depend upon any other. We can then enjoy all our relationships with the ability to give and take love without fearing loss, or becoming emotionally devastated upon the departure of our loved one from his or her body. We can love without attachment or dependency, which is much more rewarding for us and others.

**5. Confront death:** We need to ask, "what is death?" What is the nature of that energy, that power, that consciousness which, when it was in that body, caused it to think, speak, move, love, feel and create? Now that it is gone, there is a mass of cells that will soon decompose. What is life? What is its purpose? A number of us have been forced by the death of the loved one to investigate these questions. Death forces us to look deeper into the nature and purpose of life.

**6. Reexamine our life values and goals:** Contact with death awakens us to the fact that someday we too will die. This generates a number of questions. Will we have fulfilled our life purpose? Why have we come here to the earth? Why have we taken this physical body? Is our life part of some greater plan or process? If so, what does it require of us? How can we live our lives more in harmony with that purpose?

Answering these questions might motivate us to change our life style, live a more meaningful existence, improve our character, purify our love, or investigate the deeper truths of life. We may also discover that life feels more meaningful when we value others and their needs.

**7. Develop discrimination** between the body, mind and soul. The body and personality are temporary vehicles for the soul's expression here on the earth. We do not cease to exist when it breaks down any more than a car ceases to exist when our car breaks down, or a radio station ceases to exist when a radio stops functioning. Awareness that our physical existence is temporary allows us to give more importance to the spiritual aspects of life, which are eternal. We will then pay less attention to accumulating temporary objects and expand more energy toward the development of love, wisdom and self-knowledge.

## WHAT WE CAN LEARN FROM LOSS

The **fear** and the **pain** of loss are two of the most destructive human emotions. They consume tremendous portions of our emotional, mental and physical energy, and create suffering on all levels. Why is this?

Our basic life needs are **security, pleasure, freedom and affirmation**. In hope of satisfying these needs, we seek to accumulate or attach ourselves to objects, money, relationships and social or professional positions. We become attached to these, believing they give us our strength, security, freedom, contentment and self-worth or success.

We fear that if we do not have these, we will be vulnerable, and thus at the mercy of the world around us. We cling to our possessions, relationships, money and positions, believing we must have them to be well.

**Life**, however, **is change** and nothing that we see or depend upon is free from the possibility of changing or disappearing in an instant. In a split second, our money, job, spouse, parent or child can disappear. They are all merely temporary waves on the sea of life.

Adaptation and the ability to let go of the past are not only essential for evolution and growth, but also for overcoming suffering. The old must pass on in order for the new to develop. This is the law of both the material and mental worlds.

If the blood in our veins refuses to move on from where it presently is, it will damage the body. Stagnant water spoils. A vessel must be emptied in order to be filled again with a new substance. If our bodies and minds are attached to what we "are" and "have," refusing to release them, there is no possibility of growth into new and higher levels of consciousness.

The child must pass on in order to become an adult. The seed must split and cease to exist in order to become the tree. The egg must burst to become a caterpillar, and the caterpillar must perish in order to become a butterfly.

From this perspective, every loss is an excellent opportunity to discover that we have the inner power to continue on even without what we have lost, and that we are much greater than we had originally believed.

## SOME USEFUL LESSONS WE MAY LEARN FROM LOSSES IN OUR LIVES

Let us look at some possible lessons we may acquire from losing whatever is important to us, such as a watch, a wallet, important papers, jewelry, a job, a social position, money, our house, our land, our car, a camera, furniture, etc. (We have already discussed the lessons to be learned from losing a loved one.)

**1.** One possible lesson we may learn from losing or nearly losing something is to **discover the value that it has for us.** Often we do not realize how important or valuable something is to us until we no longer possess it.

**2.** Another lesson may be to discover that, **in truth, we do not need that particular object** as much as we had previously thought. We may need to realize that we have the strength to face life and be happy without it. Every attachment causes us to feel a little weaker. When we lose the object of attachment, we are given the opportunity to realize that we are stronger than we had once thought.

**3.** We can learn that these **external objects do not bring real lasting security, contentment or affirmation,** and that they are subject to change.

**4.** We may learn **how to have, use and enjoy objects without becoming attached to them or allowing them to enslave us.** The example of the bird on the branch mentioned earlier is a good one. The bird rests on the branch and enjoys its support. When a wind comes and shakes the branch, it does not experience fear because it is confident of its ability to fly and is also aware that there are plenty of other branches.

In the same way, we may enjoy what life has to offer us while remaining aware that we have the inner strength to live and be happy without these objects.

**5.** We may learn that we must **be more careful, more aware or more conscious** so that we do not lose things unnecessarily due to a lack of concentration and care.

**6.** We may be forced to **analyze the inner meaning of this loss.** What is life trying to teach us with this loss? What does this message mean about our lives, our actions and our way of living?

**7.** We may need to learn **how to try to retrieve** that which we have lost, or even perhaps fight for it, but with love and without attachment to the results of our effort. That means that while we make our best effort to regain what we have lost, we are able to accept our new reality should our effort not succeed. We can learn to protect and care for our possessions without anxiety or fear.

**8.** We can develop **faith in Divine Wisdom,** and thus accept the fact that nothing can happen which is not controlled by the just and wise powers of the universe. A faith in the Divine Plan allows us to accept that only the best for our spiritual evolution will ever be allowed to take place.

**9.** We can learn to **surrender to the will of God,** realizing that all is given and taken from this one universal source of all that exists. We come into this world naked and will leave it naked. All that we accumulate in between is simply on loan for us to use for our survival, service, and spiritual growth while on earth.

**10.** We may be forced to discover, face and **change any negative beliefs that may be provoking such losses.** We may hold beliefs such as "the world is full of evil", "I am not capable of holding a job", or "I am not capable of protecting myself," which may create unnecessary losses simply because they are merely manifestations of our belief system.

These and many other lessons can be learned from any loss. We would benefit by adopting the attitude that whatever occurs in our lives happens for a reason. We can then seek to discover what we can learn from that, making every material loss a potential emotional, mental and spiritual gain as we develop inner strength and discover how full and complete we are within ourselves without external crutches. The real secret is to **enjoy what we have without becoming dependent upon it.**

When we worry about what we do not have or what we have lost, we lose what we do have. If we stop to think how much we actually have to be grateful for, our losses will seem insignificant.

## WHAT MIGHT WE LEARN FROM A COURT CASE

Independent of the reasons we are involved in a court case, there are some basic lessons that we can learn in each situation. These lessons will not only help in our spiritual growth, but will also allow us to be more objective and efficient in our handling of the case. We will be able to face the situation with greater clarity and discrimination, thus protecting our inner peace and health.

**1.** We will be forced to **develop our mental powers** by researching and planning the case. In most situations, it is best not to leave the case completely up to our lawyer, just as it is best not to leave our health completely up to our doctor. These experts are in a position to give us good advice, but in the end, it is our life and we are responsible for making sure we are sufficiently informed, through them, to make the final decisions.

**2.** We must face and **overcome the temptation** to use false witnesses or information in order to win the case. This holds true even in cases where we may be innocent, or where the opponent is obviously using all types of falsities to prove his argument. It is much better to protect the truth and lose the case than it is lose the truth and win the case. The saying is that **"Those who protect the truth will ultimately be protected by the truth."**
Of course, in order to be protected by the truth, we might first be tested as to how far we are willing to protect it. For example, are we ready to stand by the truth, even if it means we will make less money or lose our position, our money, our family, or even our life? History is full of examples of great spiritual beings who endured great losses as they were being tested in this manner.
Today's judicial system, in which the truth is sometimes sacrificed for the personal gain of a few who have contacts and power, offers a wonderful opportunity to the soul to test its inner strength and determination to function in an honest and honorable way, even in a system which has lost its moral basis. Life is eternal. We may succeed in protecting our small temporary interests with lies, but in the end, we will be brought to court for those lies in the " higher court of life."

**3.** We will have the opportunity **to overcome negative feelings** toward our "opponent." We must remember that everything that happens in life occurs for one of two reasons:
**a.** To balance accounts for something we have done in the past.
**b.** To offer us experiences which stimulate our further spiritual development and alignment with the higher laws of life.
We must understand that our "opponent" is not responsible for this situation, for it were not that particular person, it would be another. The other person is simply

a puppet in the theater of life. Our own decisions, choices and need to evolve have attracted this situation to us, regardless of whether we can remember or are aware of them.

We may feel that a great injustice is being done because we are innocent and correct. In such a case, we need to have faith in the wisdom of divine justice that brings us these potential lessons in our spiritual growth process.

In the case that we are the ones who are bringing the other to court, we would do well to remember that, in reality, we are not the victims. Whatever has been done to us, or taken from us, has been made possible because we have created that situation through our decisions and choices until now (even if we are unaware of them).

Another may be motivated to harm or cheat us, but he or she can not manifest this unless we have created the conditions for that experience. That experience offers us some type of stimulus for our evolution.

This, however, does not mean there are no unjust actions and that we should let the wrong act go uncorrected. If we did so, society would fall apart morally, economically, emotionally, mentally and spiritually. We are taking this person's **action** to court, not the person himself. We can continue to love the person and send him healing light while simultaneously realizing that, for his good and for society's good, his act must be called into account.

This may seem like a contradiction, but although there are obviously actions and behaviors that are immoral and unjust, there are actually no victims. These immoral actions are wrong and must be corrected, but we could not be their recipients unless we have attracted them as stimuli for our growth process.

Thus, it is our obligation to bring all transgressions against the law to court, so their behavior may be corrected and that they may serve as an example for others. Still, this must be done without hate, anger, bitterness or feelings of revenge toward the person we are prosecuting.

Lawbreakers are often unfortunate victims of abuse, pain and alienation, which have subsequently brought them to a state where they are capable of harming others. They are confused and need help. Their self-image and attitudes toward life and society need to be healed.

Our prison system needs to become efficient at effecting such modifications in behavior. We need to turn our energies toward the real rehabilitation of law transgressors rather than simply containing them, punishing them and abusing them. They are victims of our society's lack of love, understanding and unity. In a sense, we, as a whole, are guilty for their acts. Their acts are the result of the inequality, alienation and indifference that abound in our society. Putting them in prison without making any attempt to correct the family, school and social conditions that created their mental state is no solution.

We must fight for our rights with all our energy and clarity because such acts must not pass uncorrected. On the other hand, we must fight impersonally, compassionately and without negative feelings toward the other. This we should seek to do regardless of whether we are the accused or the accuser.

**4.** We can use this opportunity to **develop faith in divine justice.** A court case is an opportunity to remember that there is, in fact, divine justice, and only that which is best for our mutual growth will take place.

## IN THE CASE WE LOSE

We have all heard many times that it is not important whether we win or loose, but how we play the game. Despite that, we seldom practice this philosophy in our daily lives. We want to win in every situation, and we feel very unhappy and react badly when we lose. We are also prepared to play the game in any way we must in order to win, even if this means cheating or lying.

What is really important is how we have played; whether we have played fairly, with dignity and integrity, not doing to others anything we would not like done to us.

Whether we win or not is simply not important from the spiritual point of view. This brings to mind once more the prayer of St. Francis of Assisi: **"DEAR LORD, Grant me the peace to accept what I cannot change, the courage to change what I can change, and the discrimination to know the difference between the two."**

In the event that we do lose, there are still a number of lessons we can gain from that experience.

**1. We can accept that this loss** is the best possible experience for our spiritual development. We can realize that we can continue to live happily without whatever we have lost, be it our money, our possessions, or even our freedom of movement.

**2. Love, compassion and forgiveness towards our opponent** will free us from the need for future lessons of this kind. We can realize that the other person has nothing to do with our loss, but is merely a puppet in our life. He is not responsible for our reality. We have used him to give ourselves the opportunity for these lessons.

**3. In the event that we are actually imprisoned,** we also can use this situation for our spiritual growth. We will have more time to perform spiritual disciplines, such as meditation, prayer and reading, which can bring about significant changes in our level of awareness. Sri Auribindu had his first cosmic experiences as a political prisoner of the British in India. Many have found God in prison.

If we are optimists, we will see the opportunity in every problem rather than the problem in every opportunity.

The message in this chapter is that everything that takes place during our lives is an opportunity for us to learn lessons that further our emotional, mental and spiritual growth process. Perceiving events in this light allows us to deal with them much in a more positive manner.

Technique no. 18

# REPEATING A POSITIVE WORD

## Why this is beneficial

Repeating a positive word, phrase or prayer is an ancient means of purifying and transforming the mind, and thus, belongs to another category of techniques, which we could call "spiritual exercises." This method is also very helpful for coping with emotions in the present.

Rather than allowing our mind to dwell on various problems and emotions, we can repeat a chosen word or phrase that will help us connect to a more objective, philosophical or spiritual perception of reality.

Such words or phrases give us inner strength, especially when we are faced with difficult situations. They become a source of energy and inner security.

## A simple technique for connecting with positive energies is:

**1.** We focus the mind on a positive frame of reference, such as a religious figure, spiritual truth or value such as love or peace.
**2.** Each individual can choose his or her own phrase and point of reference. Some examples might be:

**Words:** love, peace, harmony, acceptance, light, etc.

**Phrases:** "I am an eternal divine being". "I am a child of God". "I am divine creation". "I love and accept all unconditionally - including myself". "I feel safe and secure in every situation". "All exists in a divine plan."

**Prayers:** Lord Jesus Christ, have mercy on us. Loving Lord Jesus Christ, we love you and we thank you. (Any other prayer can be used according to one's religious beliefs.)

### Note:

The possibilities are limitless. We can repeat our words, phrases and prayers as we walk, drive or perform mechanical chores, such as cleaning, gardening, etc.

*Life Story no. 19*

# *GOOD, RIGHTEOUS AND SPIRITUAL*

Paul is very much identified with portraying the role of the "good, righteous and spiritual person.". That is not to say that he is not a good person, but that he bases his self-worth on this fact and wishes to appear even more "spiritual" than he is. He has been programmed to believe that he is worthy and secure only if he is (or appears to be) righteous, good and spiritual.

This belief causes him to suppress some of his natural needs and desires, in turn creating a "mask" and a "shadow." His "mask" displays the appearance of a person without needs or desires, when the truth is that he has many such feelings festering in his subconscious (shadow). He hides his "evil" secrets, including his sexual whims, even sometimes from himself.

He tends also to suppress his wife and children in the same way. He criticizes, rejects and accuses others (and himself) for mistakes, inconsistencies or "immoral behavior". He finds ways to "advertise" actions that demonstrate how good, righteous or superior he is. He also plays the role of the savior, the teacher, the counselor, the parent, etc.

Paul can be fanatical about some of his beliefs. He compares himself to others, creating for himself either feelings of guilt and inferiority or of pride and superiority. These feelings obviously prevent him from feeling unity with those around him.

**Some of the beliefs that lead him to and sustain this role are:**

**1.** I will be accepted only if I am right, good, or spiritual.
**2.** I must do what others consider right and good in order to win their approval.

**3.** If I am not good and righteous, God will punish me (He might also punish my children).

**4.** If I am, or appear to be good, righteous and/or spiritual, I am superior to others.

**5.** I am worthy only if I am superior.

**6.** I am not worthy as I am, and I have to do much in order for others to love and accept me.

**7.** A "spiritual" person does not have needs or desires.

**8.** A "spiritual" person is always kind and accommodating.

(We need here to distinguish between **being** good or spiritual and **playing** that role, or basing our self-worth or security on that. A naturally good and spiritual person does not think about being so, nor does he or she not compare him or herself with others or deem him or herself superior.)

**Some of the beliefs that might free him from this role are:**

**1.** I am worthy of love and respect exactly as I am.

**2.** My self-worth has nothing to do with others' approval.

**3.** Just as all other beings, as a divine creation, I am good and lovable as I am.

**4.** God loves me unconditionally.

**5.** All beings are equally worthy of love and respect.

**6.** My-self worth is based on my being and not on how much I do.

**7.** As a soul in the process of evolution, I accept and acknowledge my weaknesses, needs and desires while simultaneously evolving through them.

**8.** I respond as much as possible to the needs of those around me, while simultaneously feeling comfortable with not accommodating them when their desires seem inappropriate.

**9.** My self-worth is based on my inner being, my existence itself, and my inner divine nature, not on other external factors.

**10.** My self-worth is a simple function of the fact that I, as all others creatures, am a unique aspect of divine creation.

**11.** My self-worth cannot be increased nor decreased. I can never be more or less worthy of love and respect than another.

# CHAPTER 19

# FACING AND OVERCOMING LONELINESS

Most of us have experienced the pain of loneliness. We have each had moments in which we have felt misunderstood, disappointed, unsupported, deserted, isolated or alone facing the world around us.

The feeling of "loneliness" is **not** synonymous with "being alone". We might be physically alone, and yet still feel close contact and unity with others, while another can be surrounded by family, friends and society and feel a deep, painful, penetrating loneliness.

## WE ARE CREATIONS OF UNITY

Our life begins here on this planet with the union of two cells - the ovum of our mother and a sperm cell from our father. We are products of the union of two separate beings. Our physical body is the result of the attraction and love that brought those two beings into union. We are born out of a union of love.

For the first nine months of our existence, here on the physical plane, we experience total union with our mother. We share one blood stream, one digestive system and one respiratory system. Whatever happens to our mother happens to us, and whatever happens to us happens to our mother. This is true both physically and emotionally.

Then comes the traumatic experience of emerging from our warm, secure, blissful womb into the cold, foreign and frightening world. It is not enough that we have to face this strange, harsh world, but then suddenly someone cuts our umbilical cord, severing our connection to our mother. It pains. They scrub us with an irritating sponge; the room is cold, with too much light, and people act in mechanical and unfeeling ways. We are separated from our mother and suddenly find ourselves ALONE - strangers in a strange land.

Fortunately, nature has instilled adults with the tendency to be loving and nurturing toward young beings of all species. Thus, during our first months, and hopefully years, we are more likely to receive harmonious, loving vibrations than negative ones. Sadly, this is not always true. Some children are born into families in which there is a great deal of tension among its members, - i.e., parents, in-laws, other siblings, etc.

Older children may react toward us with jealousy, and parents with tension and anger, projecting their own emotional problems onto us. We become aware of the conflicts between our parents and between them and their parents. All this disappoints, confuses and disturbs us, causing us to feel insecure and vulnerable.

The less love we receive, the more insecure we feel. The more conflict we see and feel around us, the more confusion and conflict we experience within us. As products of two beings, it is difficult for us to feel inner harmony unless these two beings are in harmony with each other.

## WE HARDEN AGAINST THE WEATHER OF LIFE

As we begin to grow and mature, we begin to develop our own personality incorporating as many "emotional defense mechanisms" as we need in order to feel safe and secure. The more insecure we feel, the more defense mechanisms we develop. The greater the wall we build up around ourselves, the **more likely we are to feel alone.**

As we move into adolescence, the need to develop a personality of our own becomes a "survival need." Our parents, teachers and society confront us with their models of who they think we should be and how we should behave. In our need to assert our own individual identity, we rebel. This rebellion creates an even greater feeling of alienation and isolation from our parents, teachers and society as a whole. This, then, may lead to stronger feelings of loneliness in which we feel that **no one understands us or cares for us.** No one is able or willing to listen to us, or if they do, it is difficult for us to express what we really feel, and nearly impossible for them to understand what we feel and think because they too are consumed with what they think and feel.

We begin to realize that our parents as all other beings have their faults, weaknesses and attachments. We become disillusioned with the world. Eventually, we feel **alone,** that we must face the world alone, and realize that, just as we were born alone, that we will die alone.

These realizations, whether conscious or unconscious, cause us to develop even stronger **defense mechanisms,** which isolate us even more from others and even from ourselves. These mechanisms seek to establish a strong external ego structure so as to protect our soft, insecure, frightened, lonely self inside that hard external shell. This is similar to the delicate and beautiful rose which creates many thorns to protect itself, or the soft vulnerable turtle that would perish without its protective shell. We develop many thorns and shells, i.e., aloofness, indifference, insensitivity, aggressiveness, criticism, illness and cunning, in order to protect ourselves. These ego mechanisms create a thick wall around our psyche, isolating us from others. Although surrounded by many people, we feel lonely and distrustful.

## FACTORS WHICH INCREASE
## THE FEELING OF LONELINESS

Loneliness is increased by the following factors:
a. **A lack of trust** in the people around us,
b. A feeling of **insecurity**
c. A fear that we are **unable to cope with life's** difficulties
d. The belief **that we are not lovable.**
e. The belief that there is **no true love** in the world.

These factors are further accentuated by some of the following factors, which are present in our modern civilization.

**1.** The **idolization of individuality** in western and northern countries has led many to the heights of loneliness as indicated by the high rate of suicide and impersonal mass murders.

**2.** The **"generation gap"** has caused a general break down in communications between parents and children. The rapidly changing way of life, along with mutating values systems, makes mutual understanding difficult between the generations. This leaves both generations feeling wronged and lonely.

**3.** The **deterioration of the family structure,** in which over fifty percent of all marriages end up in divorce, has seriously undermined the feelings of security and unity of belonging to a family. The deep, sure bonds of mutual love and support have greatly diminished. Siblings might ignore each other's problems, and children often leave their parents to experience a lonely passing away in homes for the elderly. The sense of commitment in which the family protects and supports its members is less evident than it used to be.

**4.** Our **focus on money** as a source of security and happiness causes many to accumulate whatever they can even at the expense of others. This way of thinking also creates the fear that others will try to do the same at our expense, and thus we feel even more vulnerable and mistrustful, and thus even more lonely.
   This fear causes us to react in such a way that we isolate ourselves from others, increasing our loneliness. The result is an image of fifty people riding a bus, all feeling the need for sincere communication, but all being afraid to "risk" it.

**5.** Our basic obstacle to unity and communication is **ego-centeredness.** This reminds me of a cartoon by Feiffer. The cartoon character confesses the following truths:

a.     I was single and lonely.
b.     I got married and discovered that I was still lonely.
c.     We had children, and I was still lonely.
d.     I had affairs and was lonelier than ever!
e.     I got a divorce. I've never been so lonely in my life.
f.     My daughter and her husband gave me a dog.
g.     FINALLY COMPANIONSHIP.

How is it that none of those relationships were able to give this person the feeling of companionship that the dog manage to instill? The answer is simple. The dog does not have an ego with which to conflict. All human conflicts are ego conflicts. **Our ego is the wall that prevents our unity with the others**.

## HOW WE USUALLY TRY TO
## OVERCOME LONELINESS

Our feelings of insecurity, vulnerability and loneliness create a sensation of emptiness within us, which is like a hole that needs to be filled. We try in various external ways to fill that hole. In some cases, we are able to fill it for a period of time, however, as we grow emotionally, mentally and spiritually, those things, activities or people which once helped us to feel whole and meaningful, lose their power to provide us with the same contentment.

Once a play doll or a little toy car was enough to fill our minds and our time. It was our whole world, and if someone took it from us, it was the "end of the world" - a traumatic experience. Eventually, the day came when those objects naturally no longer satisfied us, and we sought other ways of filling that feeling of emptiness, or lack of wholeness or completeness.

As we mature, we will obviously become frustrated with our old "toys" and experience a feeling of emptiness until we discover our "new toy." Let us discuss some of those "toys" which we use to temporarily fill that emptiness we feel inside.

**1.** We seek union with the world around us through **owning** objects such as land, houses, clothing, cars, etc. Through owning and having as **our own,** we at least feel a **relationship with these objects** that fills our emptiness for a period of time. For some people, this has such great meaning that it is enough for them. Some find no fulfillment in owning, yet, others cannot feel satisfied no matter how much they own and their need becomes an insatiable greed.

**2.** We seek to distract the mind from its feeling of emptiness by **saturating our**

**senses with sensual inputs**. Thus, we do not allow the mind to turn inward to feel its lack of peace. We fill the senses with such inputs as foods, drink, sex, movies, TV, magazines, senseless conversation, work, drugs, tranquilizers, alcohol, coffee, tea, cigarettes, etc., all to avoid feeling our loneliness and emptiness. Often this need for sensual input creates addictions that have a negative effect on our health and our relationships.

**3.** A very common way in which we seek to remove the feeling of loneliness is to **create relationships and a sense of belonging.** We have a need to feel that we belong somewhere. That connection may be to a social group, a religious group, a political group, a group that supports a particular sports team, a family grouping, or a **personal relationship** with someone. We gain a sense of identity through belonging somewhere. Yet even after fully satisfying this need to belong, we discover that we still feel separate and lonely.

When we try to fill our emptiness by focusing all our energies on one person, thinking, "**that person must love me and give me attention in order for me to be happy,**" we make things difficult not just for ourselves, but for the other person as well.  We limit our potential for happiness and for overcoming loneliness.

The persons whom we have selected may or may not be in a position to give us the attention and love we need. They may not be attracted to us or may already be attached to someone else. They may not be able to express their love or feelings. They may become ill or even depart from the physical body.

All of the approximately five billion persons on the earth have the same need to give and take love with those around them. When we focus solely on one person and believe that **only he or she** can remove our loneliness, we ignore the other billions with whom we can communicate and exchange care and love.

Another trap on this level is the idea that sex is the basic uniting factor between a man and a woman. The sexual act can, in many cases, be an opportunity for a wonderful physical, emotional and spiritual union between two individuals, providing there also exists an **emotional and spiritual harmony** between them. Otherwise it is simply a mechanical act that leaves both parties feeling separate again some moments or hours later.

We can also experience that unity through love, devotion, touching, hugging, caring and affection. Also, non-sexual expressions of love and unity can be shared by most beings without creating the complications associated with the sexual, i.e. attachment, expectations, jealousy, etc.

**4.** Another way in which we try to fill our emptiness is to **accumulate knowledge and information about the world**. This gives us a sensation of power. The danger here is that we can develop increased false **pride** because we believe we are superior or "important" because we know more than others do. This might cause us to reject others who we believe are "ignorant." This, of course, then deepens our loneliness.

**5.** We might seek to fill our emptiness through **creative self-expression or work**. At the same time, we cultivate a deeper contact with that creative source within ourselves, thus improving our relationship with ourselves. We discover that we are not empty after all, that there is a power and fullness within ourselves.

## SEARCHING FOR OURSELVES

After seeking in various ways that perfect unity, we once felt as embryos in the womb, we are still left with a feeling that **something is missing**. We are still incomplete and have yet to find what we are looking for. The various "pieces" with which we have tried to fill the hole or our emptiness do not exactly fit. Finally, it dawns upon us: **we have been looking for our own selves all this time**.

We feel lonely because we miss our **real self,** the self for which **Socrates was searching,** the self of the **reborn Christian,** the self of the **liberated yogi,** the self of the **self-actualized being,** the **Christ within us,** the **God within us,** the **spirit,** the **soul,** our **true Self.**

We are something like the woman who could not find her necklace and frantically searched everywhere for it until she turned her attention to herself only to realize it had been hanging around her neck the entire time.

When we have tried to fill our loneliness in all the above ways and still feel a gnawing in our heart and mind for something else, we seek to know our real self. This self is beyond our personality, beyond our conditioning, beyond our sex, religion, political beliefs, beyond all that we know about ourselves.

In order to do this, we might engage in any of the many religious, philosophical or psychological systems that suit us for this work.

As discovering this ultimate solution for loneliness is a slow process, let us look at some other more tangible ways in which we can face and overcome this sense of emptiness.

## METHODS OF FACING
## AND OVERCOMING LONELINESS

**1.** Thomas Merton has said, "Depression is the height of self-indulgence." Although his statement is obviously a generalization and there are clearly other causes of depression, some chemical and /or environmental, there is some degree of truth here. We tend to feel lonely and depressed when **our attention is focused on ourselves,** our problems, our unfulfilled needs and desires, our sense of injustice, and our unhappiness. Basically, depression becomes stronger when we are unhappy with what we are or what we have and feel helpless to change them. Depression is an extreme form of loneliness in which nothing brings us happiness.

But, what about the others? We might benefit by thinking about how many other people are lonely, blind, handicapped, widowed, orphaned, seriously ill, mentally retarded, poor, homeless or on the verge of starvation. If we do this for a moment, we will instantly recognize how egotistical our feeling of loneliness is. We can realize everyone feels lonely and desires more contact with others at some point in life. Rather than concern ourselves with what others can offer us, we can think about **what we can offer** others who need us.

**2.** We can **approach others** rather than wait for others to approach us. This requires us to overcome any blockages or complexes that prevent us from easily approaching others. Some of these may be:

**a.** A fear of **rejection,** if we put ourselves in the position of the one who opens up first to the other.

**b.** A fear that **we are not lovable** or acceptable to others.

**c.** A feeling of **pride;** we cannot approach the other, but the other must approach us.

**d.** A feeling that **we have nothing to offer others.**

**e.** A feeling of **superiority** which makes us look down on others, consider them unworthy of our company, or fear the loss of our self-worth if we keep company with them.

**f.** A **lack of love and patience** on our part.

**g.** A **general fear and mistrust of others.**

We must overcome such programmings, open our hearts and allow more harmonious contact with others.

**3. Remember that everyone needs love, affection and caring.** In remembering this, we realize that our need is legitimate. On the other hand, we also realize that everyone around us desires the same thing, and thus we are no longer afraid or too proud to approach them.

**4.** When walking the street or circulating in public, we can **look into others' eyes, smile and nod our head, acknowledging their presence.** We can focus on feeling our contact with others. When we talk to someone, we can look into his or her eyes, and focus on the real self behind those eyes. We can remind ourselves that all the personalities we know are actually **immortal spirits** presently occupying physical bodies.

**5.** We can **develop a relationship with our inner Self** which exists before and after our short physical life. This is who we are when all fear subsides and we become aware of an inner voice, inner strength, and inner power. When all emotions and thoughts subside, we are in a state of **being** rather than **becoming.** This is the part of ourselves which feels whole and complete in the present moment and is not overcome with bitterness about the past and expectancy or anxiety about the future.

**This inner self is in a state of latent potentiality** just as the almond tree is latently potential within the almond seed. We simply need to nourish and attend to it, so that it may grow stronger within us.

Some ways in which we can nourish this inner self are through self-analysis, recording our dreams, prayer, meditation and creative self-expression. Techniques such as physical exercises, breathing techniques and deep relaxation may help to calm the disturbances of the mind so that the presence of the inner self is more deeply felt.

**6.** When we develop a **relationship** with the power, which we might call God, life or nature, that organizes and sustains the universe and even our own particular body, then we seldom feel alone anymore. That power or being is present wherever we are. Loneliness disappears when truth is experienced just as darkness disappears when a light is turned on.

According to some philosophies, it is difficult to distinguish between our own inner self and this power: they are sometimes considered to be the same, i.e., the "God within us".

It is a matter of personal preference as to whether we choose to develop a relationship with this divine power as something outside or inside ourselves. In either case, we considerably reduce loneliness by realizing that we are always in the presence of, and in relationship to, the Divine Being which is omnipresent in all beings and creation.

**7.** We can **join with others** who have similar interests. As we grow, we may find that our old contacts no longer satisfy us to the same degree. Our interests and needs may have changed while theirs may have remained the same. Thus, we may need to seek out new contacts with common interests.

This can be done to the extent that it does not prevent us from fulfilling our duty to our family. Our family is our responsibility, which we cannot ignore, but we can choose our friends according to our interests and needs.

One reason we may feel lonely is that we are seeking to make contacts with people who do not share our ways of thinking and feeling. Rather than look for some specific person to fill our loneliness, it might be better to join together with a group of other people who are pursuing similar goals. We will be in the presence of people with whom we can communicate.

**8.** We can face loneliness **by arranging to be alone some days** each year. One of the most effective ways to overcome the fear of something is to confront that which we fear. If we fear loneliness, we can arrange occasionally to be alone and **get to know ourselves**. In this way, we can learn to love, accept, and respect ourselves. We can discover our inner fullness. We can take a more objective look at how we are doing, where we are going, and what we want to do with our lives in the near future.

Many of us run around like madmen chasing after so called "necessities" without stopping to ask, "Is it absolutely necessary? Is it worth it? Is there any other way to achieve that which I want from life?"

Occasionally retreating from our daily activities at some home or hotel in the countryside can give us the deep rest and perspective we need in order to put order and clarity into our lives.

In conclusion, we all feel loneliness or incompleteness to a certain extent. This feeling is increased by our sense of insecurity, vulnerability, mistrust of others, and lack of self-confidence and self-acceptance. On the other hand, the world situation contributes to those feelings, creating an epidemic of **alienation and loneliness.**

We try to assuage those feelings by owning objects, pursuing sensual pleasure, creating relationships, belonging to organizations, seeking knowledge, and burying ourselves in work and creative self-expression. These activities bring momentary relief from that unpleasant empty feeling, but do not eradicate it completely.

**Only Self- knowledge or the experience of unity our Divine Source can completely satisfy that need within us.** We can work towards that goal while, at the same time, opening ourselves up to others more and more, as we develop greater inner security, self-confidence, self-knowledge and love for all beings - including ourselves.

## Technique no. 19

## REMEMBERING TRUTHS

### Why this is important

Spiritual truths and logical thoughts can spare us a great deal of emotional pain. They free us from fears that give birth to a wide variety of negative and painful emotions.

### A simple technique for developing clarity and peace is:

Whenever we find our mind trapped in negative fear - based thought processes and emotions, we can bring to mind any logical thoughts or truths that will free us from them.

Some of these thoughts are:

**a.** We are all eternal souls in the process of evolution.

**b**. Life is a school in which we are learning.

**c.** Every event that occurs in life happens for the purpose of facilitating that process of evolution.

**d.** My lesson is to love all, including myself, unconditionally.

**e.** Every problem is an opportunity to learn something and grow stronger.

**f.** I change whatever I can and accept that which I cannot.

**g.** I am a Creation of the Divine.

**h.** I am Divine Energy

**i.** There is a just and wise power governing the universe and my life.

### Note:

The truth will set us free.

*Life Story no. 20*

# WEAK, INCAPABLE
# AND DEPENDENT

Hubert feels weak and incapable. He has been programmed to feel this way by a fearful mother and a domineering and demeaning father. He has come to perceive himself as unable to face the difficulties of life.

He seeks to find others who will take responsibility for his life. At the present time, his wife has taken on this role. His fear of making mistakes causes him to appear lazy. When he fears, his legs tremble. He occasionally becomes ill in order to avoid certain responsibilities and situations. He smokes and drinks excessively so as to deny his feelings of inadequacy.

Hubert attaches himself to people he perceives as strong and able but then feels suppressed by them. He praises and flatters them to ensure their continued love and support.

He finds it difficult to be punctual and efficient towards responsibilities, disciplines, programs and agreements. He also tests other's love in various ways. He demeans himself in front of others so they will tell him that he is good and capable.

Hubert rejects his father and does not want to be like him. His mother was a prototype of weakness. Thus, the only solution was to be "weak." He made his father's words, "You will not do anything with your life," come true.

**Some beliefs that may be leading Hubert to this role are:**

**1.** I am unable to face life's difficulties.

**2.** I am incapable of fulfilling my father's expectations.

**3.** They will reject me if I try and fail. It is better not to risk it.

**4.** Life is difficult and dangerous.

**5.** I need others (parents, spouse, siblings, etc.) in order to feel safe. Without them, I am in danger.

**6.** I am weak; I am not clever or talented. I am not worthy and I will not be able to succeed.

**7.** I do not have the discrimination in order to make my own decisions. I need others to tell me what to do.

**8.** If I grow up, I will be expected to take responsibility for my life; I will be like my father.

**Some positive beliefs that will help Hubert connect with his inner strength are:**

**1.** I am totally capable of dealing with any events or responsibilities.

**2.** I am able to fulfill my goals and actualize my potential.

**3.** I am worthy of love and respect regardless of the results of my efforts.

**4.** Life is divine and just.

**5.** I have all the power and inner guidance I need to deal with life by myself.

**6.** I am strong, clever and talented. I am able to succeed.

**7.** I have the ability to make my own decisions.

**8.** I am becoming the ideal adult I would like to be.

**9.** I accept and love myself exactly as I am at this stage of my evolutionary process.

**10.** I enjoy growth and change.

**11.** I playfully face life's challenges.

# Chapter 20

# STAGES OF LOVE

Do we really love or are we simply attached to, identified with, or dependent upon specific persons? Is our love free and unconditional, or is it mixed with various conditions and demands? What is unconditional love? Is it possible for us to cultivate it? What is the difference between love and attachment? How can we determine whether what we feel is love or attachment? How can we purify our love and move into a higher level of consciousness, offering greater happiness to all, including ourselves?

These are some of the many questions that we will address and analyze in this chapter.

## WHAT IS LOVE?

Love is a very difficult word to define, perhaps because the reality of love approaches the spiritual dimensions that are beyond time and space, and thus comprehension by the human mind. Love, like all other highly spiritual realities, is more easily described by what it is **not**. Love is not fear, hurt, pain, jealousy, bitterness, hate, separateness, lust, attachment, aggressiveness, ego-centeredness, indifference, possessiveness, suppression - the list goes on.

Love, like God, peace and other spiritual realities, can be perceived more easily through the effects that it creates. We cannot see the wind, but we can see the effects of the wind, such as the leaves moving, branches swaying, or the sound of air rushing. We know wind exists by its various side effects. We know there is a primal cause (God) for creation because we perceive its effect: creation itself.

What then are the effects of love? Love creates feelings of **unity**. We feel toward others as we feel towards ourselves. We are interested in their welfare, happiness, success, health and spiritual growth as much as we are concerned about our own.

Loving others means **wanting them to be happy** regardless of what it is which makes them really happy. It breeds **understanding, compassion, forgiveness,**

**happiness, excitement, peace, joy and a desire to be helpful** in any way we can.

Love is **expansion beyond our ego limitations.** It is the ability to identify with the other, to let go of our self-interest and personal needs enough to really **hear and understand the other's needs and interests**. It means caring enough to **sacrifice** when necessary, our own pleasures and desires when the other's needs are obviously more important.

Love is the force that brings about unity and harmony. It is the "glue" of the universe. It helps persons with different egos, desires, and programmings and needs to overcome all those potentially repelling forces and unite.

Love is the force of unity that will enable our already internally existing spiritual unity and harmony to manifest itself on the mental, emotional, physical, familial, social, economic, political and international levels. We are moving toward unity (even if it seems the opposite sometimes), and the main forces are love and wisdom.

Thus, love is the greatest, the highest human quality, and it needs to be given priority over all other needs and concerns. Only in this way will we acquire peace, happiness and wellbeing on Earth.

Love needs not so much to be learned or cultivated, but rather released or brought to the surface, if you like. **We are love.** Our basic nature is love, but ignorance, fear and attachment have buried it so deep within us that it is sometimes difficult to summon or maintain. Loving others steadily, independent of their behavior, is not an easy achievement.

## LOVE VERSUS NEED

The power of attraction which we call love is expressed at many levels and in countless ways. The most basic level is that of **need**. We often use the word love when we really mean "need". We say, "I love you," but if we analyze more deeply, we learn that what we are really saying is "I need you." This is the basic message of most love songs. They lament with sadness, pain, agony and cry out "you left me, I cannot live without you. I need you."

This is not love. It is need, attachment and addiction. If it were love and the other was happier by leaving us or even happier with someone else, we would be happy for him or her, not full of sadness for ourselves. Loving others means wanting others to be happy, healthy and successful in the ways that they are guided to be. Love does not create the pain we feel when someone leaves us or rejects us. That pain is generated by our dependency upon that person for our security, pleasure or affirmation.

Love creates happiness. Needs and attachments create fear, pain and suffering.

Our love is still mixed with a considerable amount of need. Love wants to give. Need wants to take. Sometimes what we are seeking to take is very subtle and requires deep inner inquiry. Whenever we feel pain in our relationships, it is because our needs are in danger of not being satisfied. When this happens, our "love" turns to hurt, disappointment, fear, loneliness, inferiority, or bitterness, and some-times, anger, hate, rage and desire for revenge.

How can love become all these negative emotions? It cannot. The simple truth is that such an emotion never was pure love to begin with. It was an "attraction" based to some degree also on need. This does not mean that we should reject our-selves because we have seldom really loved purely. As we are not yet enlightened spiritual beings, how could we? It would be like rejecting ourselves because we do not yet have a university diploma when we are still in the first grade. It is on-ly natural that we cannot yet love unconditionally. That is our stage of evolution.

## FREEING OUR LOVE FROM NEED

The first step towards opening our hearts to real love is to accept and love our-selves exactly as we are with all our weaknesses and faults. Only then can we pro-ceed effectively.

The second step is to begin observing the feelings that are stimulated in our re-lationships. Through objective self-observation, we can determine in which situ-ations we love unconditionally and in which we are feeling attached and "loving" with specific conditions. Following are some examples that will help.

## NEEDING THOSE WHO MAKE US FEEL SECURE

We look to others for security. We look to our parents, spouses, siblings, chil-dren, employers, friends, spiritual teachers and others for security.

We **do** feel love toward these beings, but often that love is based on the fact that they offer us a sense of security. If they start behaving in ways that obstruct our feelings of security; if they decide to leave us or be with someone else, will we still love them? If our employer fires us, will we still love him? If our parents throw us out onto the street, will we still love them? Or is our love tightly woven with the need for security?

If as parents we dream that our children will become economically well off and socially accepted professionals, will we love them the same if they became street artists, beggars, or anarchists? Some parents will be able to; others will not.

The basic question is whether or not our feelings of love are steady and consis-tent regardless of the various changing behaviors of those we "love". In each case where we perceive our heart closing, we can look to discover what we fear in that situation. What might we possibly lose?

Only when we have realized total inner security, perhaps based on an inner spir-itual awakening or on our faith in God, will we be able to love without security attachments. Only when we know that we can live **without** others can we **really love** them constantly.

Society has helped us to completely confuse this matter. We believe if we love others, we must be totally dependent on them and should fear that our world would fall apart if something happens to them. This is insecurity. This is a lack of faith in God. It is a lack of faith in our own spiritual nature and our ability to deal with life. It has nothing to do with love.

Perhaps this is why the Apostle John wrote, "Where there is perfect love, there can be no fear".

## NEEDING FOR PLEASURE AND AFFIRMATION

Let us look at how our needs for pleasure and affirmation can limit our experience of love. We create relationships that give us pleasure and affirmation as well as security. We may be dependent upon the other for money, travel, clothing, sex, encouragement, compliments, humor, tasty food, a clean house, comforts, or even his or her beauty. Yet, if he or she stops providing these for us, or decides to provide them for someone else, or to divide that pleasure or affirmation between us and someone else, do we continue loving that person or do we feel hurt, disillusioned, and overcome with feelings of injustice, anger and perhaps revenge? The condition here is that *"I love you because you provide me pleasure, happiness or excitement; if you stop, my feelings change."* It is conditional love.

We may also depend on someone for affirmation. This may take various forms. One is that, *"You listen to me and do what I say. I can control you. That makes me feel powerful and worthy. If, however, you stop doing whatever I say, I will stop feeling love and unity with you."* This problem often develops between parents and children when the child moves into adolescence. It also occurs between spouses. In many countries the wife might be suppressed in the beginning, and the husband feels powerful and affirmed. If, however, she begins to think and act for herself, he begins to panic and becomes angry and sometimes aggressive. The roles may also be reversed, and it is the woman who controls and feels affirmed.

**We also feel affirmation when someone needs us, when someone is dependent upon us.** This could occur between parent and child, teacher and student, friends, or even between the "savior" and the "needy." In these cases, the needed feels worthy or perhaps superior. This is one aspect of codependency. We might also find meaning in life because someone needs us, depends on us. If however, the other doesn't want to be the child, the student or the needy one anymore, do we feel the same attraction and love? If not, our love is mixed with our **need to be needed.** We need to give, offer, and sacrifice in order to feel useful, worthy or boost our self image. If this is the case, then all that we offer in these situations, all our sacrifices, are actually for ourselves and not for the others.

That does not negate the fact that they may actually need us, or that we also have feelings of altruistic love mixed with our need to be needed. We are often motivated by two or three motives simultaneously

A third aspect of this attraction for affirmation is the situation in which we "love" those **who affirm our rightness**, either verbally by telling us we are right, or simply by belonging to the same social, political, religious, spiritual group and embracing the same belief system.

*"I love you because you agree with me, you are like me, you affirm me".* If they change beliefs and convert to another political party, religion, or spiritual group, will we feel the same closeness and "love?" Perhaps yes, perhaps no.

A fourth aspect of this affirmation principle is called "**Eros**" (in Greek "erotas") or falling in love. In this case there is a mutual (occasionally only one-sided) infatuation on the physical, sexual, emotional and sometimes mental level. This is a special attraction between two persons who excite, bring joy to and stimulate each other positively. This positive stimulation usually has to do with the needs for security, pleasure and affirmation.

This intensity of feeling seldom lasts more than a few years. The couple then has the possibility of transforming their "Eros" into a steady form of unconditional love, or facing the sadness of conflict or separation. Sooner or later, we will come face to face with the other's various negative aspects, and if we cannot love them as they are, the relationship dissolves.

Until we are able to love unconditionally, we will be unhappy, insecure and frequently in conflict with those around us. We will be able to do this only when we have matured sufficiently so as to experience inner security, inner satisfaction, inner freedom and a steady feeling of self-worth. In other words, we can love purely only those who we do not need. When we need others, we cannot love them unconditionally. This might be difficult to comprehend at first, but deep thought and observation will prove it to be true. Being able to love without conditions is a basic prerequisite for both spiritual growth and a happy life.

## SELFLESS LOVE FOR A SPECIFIC PERSON

The next stage in the evolution of love is being able to love others regardless of their behavior. Probably the closest most of us have come to experiencing this love is toward our children. There are some parents who have totally selfless love for their children. They maintain steady love for "their child" even if he or she decides to live a completely different lifestyle from that which the parents have programmed, even if he or she rejects and abuses the parents, and even if he or she becomes a dangerous criminal.

This love is not universal nor is it totally unconditional because there is one condition, that the other is "my child" and not someone else's. We might also experience this type of selfless love for a specific being when that being is "our student" or under "our care or responsibility." This type of love has to do with the role of protector or feeling responsibility for someone. **It enables us to accept all types of behavior from others and continue accepting and loving them with understanding and compassion.**

In some rare cases, we may also feel such love for persons who belong to the same grouping, i.e. nationality, religion or social class.

In these cases, we do not gain something tangible from these individuals. We do not ask them for anything. Our love is not dependent upon their abiding by a certain type of behavior or even reciprocating our love. Our love is more selfless but still specific and not universal.

## UNIVERSAL SELFLESS LOVE

The next stage is to expand our feelings of unconditional love and acceptance to even more people and eventually **to all beings, including animals, plants and insects.** This love, however, is still directed toward form. We focus on the form of these beings, thus we feel a sense of sadness when they experience suffering or unhappiness.

We perceive their form as reality. We feel love and acceptance for that person, but we still live within the illusion that the form is the reality. We forget that behind that form there is an immortal ever-blissful consciousness, which is just temporarily projecting that form toward the earth plane level. Universal consciousness is never in pain, never suffers, is never unhappy and can never die. That is the ultimate reality of the being or beings whom we love.

Those who experience this universal selfless love often **choose careers or lifestyles that allow them to serve the whole in some way**. They may join service groups such as the Peace Corps or other voluntary service organizations. They feel a need to express that love through actions which better the quality of life for those around them, especially for those who are suffering, lonely or unhappy.

Their interest expands beyond the limits of themselves and their immediate family. They begin to realize that all beings are brothers and sisters in one spiritual family of all humanity. As their awareness grows, they perceive even animals, plants and insects as belonging to "their family." They want to express this love through acts of service, care and devotion.

## SPIRITUAL UNIVERSAL LOVE

The next stage is the development of **spiritual universal love** where w**isdom or spiritual discrimination** is now added to our love. We now see all forms as various manifestations of one unchanging, ever blissful, divine consciousness.

Although we continue to help and serve wherever we can, we do not feel unhappy about their pain, suffering or unhappiness. We realize that the real being behind that form has chosen to pass through that experience because it is exactly the next stimulus which he or she needs for his or her spiritual growth process. We realize now that we are all passing through the precise experiences, pleasant and unpleasant, which we need in order to wake up from our dream of this illusory material reality.

**Although we are not affected by the suffering we see, we are even more wholly dedicated toward eliminating it.** Thus, we love and accept all beings as they are while we direct our energies toward facilitating this process of our mutual spiritual unfoldment. Each of us moves forward in his or her own unique way.

In the past, we may have tried to solve people's problems for them. Now we realize that the most effective forms of help we can offer are unconditional love and education concerning the true spiritual nature of our being.

We now realize that the **main solution for the world's economic, political and social problems is education** concerning the spiritual truths of our immortal nature and our inherent oneness with all beings. When we understand, believe and experience this totally, we will be healthy, happy and in harmony with all those around us.

We experience such **"wise love"** or "loving wisdom" from the highest spiritual teachers. It is sometimes difficult to understand their love and caring, which at times to the beginner, may seem like indifference, especially when we pass through tests and expect sympathy and emotional reactions. It is difficult for some to realize that it is sometimes more loving to allow someone to suffer a little more so he or she can find the solution him or herself and grow stronger and freer from ignorance. Only a realized being can know, however, when "not to help" externally because this would be the most loving act for a specific person.

Many parents would do well to learn this form of discrimination. They would help their children far more if they refrain from solving their problems every time they are in trouble. No one should, however, misconceive that this text is suggesting that we should not help those who are in need. We must help, but we must also ask ourselves what the most appropriate help would be in each situation.

**The greatest gift, the most precious help we can offer to those we love, is to help them get in touch with the power and wisdom that exist within them.** This, at times, means helping, and at others, means letting them struggle by themselves while we mentally pray for them and send them light.

For an awakened spiritual being to see someone cry about some unhappy event in his life or fear some future possibility, might be like our watching a small child cry about a toy that has broken or express fear of the "boogie man." We sympathize with the child. We love it and we want to help it, but we cannot really be worried.

Those who experience this level of love sometimes do not exhibit the emotional display which others may be used to interpreting as indications of love. As we grow spiritually, we begin to understand, however, that real love is a love for the soul within the other, which is seeking to free itself from ignorance and the illusion of weakness and fear.

These spiritually awakened beings offer help on other levels through their positive thought forms, prayers or sometimes, direct contact on the astral level, usually in dreams. In this way, help is given without undermining the others' self-confidence.

## LOVING THE WAVE OR THE OCEAN

When we limit our love to a specific person (we do not mean sexually, but rather emotionally, mentally and spiritually), it is difficult to experience love in its highest expression. We love this person and not others. We tend to focus on a specific person, "loving" them because they offer us security, pleasure or affirmation; or because we consider them to be "ours."

**Pure love is universal**. It can express itself toward any particular being, but it cannot limit itself to that being or group of beings. If it does, then it is love mixed with conditions. Each individual is one of the countless waves on an ocean of consciousness. The ocean is God, the Universal Consciousness, which is temporarily taking the form of those specific waves and then disappearing into the formlessness of the ocean again before reappearing as billions of others. All waves are expressions of the one ocean.

When we single one specific wave out the ocean of beings and limit our love to that, we are, in essence, loving an illusion. That being which we love is just a temporary manifestation of the one Universal Being which manifests as all the other beings simultaneously. That form on which we focus is a temporary physical, emotional, mental manifestation that will dissolve back into the ocean. When we love the **water** in that wave, that is, **its spiritual essence**, the spirit within, we begin to love all waves. The same water is in all the waves. The same spiritual essence is in all beings.

Then we love the spiritual essence in others and not only their form or the specific benefits that we receive from them. We love the spirit within. Our love now becomes both unconditional and universal. It is unconditional because it does not depend on what others do or do not do, and universal because we start to love more and more people independent of their appearance, character and other superficial factors. We love the spirit within them. We as spirit are one with the spirit, which is within them.

So we can love the wave or we can love the ocean and thus all the waves. This is our choice.

**Love is like the gold ore** that is brought up from the earth; it is mixed with other metals (emotions, needs). Our job is to purify that gold through our efforts to love unconditionally in all of our relationships, no matter what the other does or does not do. Only then will we truly be happy.

## Technique no. 20

# MEDITATION

### Why this is so beneficial

Regular meditation is a way to transcend our emotions and experience the inner peace that is our real nature.

No matter how upset or depressed we may feel, our inner self is always in a state of peace. Regular meditation helps to bring that peace more and more into our daily life so that stimuli which used to bother us lose their power to do so.

People from all walks of life, in all countries of the world belonging to all possible religions, meditate for a wide variety of reasons. The same technique offers something different to each according to his or her needs and motives. Some of the motives for which people meditate today are:

**1.** To **relax** the body and mind, and rejuvenate one's flow of energy in order to more effectively face the responsibilities of one's demanding and active life.
**2.** To **heal** illnesses (especially psychosomatic ones).
**3.** To **overcome** emotional problems.
**4.** To develop a more relaxed and **positive view** of life.
**5.** To develop a peaceful and more **clearly functioning mind.**
**6.** To attain a greater ability to **penetrate the core** of problems and find inspirational solutions. Scientists and businessmen have found this especially useful.
**7.** To tune into **creative inspirations** for various forms of artistic expression.
**8.** To **free oneself** from **addictions,** such as cigarettes, alcohol, narcotics and tranquilizers.
**9.** To **purify one's character.**
**10.** To develop **will-power.**
**11.** As a method of **self-observation** and **self-discovery.**
**12.** To develop the **latent powers** of the mind.
**13.** To develop an **inner relationship with the Divine.**
**14.** For **spiritual growth**, self-knowledge or enlightenment.
**15.** To **transcend the identification with the body** and mind, and experience spiritual realities.

### Note:

Meditation should be learned from an experienced teacher.
Many lives have been transformed by this technique.

*Life Story 21*

# THE REBEL, THE REVOLUTIONARY, THE ANTAGONIST.

Jake is a "rebel." He believes others want to control him and prevent him from doing what he would like to do. He easily feels suppressed and reacts defensively so as to protect his freedom, often from imaginary dangers. When he fears that his freedom is in danger, he becomes defensive and aggressive, often demeaning or hurting others. He is seldom on time and frequently does not keep his word. Doing so for him would mean "not being free."

As a child, he was, in fact, suppressed by both parents, and as a result, has now developed this sensitivity.

This has caused his professional life as well as his personal relationships to suffer. Although, he does not want to push people away, nor does he want to hurt them, his behavior often does so. He is the victim of his own reflex defense mechanisms that function in order to "protect his freedom." He is unable to think about what he is doing or control himself when he gets into these states of "self protection."

His family and friends understand him only to a certain extent and are annoyed by his behavior. Many have ceased to ask anything of him because he might react angrily, something they wish to avoid.

He realizes this is happening, feels badly about it, but cannot change it nor admit it to the others. He also has a tendency to feel easily wronged, in which case, he again becomes aggressive and violent in his attempt to protect his "rights."

He tends to be uncooperative and oscillates between being aloof and intimidating toward those around him, trapping both himself and those around him in a constant state of tension.

**Some beliefs that lead Jake to this behavior are:**

**1.** My freedom and rights are in danger.

**2:** I have to fight for my freedom and justice.

**3:** I need others, but they put me in danger.

**4.** Others want to control me.

**5.** I will lose my freedom, self-worth and happiness if I do what others want from me.

**6.** When others agree I am right, I am worthy and safe.

**7.** I am not loved; thus I must protect myself from others.

**8.** Relationships are a war of control. If I do not fight, I will lose my freedom.

**9.** If I admit that they are right they will use this against me on another occasion.

**10.** People are hypocritical and are underhanded; I cannot trust them.

**Some positive beliefs that will help him discover his inner peace and ability to cooperate are:**

**1.** I am free to be myself in every situation.

**2:** I can protect freedom and justice with love and understanding.

**3:** I am complete in myself and feel totally safe with others.

**4.** Only I can control myself.

**5.** l am free to do what my conscience tells me.

**6.** I am worthy of love and respect regardless of others' opinions.

**7.** I am loved and safe with all.

**8.** My freedom is in my control.

**9.** The truth creates harmonious relationships of love and respect.

**10.** All are expressions of the Divine.

**Some positive beliefs which will help those around him to deal with him more effectively:**

**1.** Jake behaves in this way because he is afraid of being controlled or of being wronged.

**2.** He needs our love and understanding.

**3.** We do not help him when we allow him to behave in disrespectful ways.

**4.** We need to love him and accept him while assertively demanding that he behave toward us, as he would like us to behave toward him.

# CHAPTER 21

# FINDING OUR ROLE IN LIFE

Many of us are discontented with our work and / or our lifestyle, but few of us can identify what it is we really want. Fewer still have the courage to make the changes necessary to find happiness and fulfillment.

Although most of us live with comforts only kings enjoyed hundreds of years ago, statistics show that increasingly more people experience disillusionment and depression. We might have money and material security, but we lack a sense of meaning in our professional and social lives.

I, for one, experienced such a crisis at the age of twenty-four having worked for two years as a chemical engineer in a large industrial chemical plant. I had everything society had convinced me I needed to be happy, but I was completely miserable. I decided to find a more meaningful occupation. This is not to say that such a job could not be meaningful to someone else. Such jobs obviously have great value for society and are interesting and fulfilling for many. It simply was not what I personally had come to do on this earth. **What may be the perfect role for one person may be boring and meaningless for another.**

Each of us has incarnated to play a specific role in this theater of life. When we find our special role and play it with all our heart, we experience contentment and happiness. When we do not remember our life purpose, or do not have the courage to live it, we experience discontent and emptiness. Unless we connect to our life purpose, our lives are often mechanical and lacking in essence.

Have you ever walked into a room to get something, but upon arriving in that room, have forgotten what you came to get? I have. I have also found that when I turn around and start heading in the direction from which I was coming, I remember what it was I had been seeking. This is true of our lives here on the earth.

We are immortal souls who have incarnated temporarily to evolve, create and serve. Upon arrival, however, we forget why we came, and waste our lives occupying ourselves with superficial pleasures and material pursuits.

Eventually, for our own good, through some series of events, often unpleasant and challenging, we are forced to look inward and remember our life purpose.

## THE EARTH SYMPHONY

Collectively, we are like members of a great universal orchestra. Each has his or her part to play. The harmony of the universal piece we are playing (called life) demands two basic requirements from each member of the orchestra. Each must first **know his part,** and secondly, must be **capable of playing it**.

All animals and plants naturally and instinctively play their parts in this harmony. They have no choice.

We, on the other hand, blessed with **free will,** have the choice to play our part or not. We also have the responsibility to develop the inner qualities necessary to assume our role.

At the present time, we may say that the Earth Symphony Orchestra is considerably discordant. Many of us are playing a piece dictated by our own ego rather than what is best for the good of the whole. Few of us have found our real part in this symphony, and out of discontent, are competing rather than co-operating with the others. Thus, finding our role in life is not only imperative **for our own happiness,** but also **for social and world harmony.**

In some cases, we may need to make choices between the following:
a. **Money** or **meaningfulness**
b. **Comfort** or **creativity**
c. **Security** or **evolution**
d. **Social "success"** or **social responsibility**
e. **Superficial happiness** or real **inner contentment**
f. **Satisfying** others' expectations or our **own inner voice** of wisdom.
We need to choose wisely.

Let us examine what we can do to regain contact with our life purpose.

## FREEDOM FROM SOCIAL PROGRAMMING

**We will need to free ourselves from our social conditioning concerning what kind of work has value.** Society puts a certain value on each profession. This is usually based on the amount of money, prestige or power it can generate. This money, prestige and power, however, may not make us happy. Society's formula for success is based on a rather superficial view of man's nature.

We are programmed as young children to feel economically insecure. We are also programmed to place the utmost importance on what others think of us. We seek their acceptance, respect and admiration. Such programming leads to anxiety, fear, nervous tension, and illness.

In the process of listening to our inner voice, we may find we are confronted by criticism from family and relatives who perhaps feel intimidated by our lifestyle changes. Our changes could force them to either doubt their presumptions about life or reject us. The second is easier for them. In such cases, we will need sufficient inner strength to remain unaffected by their reactions. At the same time, we need to have enough love to forgive them and try to help them understand that we are not running away from them or from life, but just **asking for the freedom to pursue that which fulfills us**.

After passing through a period of self-examination, we may also find that we are **actually doing** that which we were born to do. In such a case, we most likely will feel fulfilled. There is, however, the possibility that we may not yet have connected with the truths which would allow us to enjoy that purpose and perform it with love and dedication.

Often the simplest roles can offer us the greatest spiritual lessons. Take, for example, the roles of motherhood or fatherhood. Not much importance is given to them today because many feel that working in an office has more prestige or creativity. **Yet, there is no more important role than that of parenthood.** The future of the world depends on the quality of today's children. As adults, their inner world, quality of being and behavior are clearly a product of how much attention and love they receive as children. Many parents believe they can offer their children more by working more so as to offer them a better education. **A person becomes great not because of his education, but because of his character.**

## OVERCOMING FEAR

**We will need to overcome our fears of such things as:**
1. Failure
2. What others think.
3. That we may not make it financially
4. That we may not be perfect in what we do
5. That we might make a mistake.

We are all in a process of evolution. If we were perfect, we would not have incarnated. Making mistakes is natural when we are learning and creating. It is important to understand that we are worthy and lovable even though we are not perfect.

We must also overcome various fears of **specific objects** and situations, such as airplanes, elevators, boats, hospitals, dust, microbes, certain kinds of people, animals, etc. These can be obstacles towards fulfilling our life purpose.

As expressions of divine consciousness, we want to become **effective instruments of that consciousness,** able to play any part that serves the benefit of the whole. Our fears are an obstacle to that effectiveness.

## SUCCESS IS NOT REQUIRED

**It is imperative that we free ourselves from excessive concentration on success as a measure of our self-worth and effectiveness.** It is **not** important to succeed. It **is** important to have pure **motives** and to **try** to the best of our ability. The results of any endeavor are affected by a number of other factors that are often unrelated to our efforts.

Think of the greatest examples of courage in history. Did they succeed in our terms? Did Jesus succeed? How many have lived their lives according to His messages throughout the last two thousand years? He knew that few would really be able to live as He requested. Yet, He gave all of His life and finally His body itself to His purpose, to fulfill His role.

Gandhi, Martin Luther King, Socrates, did they succeed? They were all killed by the societies in which they lived.

Success is not required of us. We need only ask ourselves whether we believe that what we want to do will offer something, however small, to the welfare and evolution of the whole.

Our life purpose might manifest itself in many ways, such as building houses, governing a country, running a business, researching scientifically, protecting the law, cleaning the streets, raising children, educating people, creating beauty through art, music and dance, cooking wholesome food, putting order and cleanliness into an environment, or listening to someone's problems. The list is endless.

It might be useful here to discuss the Sanskrit word **dharma.** It is an interesting term that encompasses many concepts simultaneously. A dharmic act is one that is in harmony with the laws of the universe, meaning that it benefits the whole and does not harm anyone. It is in alignment with the law, "Do not do to others what you would not like others to do to you," and on the other hand more positively, actively "do to others that which you would like others to do to you." All roles, which are in harmony with the universe, will be in harmony with these two guidelines.

No work, however, is inherently dharmic or in harmony with the universe. What makes an act or role dharmic is whether or not **our motive is selfless** and whether **we are detached from the result.**

Thus, a dharmic act is one in which we are **free from attachment to personal gain or any specific result.** We would even be willing to perform the act or service without any form of reward. **We know we have found our life purpose when the reward is the joy of performing the action itself.**

Our life purpose is an activity we would be happy to do even if we were not paid, although we logically accept payment if we need such for our survival and evolution. Doing such work brings us feelings of joy, meaning and satisfaction.

## DEALING WITH FEAR OF THE FUTURE

Many believe that we have an obligation to leave large amounts of money and belongings for our children. Yet, in some cases, such actions might undermine the child's inner resources as the child is not allowed to experience his or her own inner creative power, and thus, is likely to doubt it. Such actions stem from the belief that our children are incapable of surviving without our help.

Most religious texts promise that all we need will be provided as long as we align ourselves with the benefit of the whole. If we had more faith in the divine and our loved ones, our money and time could be better directed toward social works which would better the condition of society as a whole.

Also, this type of thinking is based on a restricted concept of family, that only those who are related to us by blood are our family. This is a limited view of who we really are. As our sense of family begins to include more and more beings, we will manifest a much more beautiful reality for all of us.

## CONTACT WITH OUR INNER VOICE

**We will need to develop a deeper contact with our inner voice through prayer, silence, and meditation.** When our minds are cleared of the various issues, needs and fears, we will hear the "small voice" of **inner wisdom**. We know, within ourselves, the role that we have come to play, but we are too full of others' opinions to hear ourselves. We would do well to take a few days retreat each year in order to get in touch with our deeper feelings, needs and values. Daily meditation in the morning and evening also contribute greatly to the development and maintenance of this contact with our inner voice.

## TUNING UP OUR INSTRUMENT

We mentioned that the second prerequisite for playing our part in the earth symphony is to be **capable** of playing the part. **This** requires that **we tune up our instruments of expression** here on the earth, that is the body and the mind. Even if we know our role, if we are constantly ill, tired, nervous, fearful or upset, we will not be able to play it effectively.

We can employ various effective techniques for the purpose of developing a healthy body and clear mind such as a healthy natural diet, exercises, breathing techniques, deep relaxation and positive thinking. With daily practice of these techniques, our bodies and minds will be capable of expressing our inner beauty and creativity.

Our first responsibility is to tune our own instruments. No musician would dare start playing his part without tuning up his instrument and harmonizing it with the others. We must realize that exercises, breathing, relaxation and meditation are essential steps, which must be taken, if we want to play our roles effectively and harmoniously.

## SURRENDER TO THE DIVINE

**An instrument must surrender completely to its player.** We are instruments in the hands of the Divine Musician. If we say to this Cosmic Musician, «no, I do not want to play that melody, I don't like it, I want a better part, a lead role,» we are not much use.

Finding our role in life means being open to whatever role is useful to the universe at each place and time. We need to let go of egocentric needs and realize that at some times we will be called upon to do great works, and at others, we will be assigned simple tasks which seem unimportant to us. Regardless of their size and scope all are important for the harmony of the whole.

We may need to pass the **test of humility** and surrender to the divine in our search for our role. Jesus washed his disciples' feet as a message that humility is absolutely necessary for entering stages of higher consciousness.

The ego thrives on the three lower stages of consciousness that have to do with security, pleasure, and affirmation. When we feel our own inner worth, we are not concerned about whether we might find greater recognition through our role in life.

In searching for our role in life, we need to ask, "How can I improve the quality of life on Earth before leaving? What can I do to make life healthier, happier, and more harmonious for myself and those who live around me?"

## PRAY FOR GUIDANCE

**We can pray for purification and guidance as instruments of divine harmony here on earth.** Through prayer and sincerity, we can become **transformers** of spiritual energy into beneficial works here on the material level. Just as plants take the light energy of the sun and use it to create sugar, starch and other forms of food, we too can take spiritual energy and use it to manifest thoughts, ideas, words and actions which have the potential to make this world a better place.

Through our daily meditations, we can receive spiritual energy, which we can then share with those around us in the form of love, compassion, understanding and service. This will give us happiness and contentment, and because life is a mirror, we will be surrounded by love and harmony.

## BELIEF IN OURSELVES

We need to believe in our inner feelings. We may make mistakes in the beginning. We may go down some dead ends or go to extremes. The only way to get in touch with our inner voice is to believe in it and act upon it. At times, it will be the voice of the ego, but gradually we will develop discrimination and will be able to tell the one voice from the other.

We are here to perform certain functions designed benefit ourselves and the world simultaneously. We will be happy only when we connect with our specific roles. Those who already have will know because they are happy, fulfilled and in harmony with themselves and the environment.

This does not mean that everyone will love us, but that we will love them regardless of their feelings towards us. The best indication as to whether we have found our role in life is if we are happy and content, and enjoy waking up each morning because what we plan to do has real meaning for us.

## USING OUR TALENTS

**We can get in touch with and develop our inherent talents.** They will guide us to what we have come to do. Our talents are the tools that we bring into this incarnation to perform the specific tasks associated with our role. Recognizing and developing our talents will help us discover the role we are destined to assume.

Let us summarize the steps toward finding our role in life:


**1. Free ourselves from social conditioning.**

**2. Overcome fears and limiting beliefs.**

**3. Let go of our attachment to results.**

**4. Cultivate contact with our inner voice.**

**5. Develop physical and mental harmony.**

**6. Surrender to the divine will.**

**7. Pray daily to become an instrument.**

**8. Follow our intuition.**

**9. Get in touch with and develop our personal talents.**

**Technique no. 21**

# RESOLVING EMOTIONS
# BACK TO THEIR SOURCE

## Why this is important

Emotions are the result of our identification with the body and the personality. All suffering and negativity is based ultimately on attachment, aversion, or fear. In order to free ourselves from pain, we will need to identify which attachment, aversion or fear is causing our unpleasant emotion.

Take, for example, jealousy. We perceive our spouse showing attention to another. We experience fear, jealousy and anger. Why? We may be attached to our spouse as a source of emotional, financial and social security. We might be attached to him or her as an only source of security, self-worth and happiness. In this case, we do not experience our own spiritual nature, namely our inner self-worth, security and fulfillment, which have absolutely nothing to do with our spouse's interests or behavior.

Of course, we are all naturally vulnerable to such emotions, but they are the result of our social programming. We have very little awareness of our true nature and thus seek security, self worth and fulfillment through others' attention, material possessions, activities and situations.

This is natural, but it does cause fear, unhappiness, pain, and jealousy. Our needs and attachments need to be transformed into preferences.

The emotion of jealousy is generated ultimately by the lack of understanding of who we really are. When we will have experienced ourselves as spiritual beings temporarily occupying the body in order to learn to manifest ever more fully our inherent beauty, power and goodness, we will feel no fear or jealousy.

**Overcoming fear by remembering and experiencing our true nature** is one of our main steps in the process of Self-Actualization.

Emotions flow temporarily through us just as various objects flow through a certain section of the riverbanks. They come and go, but we, as the witnesses, remain the same.

We can learn to avoid identifying with the emotion, realizing it is just a temporary mental state and not the totality of our being. We can accept its existence in the river of our mind but give it the same attention we would give to a leaf floating on the river. We do not run after it and attach ourselves to it, nor do we deny its existence or try to prevent it from flowing onwards and away.

### When we are suffering, the ultimate solution is to:

**1.** Search inwardly to discover which **attachment, aversion** or **ego identification** is causing that suffering.

**2.** Determine the **belief** that is creating those attachments or fears.

**3. Remember** that **we are not this temporary personality** or the roles it currently plays.

**4. Identify with our higher soul nature** and connect to our inner strength and self worth, regardless of what is happening with the personality.

### Note:

This is the basis of real change.

Only when we transform our belief system
and let go of our identification
with the roles we are playing
will we find inner peace.

*Life Story No. 22*


# THE PARENT, THE SAVIOR,
# THE TEACHER, THE RESPONSIBLE


Anthony plays the role of "savior." He feels responsible for just about every-one's reality. He believes he must come to their rescue and keep them well and happy. He cannot rest when someone he feels responsible for is not well or hap-py because he feels he has failed in his "role." Others can easily use or control him by making him feel responsible for the fact that they are not well or happy.

He has difficulty identifying his own needs when he is with others. In this role others' needs are more important than his. He would never want to express a need that would prevent others from getting what they want. Playing the savior often causes him to become the "victim" of those he is trying to "save."

He is so preoccupied with other people's problems that he seldom recognizes or confesses his own.

His family complains that he gives more time to solving other people's prob-lems than theirs. He does feel responsible for his own family, but feels a greater need to solve others' problems, as he receives greater satisfaction of recognition and self-worth from that.

He often feels used, tired and resentful that he spends so much time on others and they rarely reciprocate. He worries about others and becomes stressed about their situations and difficulties. He advises them and he tries to control them, ex-erting pressure on them (for "their own good," or to prevent them making a mis-take and thus possibly ruining his "results").

He criticizes and rejects others when they make mistakes or when they do not follow his directions or orders. He gives advice even to those who do not ask for it and feels disappointed when they do not follow it. He attracts to himself peo-ple with problems and rejects himself for not being able to "save" them. He finds it difficult to confess or express his weaknesses, his needs, his fears or his own problems. He fears, that in doing so, others will see his faults and lose respect for him.

As a child, he was programmed to believe he was responsible for his siblings, a role his mother had also played.

**Some beliefs that engage him in this role:**

**1.** I am responsible for others' reality.

**2.** Without me, others cannot progress, cannot be well.

**3.** It's my fault if others are not well.

**4.** If I am not able to create a perfect reality for them, I have failed in my role and am not worthy.

**5.** If others are not happy with me, I have failed and I am not worthy.

**6.** If others do not trust me, I am not worthy.

**7.** If others do not listen to me, do not obey me, do not follow my advice, I am incapable in this role and I am unworthy.

**8.** If I am no good in my role, I will not be respected and will be unworthy of their esteem. I will end up alone and will be in danger.

**9.** If I am not in control of things around me, anything can go wrong. I cannot trust others. If I am not in control, I am in danger.

**10.** If I show weakness or need, or if I have vices, I am in danger because:
**a.** I will be rejected, unwanted.
**b.** My weaknesses will be used as a means to hurt me.

**11.** I am worthy only if I am in the position of authority, i.e. teacher, savior, parent. Only then can I feel safe and secure.

**12.** If I am needed (as a teacher, parent, savior), I will not be abandoned. I will not be alone.

## Some beliefs which can free him from this role:

**1:** We are all 100% responsible for our own reality.

**2:** We are all guided from within.

**3:** The others are totally responsible for the reality they create.

**4.** My self-worth is totally independent of what is happening with others.

**5.** My self-worth is independent of other people's ability to trust me or not.

**6.** I am responsible only for my efforts and not for the results in any endeavor.

**7.** I deserve love and respect exactly as I am.

**8.** I trust others and the Divine.

**9.** I feel more united with others when I share my weaknesses and faults with them.

**10.** I am worthy of love and respect because of my being, not because of any role I play.

## Those around Anthony can:

**1.** Understand that he is seeking his self-worth and inner security by playing this role.

**2.** Take responsibility for their own reality.

**3.** Gently refuse to allow him to overwhelm them and take control of their own lives.

**4.** Lovingly assert their need to take responsibility for their own decisions and accept the consequences of those decisions.

## CHAPTER 22

# TECHNIQUES FOR RECONCILING PERSONAS OR SUB-PERSONALITIES

We occasionally experience internally conflicting needs, desires or beliefs. In such inner conflicts, when our "sub-personalities" or "personas" have conflicting needs, we are not sure what to do or which decision to make.

Some examples of those conflicts are listed below. As you read through them, consider whether or not you have any similar conflicts.

### SOME SAMPLE CONFLICTS

Let us look at some examples of the inner conflicts that may disturb our peace.

**1.** One part of ourselves may feel we need to spend more time on our **professional life** while another part may believe we should spend more time with our **family**.

**2.** A part of ourselves may want to open up to a **conscious love** relationship, while another part **fears** being abandoned, hurt, suppressed, manipulated, or being unable to be ourselves in that relationship.

**3.** One part of ourselves may want to give those around us (children, spouses, friends) total **freedom** to pursue their happiness in their own ways, while another part **fears losing control.**

**4.** The part of ourselves that wants to **please others** may come into direct conflict with our **desire to satisfy our own needs**.

**5.** Part of ourselves may want **others to support us,** while the other feels **restricted** by their support or advice.

**6.** One part of ourselves may **want spiritual growth**, while another may feel the need for **material security**.

**7.** One part of ourselves may want to **help** loved ones or friends, but the other may feel that perhaps we are doing them harm by continuously bailing them out and not letting them **solve their own problems.**

**8.** One part of ourselves may feel a need to **protect the planet** by living a simple life with very little consumption of energy and products, while another part may want to enjoy all the **comforts** of an energy consuming, pollution producing lifestyle.

**9.** One part of ourselves may want to take a new **job** or leave a job that we have, while another part wants the **opposite** for different reasons.

**10.** One part of ourselves may believe in **cooperating** with others, while another finds that **difficult**.

**11.** One part of ourselves may have a desire for various objects or situations as a source of **pleasure,** while another part may feel, this is a **sin**, or that we are **not spiritual** if we partake of such pleasures. It may feel this type of pleasure seeking is a **waste of time** and **energy** considering our spiritual goals.

**12.** One part of ourselves may feel the need to have an **exclusive relationship** in which our happiness and security depend upon another person (usually a mate). Another part may find this an obstacle toward its need for **independence**, self-sufficiency, and freedom.

**13.** Our need for **personal love** may conflict with our need to develop **universal love**.

**14.** Our need to **forgive** may conflict with our need to hold on to **negative feelings** toward someone.

**15.** Our need to employ various **disciplines** may conflict with our need to feel **free** to do whatever we please whenever we choose.

**16.** Our need to **follow** our **inner voice** may conflict with our need to be **like others** and be **accepted** by them.

**17.** Our need to **express our feelings** as they are may conflict with our need **not to hurt anyone**.

**18.** Our need to **express our real feelings** and thoughts might clash with our need to have the others' **acceptance.**

**19.** Our need to **follow a spiritual guide** might conflict with our need to **rebel** against all types of advice or control.

**20.** Our **need to control persons** and situations in order to feel secure may conflict with our need to **let things flow** and allow others to act freely.

**21.** Our need **never to show weakness** may conflict with our need to **share our weaknesses** with others or seek their help.

**22.** Our desire **not to ask anything** from others may conflict with our need to have their **help** and **support**.

**23.** Our need for a **stable routine** for our balance and growth may conflict with our need for **variety** and **change**.

**24.** Our need to **play our familiar emotional relationship games** may conflict with our desire to **get free** ourselves from them.

**25.** One part of us wants to **face and overcome our fears** and blockages while another prefers to **avoid** and ignore them.

There are certainly conflicts, which we haven't mentioned, but most will fall into these categories.

## HOW ARE THESE PERSONAS CREATED?

Our various **emotional survival mechanisms** can lead to the development of diverse personas or sub-personalities within our personality structure (we are not talking here about clinical illness such as multiple personality syndrome).

In response to early childhood experiences (and if you believe so, previous life experiences), we develop various inner emotional responses in an effort to maintain our feelings of security, self-worth, power and freedom. These then grow in their own separate ways, manifesting as **parts** of our personality that have their own personal beliefs, logic and identity and power. We might call these roles "personas," or "sub-personalities." Throughout this discussion we will refer to them as personas.

Each persona has it own core belief that creates and sustains its existence in our larger identity. This core belief will coincide with our need for security, pleasure, affirmation or freedom, or in a few special cases, other less common needs, such as the need to be useful, or to acquire self-knowledge or enlightenment. In some cases, the basic needs may be distorted and work in conflict with survival or growth, as for example, with the need to harm ourselves or others.

In most cases, however, these personas are created by our needs to establish our safety and self-worth, usually through other persons or possessions.

Let us look at some of our more common reactions.

### a. ADDICTION - PRESERVATION

**1.** In this type of reaction, we seek to **maintain that which is familiar**. This means we adopt a role which we experienced as a child, such as the victim, the abused, the ignored, the fearful, the one who makes mistakes, the unintelligent, the rejected, the uninteresting, etc, or perhaps the responsible one, the good child, the strong one, the intelligent one, or the one who received attention for his or her appearance.

If we do not go through a process of conscious transformation, we will, for the rest of our lives identify with these situations or roles. We will continue to evaluate ourselves in terms of those criteria we learned as children.

Although many of us swore as children we would never act like our parents, we find ourselves behaving in the same way toward our children.

**2.** Another possibility is to play the same game but to assume the **opposite role,** perhaps becoming the oppressor, the unattractive, the unintelligent, or the irresponsible one. Victims become oppressors. The weak become "strong." The fearful become "fearless," etc.

**3.** We might seek to play various **roles that will appeal** to those around us, so as to appear "successful," "good," or "acceptable" in their eyes. We may find ourselves adopting such roles as the "yes person," the successful businessperson, the socially "in," or the intelligent and informed.

**4.** If we have become used to being rejected or demeaned, we may proceed to take on this role toward ourselves by **degrading ourselves** when there is no one else to do so. We may do this inwardly as we mentally undermine our self-worth continually. In other cases, we may undermine ourselves openly before others so they will respond with positive comments toward us.

### b. RETREAT - CLOSING IN

**1.** In this type of reaction, we become emotionally **blocked** toward any situations that may have hurt us as children. When confronted with such situations, we find ways to avoid contact with any stimuli that might cause us pain. We might ignore or deny that the situation exists or sink into depression in order to avoid dealing with it.

**2.** We might **isolate ourselves emotionally** in various ways, such as through over working, drinking, eating, taking drugs, being incessantly active, reading, watching TV or by avoiding emotional contact.

**3.** We may develop a distrustful stance toward life and avoid **being open or sincere** with anyone.

**4.** We may lose trust in our own self and thus fear activity, change, or growth, perhaps becoming **totally dependent** upon one or more persons.

### c. AGGRESSION

**1.** We may react by becoming an **aggressive or offensive personality,** seeking to protect ourselves by keeping others at a distance through sarcasm, criticism, rejection, condemnation, and behavior that generally demeans or threatens others.

**2.** We might take on **antagonistic roles** where we compete for our self-worth and power in various ways with those around us.

### d. NEGATIVITY - REJECTION

**1.** We might adopt roles that **abandon every effort** and leave us living without goals, responsibilities or purpose. Some feel safer this way because there can be no failure when there is no endeavor. This may occur in situations where we have very dynamic parents who make us fear that we will never be able to rise to their heights of achievement. Consequently, we give up all effort and "drop out of the game."

**2.** Another reaction is to become the **rebel** who rejects society and its values not only by dropping out, but often by rejecting and actively resisting, or even undermining, the status quo. Such persons may also become anarchists. Our need to rebel can become so strong that we might even refuse to participate in activities we ourselves would enjoy because society, or more specifically, our parents accept that same activity.

### e. SELF DESTRUCTION

**1.** Some of us, having interpreted that we are unworthy, may decide we must **harm or destroy ourselves** through alcohol, drugs, overeating, broken relationships, financial disaster, etc. We might do the same simply to get back at our parents or others whom we feel are responsible for our unhappiness. Destroying ourselves is one way to satisfy our need for revenge toward them.

**2.** In other cases, this reaction may not be so intense, but simply act as a mechanism that would **prevent us from successfully maintaining positive disciplines** for any significant period of time. We become unable to make positive efforts for self-betterment.

These various reactions to similar childhood experiences cause us to develop our own unique mechanisms for "protecting" ourselves and our needs.

## MOTIVES

We can generalize that these reactions have following motivations:

**1.** Attempting to **protect ourselves** from possible dangers. (We must remember that what is known and habitual, even if unpleasant, often feels safer than the unknown, even if that unknown holds the promise of happiness.)

**2.** To **satisfy** various **needs:** security, safety, freedom, pleasure, affirmation, power, esteem, expression of inner impulses, love, meaning, evolution, etc.

**3.** To **prevent pain**: fear, hurt, rejection, or the loss of important persons, possessions or positions.

**4.** To **hide** from what might cause rejection: weakness, fear, needs, real feelings, beliefs, etc.

**5.** To **ensure affirmation** by being what we believe others want us to be in order to for them to accept us.

**6.** To provide avenues for **creativity** and productivity.

**7.** To enable us to move forward in the **evolutionary process**

These reactions lead to what we earlier called roles, personas or sub-personalities.

## AN ABBREVIATED LIST
## OF SOME BASIC PERSONAS

Here we supply you with a short list of personas and their core beliefs. We have grouped the personas under various names. Perhaps, in some cases, only one or two of the names might be applicable.

**1. The Good, Righteous, Spiritual Person**
  **a.** I am worthy and safe if I am (or appear to be) good, right or spiritual.
**2. The Perfect, Capable, Strong Person**
  **a.** I am worthy and safe if I am (or appear to be) perfect, strong or capable.
**3. The Victim, Abused, Unjustly Persecuted**
  **a.** Others create my reality; they are to blame for my situation.

**b.** The wronged person is right and worthy because the wrong -doer is wrong and evil.

**c.** I am not worthy of something better than this.

### 4. The Weak, Incapable, Fearful, Dependent, Child

**a.** I am not capable of coping with life by myself.

**b.** Life is difficult.

### 5. The Guilty, Sinner, Bad, Unworthy

**a.** I am guilty, unworthy, evil, a sinner.

**b.** I do not deserve love, acceptance or help from others or God.

**c.** I am in danger (without protection, vulnerable to punishment)

### 6. The Parent, Teacher, Savior, Responsible for others and everything

**a.** I am responsible for others' reality, including their happiness, health, security, success, well being.

**b.** Others cannot proceed or take care of themselves without me.

**c.** If others are not well, I am to blame and have failed.

### 7. The Rebel, Reactionary, Challenger, Competitor

**a.** My freedom is in danger.

**b.** I must fight for my freedom, safety or self-worth.

**c.** I actually need others.

### 8. The Intelligent, Informed, Superior, Counselor

**a.** He who knows more is superior.

**b.** If I show them that I know more than they do, they will love me and I will be worthy and safe.

### 9. The Indifferent, Irresponsible, Free-Moving, Disruptive, Insensitive, Lazy

**a.** Whoever has responsibilities and / or does not fulfill them is in danger.

**b.** I will suffer or fail if I take on responsibilities.

### 10. The Intimidator, General, Dictator, Aggressor, Abuser

**a.** My safety and / or self worth are in danger.

**b.** I must protect myself and others in the battle of life.

**c.** Power and the offensive are the solutions.

### 11. The **Interrogator, Critic, Mr. Right**

**a.** I am worthy when others are wrong.

**b.** Others must answer to my questions.

**c.** My self worth depends upon my being right and others being wrong.

### 12. The **Aloof, Distant, Loner, Silent One**

**a.** I can protect myself from others by not emotionally interacting with them.

**b.** I am worthy when others seek my attention.

### 11. The **Spouse, Husband, Wife**

**a.** My self worth is dependent upon how well I am accepted and recognized in the role of the spouse.

**b.** I must be accepted as a spouse in order to be worthy and safe.

### 12. The **Woman, Man**

**a.** My self-worth is measured by how much I am accepted in the role of a woman / man.

   **b.** My self worth is decided by how much I am respected and desired by the opposite sex.

   Any particular person may, however, in his self-analysis break these major roles into a wide variety of parts, which differ in numerous ways.

   Here is a list of personas along with their "motto" offered by Gay and Kathlyn Hendricks in their book ***Conscious Loving.***

   **1.** Conscientious: Do the right thing
   **2.** Super Competent: Here, let me do it
   **3.** Devoted: I'll always be there for you
   **4.** Drama Queen / King: You would not believe the day I've had.
   **5.** Ramblin' Guy / Gal: Don't fence me in.
   **6.** Victim: Poor me
   **7.** Performer: The show must go on.  Look at me
   **8.** Critic:  I tell you what is wrong - even if you don't ask.
   **9.** Loner: By myself.
   **10.** Space out: Huh?
   **11.** Mr. / Ms. Nice Guy: I must
   **12.** Dependent: I need you.
   **13.** Mr. Sick / Ms. Accidents: I am not well.
   **14.** Caretaker: Let me help you.
   **15.** Stoic: I can take it.
   **16.** Peter Pan / Tinkerbell: I'll never grow up.
   **17.** Hostile: Out of my way.
   **18.** Self-righteous: I am higher than the rest.
   **19.** Chameleon: Whatever you say.
   **20.** True believer: This is it. I know the truth.
   **21.** Shy: Please don't notice me.
   **22.** Flamboyant: This is the latest thing.
   **23.** Martyr: I'll sacrifice myself.
   **24.** Rebel: I don't agree.

   Here is another list created by a person looking into himself. See if you can discover any of your own roles.

   Poor unloved child
   Bad unworthy child
   Good obedient boy
   Playful prankster
   Fascinated wonderer
   Efficient worker

Righteous rebel
Unemotional stoic
Anxious worrier
Macho man
Understanding listener
Efficient organizer
Cooperating server
Disciplined meditator
Sacrificing hero
Intelligent problem solver
Unjustly persecuted victim
 Socializer
Loving friend
Joyful creator
Erotic dancer
Chooser of goodness
Holy -pure - monk
Seeker of enlightenment
Savior - teacher
Disappointed one
Responsible for everyone
Loving son
Loving husband
Loving father
Seeker of truth
Scientist
Body maintainer
Righteous critic
Enjoyer of senses
Writer of book
Universal philosopher
Child of the universe

We can see there are various ways of understanding and labeling these personas.
It is not so important what we name them, but that we recognize their existence
and then learn to identify them, understand them, accept them and gradually help
them to function harmoniously within us.

## THE SPIRITUAL AND MATERIAL EGO

These roles or personas, which develop subconsciously, create a variety of beliefs and subsequent needs and emotions. Most of our personas manage to cooperate enough so that we can function without serious inner turmoil, but there are

times in our lives when we experience inner conflicts in which two or more parts of our being have conflicting needs.

Many of these conflicts have to do with the differing needs between our "spiritual" personas and our "material" personas. We place these words in quotation marks because all personas live in ignorance, and thus are all material. The so-called "spiritual" personas are **trying** to be spiritual, or in some cases, only to **appear** spiritual.

One part of ourselves wants to improve our character and lifestyle, and proceed spiritually, while the other might prefer to remain in the familiar, conditioned types of behavior and activities where it finds security, pleasure and affirmation. Let's call the first part the **spiritual** ego and the second the **material** ego. We want these two to meet, to open up to each other and become one.

We do not intend to imply that the spiritual ego is higher or more spiritual than the material ego. In some cases, the opposite may be true, as the spiritual ego might be simply seeking security, pleasure and affirmation in other ways. The spiritual ego may occasionally be even more afraid or attached to persons and situations than the material ego; however, this is not always the case.

## WHAT WE CAN DO
## ABOUT INNER CONFLICTS

**1. We first need to get to know** these various **parts** of ourselves by keeping a **daily diary** in which we refer to them by names that represent their particular qualities needs or emotions.

**2.** We can keep a **separate page for each persona** in which we list its particular needs, desires, fears, emotions, reactions and beliefs.

**3.** We then need to **discover** for each persona the **core belief** that creates, sustains and drives it.

**4.** We must **accept each persona** as a natural development in our evolution process. Regardless of whether there is use for its continued existence, at some point, it served some purpose in our search for security, self-worth, freedom and equilibrium.

We can perceive each persona as one of our children, whom we accept and love regardless of its immaturity. Our purpose is to now educate that persona and help it to manifest its higher potential.

**5. We can then allow each persona to express itself** in its own unique way through dance, writing, drawing, work, etc.

**6.** We then move on to let them **communicate between themselves**.

**a.** By writing a dialogue like a one act play in which they communicate back and forth expressing: **complaints, needs, feelings, beliefs, as well as questions which they have for each other.**

In this conversation questions are asked and then answered by the other party, or perhaps arguments or accusations made on the one part to be rebutted by the other. Attempts are made by each part to get what it needs from the other.

The ultimate purpose is to create an atmosphere of communication, understanding and cooperation between these two personas with conflicting needs.

**b.** The same process can then be done **verbally as described below.**

## THE INNER DIALOGUE

**Attention**: This work can some times be disturbing or confusing, and thus it is best done with the help of a professional experienced in this type of analysis, dialoguing and psychodrama.

Before moving on to perform the dialogue, it would be beneficial to fill out the following questionnaire which will help us establish a clearer understanding of which personas we want to reconcile and what their real needs, emotions and beliefs are.

## ANALYZING OUR CONFLICTING PERSONAS

Now separately, for each conflicting part of yourself, answer the following questions.

a. For **Part "A",** which I have named _____
  **1.** Its has the following **needs, desires and attachments**

_____

  **2.** When its needs are not fulfilled, it has the following **emotions:**
_____

  **3.** It has the following **beliefs** that cause it to have those needs and emotions.

_____

  **4.** This part of myself would like to communicate the following to part **"B".**

_____

  **5.** Toward the part of me labeled "A" and named _____,
**I personally experience the following feelings.**_____

b. For **Part "B",** which I have **named** _____
  **1.** It has the following **needs, desires and attachments**

_____

  **2.** When its needs are not fulfilled, it has the following **emotions:**

_____

**3.** It has the following **beliefs** that cause it to have those needs and emotions:

_____

**4.** This part of myself would like to communicate the following to part **"A"**:

_____

    **5. T**owards the part of me labeled **"B"** and named _____,
**I personally experience the following feelings:**_____

Having established this information, we are now ready to allow these two personas to communicate. As mentioned earlier, this dialogue can be done as a written exercise or verbally in the presence of a facilitator.

In the case that we do it verbally, we will place two chairs, pillows or benches opposite each other. We sit on the one chair and assume one of the two roles. We imagine that the other persona is sitting in the opposite chair or on the opposite pillow.

We start the conversation by speaking on behalf of the persona 'A' explaining to persona 'B'

**a.** How he or she feels.

**b.** What his or her needs and desires are.

**c.** What his or her beliefs are which make him or her feel that way.

This persona may also ask the other (supposedly sitting in the opposite position) questions concerning its beliefs, emotions and behaviors in an attempt to understand it more deeply.

We then change positions, now sitting in the other chair and give the opposite side an opportunity to speak about itself, how it feels and what it needs as well as to ask and answer questions.

These two parts will speak back and forth as we get up and change positions whenever we change roles (it is important to change positions in order to help change mind-set and psychology).

This conversation goes on like any other conversation, as each persona asks questions and we change positions and each answers questions posed by the other persona. Each persona may accuse or perhaps express feelings of tenderness and love, or plead and ask for help or even ask deeper questions which help the one part of ourselves understand the other part more deeply and clearly.

The conversation goes on until we have sat in **both** positions **consecutively** and have nothing more to say or ask from either point of view. This is important because we may feel we have nothing more to say from the one side, but when we sit on the other side and ask a question, it may open up an entirely new discussion, which could last another half an hour and involve many more changes in position.

Once we have completed this dialogue, we then take a position in the middle, to the side of the two previous sitting positions, and imagine we are our **higher self**, or that we are an enlightened spiritual guide. We then give advice to each persona separately, explaining what each needs to understand or do in order to live in greater harmony with the other and to proceed more effectively with less conflict along the path of spiritual growth or self-improvement.

Whether we perform this exercise verbally or in written form, I am sure each persona will find it very useful in resolving conflicts which are often serious obstacles to achieving our inner peace, establishing harmonious relationships, and moving forth in the evolutionary progress.

## DIALOGUING WITH OUR EMOTIONS

This technique can be done in the previously explained manner. The main difference is that we speak with a part of ourselves which is prone toward feeling a certain emotion, such as fear, hurt, anger, guilt, injustice, bitterness, jealousy, depression etc.

We identify that part of ourselves, which is burdened with the bothersome emotion then ask it questions or express our needs. Next, we change positions and answer the questions or express our needs on behalf of that specific part of ourselves.

We might want to ask some of the following questions:
1. What exactly do you feel?
2. Under what circumstances do you feel that way?
3. When did you first feel that way?
4. What has happened in our past that causes you feel that way?
5. What beliefs do you hold which make you feel that way?
6. If at this moment you stopped experiencing that emotion, how would you feel?
7. **What exactly do you want** (in order to feel better):
    **a.** From the others, and from whom in particular?
    **b.** From me (the central personality)?
    **c.** From God?
8. If you do not get what you want from others, what do you imagine will happen?
9. If you cannot get what you want from others, would you be willing to receive that which you want from me (your own self) or from God?
10. What can I do you help you?
11. By what name would you like to be called when I need to communicate with you?

In this way, we will begin to understand more clearly why that part of ourselves feels that emotion which is bothering us. We will also gain some distance from and objectivity toward that part of ourselves, thus strengthening the witness who is free from that emotion. It is essential, however, to accept and love that part of ourselves as we educate it.

## CONFLICTS BETWEEN THE
## SPIRITUAL AND MATERIAL PERSONAS

We mentioned previously that these conflicts often occur between two groups of personas called the "spiritual" and "material."

The spiritual ego feels the conflict most intensely (if we didn't desire spiritual growth or self-improvement we would not have a conflict), and usually creates feelings of self rejection, failure and guilt when we are unable to satisfy its need to feel that it is "spiritual" and "worthy."

Also, when we do not feel worthy, we do not feel safe. This occurs because many of us are programmed to believe whoever is not "good" or worthy in God's eyes is not safe, as he does not "deserve" God's love and protection. Making matters worse is the fact that we might also be programmed to feel we deserve punishment.

These are obviously not the highest reasons to want to improve ourselves. They are, in fact, rather selfish motives. If we want to change to ensure our safety, or so others will accept us, we are simply replacing the material ego with the spiritual ego. Nothing has really changed. In some cases, our need to fulfill these spiritual "requirements" for our self-acceptance has to do with our need to feel we are **more** spiritual than others. Thus, we simply replace the need for affirmation and superiority on a material level with the same need on the spiritual level.

**It is important to realize that our self-worth is permanent and divine.** We cannot be worth more or less in God's eyes. We are divine consciousness itself in the process of evolving our ability to express our divinity on the material planes. Our inherent spiritual value is not changed by our actions or spiritual growth. What is changed is our ability to express those values mentally, emotionally and physically.

Trying to be a better person because we believe it will encourage God to love us more is also an insufficient motive for growth. Desiring to become a clearer channel for divine energies of love, peace, harmony, justice and happiness is a much better motive. Seeking to purify ourselves so we can experience that Divine Consciousness in every being and event that we encounter, is a useful motive. Seeking to remove all mental, emotional and physical obstacles so that we can cultivate pure love, simplicity and selflessness, is also useful.

Such motives are free from the game of who is spiritual and who is not, or who is more spiritual, or who is good and who is bad, and whom God loves and whom God does not love. They are based on the presumption that God is a much higher type of consciousness, and thus is incapable of not loving anyone no matter what that person might ever do. This seems only logical since the Divine Being has asked us, mere humans, to love even our enemies and those who ignore and harm us. Is it possible then that It is incapable of doing so?

This type of thinking also removes us from the game of spiritual pride in which we feel that we are higher, more important, or more favored by God than others. It also frees us from feeling we are lower, less important or less favored by God than others.

The **material ego**, on the other hand, tends to react in such situations to the rejection and pressure it receives from the spiritual ego by rebelling and sabotaging its various efforts toward discipline, self-control and self-improvement. Thus, the more we pressure ourselves, the more our material ego reacts and rebels. In such cases, we experience instability in our spiritual or self-improvement efforts. In these cases, we usually play the roles of parent and child with our own selves. The parent in us rejects the child in us for not being a "good child," and the child then reacts so as to undermine the parents' effort toward control.

In order to move more effectively toward our goal of spiritual transformation, these inner conflicts must be dealt with in a more mature manner. Rather than communicating within ourselves as child and parent, it would be more useful to develop a mature adult to adult system of conversation or dialogue.

## QUESTIONNAIRE FOR
## "SPIRITUAL" vs. "MATERIAL" CONFLICTS

The following technique is best done with the guidance of a facilitator or as a written exercise.

Our purpose is to allow these two parts of ourselves a chance to reflect upon what they really want, need, and desire, and then express all of this to the other part. It is best for one to begin with a written analysis. Here are some questions that may help:

### Questions for the Spiritual Ego:

**1.** What does it feel when it is unable to achieve or maintain a particular goal?

**2.** In which particular situations does it feel that? Give some examples.

**3.** What does it believe about those situations, and particularly about itself, which causes it to have the feelings which it mentioned in answer to question 1.

**4.** Why does it believe those beliefs? Upon what basic beliefs are they founded?

**5.** What are its needs and desires?

**6.** What specifically does it ask from the Material Ego?

**7.** What can it do in order to have a better relationship with its Material Ego or inner child, and thus, proceed with greater unity and stability?

### Questions for the Material Ego:

**1.** What does it need and desire in order to feel secure, happy and worthy? Let it make a list of what its needs (objects, persons, situations, behaviors from itself and others, etc.).

**2.** Why does it believe that it needs each specific thing? Let it answer, in regard to each, what it believes will happen if it is unable to fulfill each of those needs or desires.

**3.** What are the basic beliefs which underlay its dependency on these specific needs and desires?

**4.** What specifically does it ask from the spiritual ego in order to feel more unity with it, to establish greater cooperation between them and greater happiness for both?

**5.** What can the Material Ego do in order to create greater unity and harmony, since they both live must share the same body and mind?

After answering these questions in written form, we can then engage in a verbal dialogue between these two parts of our selves.

## TRANSCENDING THE PERSONAS

The eventual goal is to transcend these separate parts and experience our complete self, which encompasses all the personas but is limited or controlled by none. Only then can we be one whole, unified being. This is done mostly through meditation and by pursuing a simple, moral life.

This can be aided by daily relaxation techniques in which we communicate with these parts of our being in a loving way and educate them with the help of spiritual truths.

A second way is to transcend these parts is through daily meditation. This can be studied in detail in the book **THE ART OF MEDITATION** by the same author. Through meditation, we eventually become the detached witness of all these parts, allowing ourselves to view them objectively.

Those interested in more information about reconciling inner conflicts will be interested in the book: **SARAM - the Adventures of a Soul and an Insight in the Male Psyche** by the same author.

More information can be found on our web site.

## Technique no. 22

## SELFLESS SERVICE

### Why this is so important

Selfless service to those in need frees us from our ego centered thoughts and exaggerated importance to our problems, and thus from the major source of our pain

Selfless service can transform stagnant and misdirected energy into service that benefits others. Acting with the intention of helping others is a way to channel energy, which might otherwise stagnate within and develop into negative alienating emotions.

Work that brings a sense of fulfillment and meaning to a person's life is an essential ingredient in creating a life of peace and contentment.
This work is best performed out of love for those whom we are serving, as opposed to desire for rewards, material or mental, such as gratitude on the part of the other.

Obviously, our service must never undermine the others' sense of responsibility or inner strength. We need help only those who presently cannot help themselves.

Equally, we must be very careful not to develop a "service ego" in which we feel superior to others because we are helping. Also, service should never be a form of escapism.

### How to get started

There are an abundance of volunteer groups to which we can offer our support. Each of us will need to decide what cause interests us most. Some possibilities might be:

**1.** Visiting orphans.

**2.** Visiting old people's homes or old people in their homes.

**3.** Visiting the ill.

**4.** Participating in animal protection activities.

**5.** Participating in forestry protection activities.

**6.** Recording books on tape for the visually handicapped.

**7.** Cooking for or otherwise helping the homeless.

**8.** Donating money to various causes

If we possess any special skills, we might be able to serve in more specific ways such as:

**1.** Providing voluntary medical or dental care.

**2.** Providing voluntary legal service.

**3.** Providing voluntary psychological support.

### Note:

Our problem is separateness.

Our solution is unity.

*Life Story 23*

## THE GUILTY, THE SINNER,
## THE BAD, THE EVIL ONE

Susan tends to feel guilty. She has been programmed to believe that she is an unworthy, evil sinner. This causes her to incessantly seek her affirmation of her self-worth through others. She spends tremendous amounts of energy attempting to prove her self-worth through her professional endeavors and her service to others. She is unable to say "no." She cannot bear the idea that someone exists who does not thinking highly of her. Even one person, who questions her sincerity or does not respect her, causes her self-doubt mechanisms to shift into overdrive.

She needs to make her actions, achievements and service known to others, sometimes overtly, sometime inconspicuously. She has no tolerance for her own or others' mistakes. She cannot admit her mistakes or faults because to do so would to indicate that she is not worthy.

She also needs to find as many faults as possible in others. The more faults she finds, the more her own self-worth is verified. The more she is the victim of others' mistakes, laziness or irresponsibility, the more affirmed she feels.

She seeks out situations in which she can be the martyr who does what the others neglect to do and again affirms that she is good and the others are not. She consistently undermines her own happiness and wellbeing. She does not feel she deserves any lasting happiness. Also, being happy means she is not the victim, diminishing the feeling of being a "good" person that she gets from being unhappy.

Her behavior is, of course, frustrating for those around her. She feels easily hurt, demeaned or rejected. She is antagonistic and competitive. She needs to be affirmed frequently and will often be critical of others. Her behavior towards those from whom she needs affirmation differs from than toward those from whom she does not. She easily becomes angry and intimidating, or in some cases, might retreat, once again feeling like the victim.

She does not allow herself time for self-care because she does not believe she deserves to spend time on herself.

Pushing herself relentlessly, she has little patience for those who do not push themselves. She tends to tests others' love, not believing they have the capacity to honestly love her. This can be very trying for those who do in fact love her.

In general she creates tension in her environment.

## Some childhood experiences which may have lead her to this role are that:

1. She received the message that she was bad, unworthy and guilty, and was rejected in various ways when she did not do what her parents asked or did not fulfill their needs.

2. Her parents had similar feelings about themselves.

3. As a girl, her needs were given less importance than the needs of her male siblings.

4. She was told that God does not pardon, but rather, punishes the guilty.

5. She was made to feel guilty about her sexuality and contact with boys in adolescence.

6. She was sexually approached by a male in the family, a trauma the family never honestly faced, but instead chose to deny, causing her to take the blame on herself for what had happened.

## Some beliefs that may cause her to behave in these ways:

1: I am guilty, I am a sinful, and I am no good.

2: I am unworthy of love, acceptance, or help from man or God.

3. If I am the victim, then I am worthy

4. I have sinned.

5. Others did not give me love and affection, so I must be unworthy.

6. My sexuality is a sin.

7. Whoever makes mistakes is guilty, a sinner and unworthy of love.

8. I am guilty when others criticize or accuse me, or when they complain or are not happy.

9. I am unworthy when others work harder than I do.

10. I am unworthy when I do not reach my goals.

11. I must do much more than others in order to be worthy.

**12.** When I am criticized or someone raises his voice at me, I am in danger and unworthy.

**13.** I must be perfect (in cleanliness, tidiness, order, appearance) to deserve love and acceptance.

### Some beliefs that might liberate her from these behaviors are:

**1:** I am a good and worthy person.

**2:** I am worthy of love and respect exactly as I am.

**3.** I am worthy even when others are good and capable.

**4.** I am a creation of the divine.

**5.** I am worthy of love and respect even when others are not capable of giving them to me.

**6.** My sexuality is an aspect of my divine nature.

**7.** Mistakes are a natural aspect of any creative or growth process.

**8.** I am worthy of love and respect regardless of others' behavior.

**9.** My self-worth has nothing to do with my or others' achievements.

**10.** I feel safe and secure in all situations.

**11.** As beings in evolution, we all deserve love and respect, even when we are not perfect.

### Those around her will be able to maintain their peace and love by:

**1.** Giving her love and affirmation.

**2.** Understanding her need to talk about herself and find fault with others without getting caught up in it.

**3.** Being firm and loving with her when she seeks to find fault in others, and not allowing her to perpetuate this illusion.

# CHAPTER 23

# HEALING THE INNER CHILD

**Note:**

The work described in this chapter usually requires
guidance by a person experienced in this work.

Our inner child is that part of our subconscious that still feels, thinks and behaves in the ways we learned as children. Our emotional life is largely dictated by the feelings, beliefs and needs generated by our childhood experiences.

We have become split personalities who function with two minds. One is logical while the other still perceives life through the eyes of the children that once we were. While one knows logically that we have no reason to fear or doubt ourselves, the other continues to experience anxiety, fear, guilt and self-doubt. While we know cognitively that we have the ability to deal with life, a part of ourselves continues to be fearful, jealous and angry.

We may not be consciously aware that our inner child feels vulnerable, lonely, fearful, angry or hurt, yet, these emotions are very visible in the form of our fears and defensive reactions. Our hidden emotions are also quite evident in our tensions and psychosomatic illnesses.

On the other hand, our inner child and other aspects of our subconscious are a rich and abundant source of inspiration, joy, creativity and love for life.

We need to establish contact with our inner child and learn to accept and love it as it is, while at the same time educating it concerning the truth of its divine nature. We can then heal our inner child of its traumas and misconceptions while simultaneously recovering from it our innocence, joy and inner connection with life.

Regardless of which techniques we employ in relationship to the inner child, it is essential that we develop a relationship with it by communicating daily. We suggest the following technique.

## DAILY COMMUNICATION WITH THE CHILD WITHIN

**1.** Sit or lie down with the spine straight.

**2.** Relax the entire body and mind through your preferred relaxation or concentration technique.

**3.** Imagine the inner child and communicate with it. (It might appear at any age.)

    **a.** Ask it how it **feels**.

    **b.** Ask if it has some **needs** it would like to satisfy.

    **c.** Speak to it about your **needs as an adult**.

**4.** Give it **positive reinforcement.** Our child needs to hear about love, security and self-worth.

**5.** Mentally **embrace** the child and hold it with **tenderness** and **love**.

    **a.** Feel (imagine) the child in your arms.

    **b. Identify with the small body** and feel yourself inside the embrace accepting the love and tenderness offered to you.

    **c.** Become one with the child.

This technique can be performed as a prelude to any meditation, relaxation technique, prayer or positive projection technique, or alone as it is. Once mastered, it takes only five minutes.

## DISCOVERING OUR PAST

Our first step will be to discover the events that might have programmed our inner child to be overly sensitive to situations or stimuli, which we now objectively realize, are not worth losing our peace over. In studying the following list of possible childhood experiences, we might find some experiences described exactly as we remember them, while others may remind us of experiences that are somehow different than the ones described. Some memories or associations may take time to come. We may be reminded of something else of which we would like to take note.

## LIST OF CHILDHOOD EXPERIENCES

Note: After each experience, you will find a list of numbers with the letter "B" referring to the list of possible beliefs, subconscious conclusions of the child, which may have been programmed into our childhood mind because of these experiences. This list can be found on our web site *www.HolisticHarmony.com*. The numbers here refer to the numbers of the beliefs on that list.

Wherever the questions refer to our parents or other persons of our childhood, we must also think of stepmothers, stepfathers, grandparents, uncles, aunts, brothers and sisters, cousins, teachers and any other persons who existed in our lives as a child up to the age of 18.

**1.** Was there someone who became **angry** with you, scolded you, rejected you or accused you? Who and when? B=(1,2,3,4,5,6,7,13,14,15,16,70,142,143).

**2.** Were there people in your family **who fought among themselves** or rejected or hurt one another? Who and when? B=(1,2,3,4,5,6,143).

**3.** Have you ever experienced the feeling of **abandonment**? Were you ever left alone? Have you ever felt that others didn't understand you, or that you would receive no support? When? By whom? How?
B= (1,4,8,9,10,11,12,13,14,15,16,70,142).

**4.** Did you ever feel the **need for more affection**, tenderness or expression of love? From whom and when (during which periods of your life)? B= (1,13,14, 15,16,142).

**5.** Were there persons in your environment who were **often ill** or who often spoke of illness? Did they ever **blame you** for their illness or did you ever feel guilty concerning their illness? Who and when?
B= (17,18,19,20,21,22).

**6.** Did you ever experience the feeling of **humiliation** in the presence of others or in connection with others? In which cases?
B= (1,4,5,8,14,23,24,25,70,143).

**7.** Were you ever **compared to others** as to whether you were less or more capable or worthy? To whom, in which instances, and in connection with which abilities or character traits? B= (1,23,24,25,26,70,143).

**8.** Have you ever **lost a loved one**? Who and when?
B= (7,8,9,10,11,12,14,15,17, 18,21,27,28,2,142).

**9.** Did anyone ever **approach you sexually** without your consent? Who, when, and how did you feel? B=(1,30,31,32,33, 34,136,142).

**10.** Were you ever aware of your parents or anyone **else making love**? Who and when? How did you feel and what did you think?
B= (33,34,35,36,37).

**11.** Did your parents ever state that you were the only reason they stayed together, and that this had been a big sacrifice on their part? Did they ever tell you they had sacrificed a great deal for your sake, and that **you were indebted to them**? Who? When? About what matters? What exactly do you believe you owe them?

B= (1,6,38,39,40,41,41,42,43,141,143).

**12.** Did anyone **ever accuse you of being the cause of his or her unhappiness,** illness or problems? Who accused you and about what exactly? What did they mean by saying that it was your fault? What does this statement mean to you? According to them, what should you have done?
B= (38,39,40,41,42,43,44,45,46,47, 48,49,50,51,52.53,54,141,143).

**13.** Did anyone ever say **you would never achieve anything** in your life, that you are lazy, incompetent, or dumb? Who, when and concerning what matters?
B= (55,56,57,58,59,60,141,142,143).

**14.** Were you ever caught **playing with your genitals** (alone or with others), and did anyone make you feel guilty about that? Who? When? What was their message? B= (61,62,63).

**15.** Did anyone **speak about guilt and punishment** from a person, a parent, the police or God? Who? When? About what types of guilt and what type of punishment? B= (1,62,63,64,65,141,142,143).

**16.** Did any **teacher ever make you feel humiliated** in front of other children? When? How? Concerning what? B= (66,67,68,69,142,143).

**17.** Did you ever **feel rejection or inferiority** in the company of other children? By whom? Inferior by what criteria?
B= (23,24,25,26,70,142,143).

**18.** Were you **ever told you were responsible for the general well being of your siblings or others**, and that whatever happened to them was your responsibility? Who did? About whom? Concerning what matters were you responsible?
B= (44,45,46,47,48,49,50,51,52,53, 54,141,143).

**19.** Were you ever made to understand in some way (negative or positive) that **in order for someone to be acceptable and lovable**, one must: B= (141,142,143).
___a. Be **better** than the others?
___b. Be **first** at everything?
___c. Be **perfect**, without faults?
___d. Be **intelligent** and clever?
___e.  Be **handsome / beautiful**?
___f.  Have **perfect order** and cleanliness at home?
___g.  Have **great success** in his/her love life?
___h.  Be **financially and socially successful**?
___i.  Be **accepted by everyone**?

___**j.** Be **active in many ways**? Achieve many things?

___**k.** Always **satisfy the needs of others**?

___**l.** **Never say "no"** to others?

___**m. Never express** his/her personal **needs**?

**20.** Did anyone ever make you believe in some way that you were **incapable of thinking**, making decisions, or achieving things by yourself, and that you would always need to depend on others? Who passed on this message to you? About what matters were you supposedly "incapable" of making decisions or handling life properly?
B= (91,92,93,94,142,143).

**21.** Did you ever have **role models** (parents, older siblings or others) who were, or still are, **so dynamic** and competent that you felt:
B= (95,96,97,98,141,142,143).

**a.** The **need to be like them**?

**b.** The need to **prove your worth**, to reach or even surpass these models?

**c. Despair**, self-rejection, abandonment of effort, self-destructive tendencies (possibly subconscious), because you believed you could never measure up to them?

In connection with whom has any of this occurred (a, b or c) and with what criteria of success?

**22.** Has there ever been in your environment **someone with unexpected, un-predictable, nervous or even schizophrenic behavior** (possibly alcohol or drug induced) making it difficult for you to anticipate what he or she might do next? Have they engaged in violent behavior (physical or psychological)? By whom, and what was the behavior like? B=(1,2,3,4,5,6,7,8,11,12,13,14,15,16,99,100,101,102,103,104,105,106,107,108,135,142)

**23.** Have you felt rejection towards **or shame concerning one of your parents**? For whom and why? B= (109,110,111,112,142,143).

**24.** Did you ever make the discovery that one of your parents had an **extra-marital affair**? When and under what circumstances? How did you feel about that? B= (83,104,109,110,111,112).

**25.** Did anyone often speak to you about **a vengeful, punishing God** or about the "**Devil**?" Who did, and in what context?
B= (1,62,63,64,65,113,114,135,141,142,143).

**26.** Did you ever feel that someone told you one thing but did another, that there was **no consistency in their words**, that they had a double standard - one for themselves and another for others - or that they were hypocritical, false and deceptive? Who and when? Concerning what topics? B= (115,116, 117,118,119,120,121).

**27.** Upon what was your **parents' security based**?
___**a)** on money?
___**b)** on the others' opinions?
___**c)** on education?
___**d)** on personal power?
___**e)** on the unity of the family?
___**f)** on property?
___**g)** on one's spouse?
___**h)** other? _____
B= (122,123,124,125,126,127,128,129,142,143).

**28.** Were you a **spoiled child** who always got whatever you wanted, and to whom no one ever refused a favor? B= (131,132,142).

**29.** Did anyone **suppress your freedom** of movement and expression? Did they force you to do things you did not want to do? (study, visits, dress). Did they forbid you to do things you wanted to do? What were you forced to do or prevented from doing?
B= (135,136,137,138,142,143).

**30. (FOR WOMEN).** Did anyone in some way try to make you believe that **since you are a girl**:
**a.** You are worth less than a man?
**b.** You are not safe without a man?
**c.** Sex is dirty (a sin)?
**d.** You must be married in order to be socially accepted?
**e.** You are less competent than men?
**f.** Your only mission is to serve others?
**g.** You must not express your needs, feelings or opinions?
**h.** You must submit yourself to your husband?
**i.** You must be attractive to be acceptable?
B= (133 a,b,c,d,e,f,g,h,i,j,k,l,m,n,o, 141,142.143).

**31. (FOR MEN).** Did anyone in some way try to make you believe that since you are a boy:
**a.** You must be strong?
**b.** You must be superior, more competent, stronger and more intelligent than your wife?
**c.** Your self-worth is measured according to the success of your love life or the

number of your sexual conquests?

**d.** Your worth is measured according to your professional (financial) success?

**e.** You must compare yourself with other men?

B= (134 a,b,c,d,e,f,g,h,i,j,k,l, 141,142,143).

## ADDITIONAL AIDS FOR THE
## SEARCH INTO THE CHILDHOOD YEARS

In addition to this list of childhood experiences, we can also search the past in the following ways:

**1.** Through childhood **regressions:** Guided by a well-trained professional, we can re-experience memories of the past.

**2.** By **writing the story of our childhood** years, we can strengthen our contact with the details of the past. This can be written in the first person, but even better in the third person, as if we are chronicling the life of some other person. This enables us to be more objective and honest in our observations. We will discover patterns of behavior that we tend to repeat throughout the years. We will find the experiences that have marked our subconscious, creating our emotional mechanisms.

This life story need not be detailed in chronological order. Each day, we can add whatever we remember in any order.

The first comment made by many people is, " I don't remember anything before the age of ten. How will I do this?" This is no problem. As we start to write, the subconscious will be awakened and memories will start flowing forth. The more we write, the more the memories will be activated.

Placing old **photographs** before us as we write will help, as will asking parents, grandparents, uncles, aunts and older brothers and sisters what they can remember. We are not obligated to accept their interpretation of the past, but their words may trigger other memories.

Best results will be obtained if we dedicate at least twenty minutes daily to this process for at least three months.

The **basic guidelines** for writing the story of our childhood years are:

**a.** Add whatever additional memories you remember each day.

**b.** It need not to be in chronological order.

**c.** We can write in the third or first person.

**d.** Ask others (parents, uncles, aunts, siblings, grandparents) what they remember.

**e.** Look at old pictures.

### 3. A questionnaire for getting acquainted with the inner child

Answering these questions will assist our investigation into the messages we might have received in our childhood years. Complete the following sentences with at least three answers for each if possible. Also, try to remember exactly what happened which caused you to come to those assumptions.

    **a.** As a child, I heard that my most significant faults were.....
    **b.** As a child, I felt guilty about/for....
    **c.** Some messages I received about God were...
    **d.** Some messages I received about sex were...
    **e.** Some messages I received about money were...
    **f.** I felt rejection when...
    **g.** I felt fear when…
    **h.** I felt shame or inferiority when...
    **i.** I felt abandonment when

## 4. A deeper questionnaire concerning our beliefs

The following questionnaire will give us supplementary information concerning the programmings we developed in those early years. Please answer as honestly as you can, allowing enough time to establish contact with the various parts of your personality. Do not be surprised by needs, desires, beliefs and feelings that seem to conflict or be contradictory. This is quite common and natural for a person in the process of evolution who is passing through changes in his values, beliefs and needs.

Give three or more answers to each question.

### A. The basis for our feelings of security.

1. The three positive human characteristics which I value most are ...
2. The three negative human characteristics that I find most unacceptable are...
3. I love and accept myself more when ....
4. I feel guilty when ...
5. I have negative feelings when...
6. I feel happy when ...
7. I feel insecure when...
8. I feel secure when...
9. I do not believe I can ....
10. If my house were on fire and I could save only three objects (excluding people or animals), they would be.....
11. My three strongest fears are....

### B. How I perceive others and how I believe they perceive me.

12. How I believe my spouse or love partner perceives me. (Or previous spouse

or love partner. Or all spouses and love partners we have had until now.)

13. Three of my spouse's (love partner's) positive traits are ...
14. Three of my spouse's (love partner's) negative traits are...
15. How I believe my parents perceive me....
16. My parents always told me that I was unable to ...
17. The criticism I heard most often from my parents was...
18. Three of my father's positive qualities were/are...
19. Three of my father's negative qualities were/are...
20. Three of my mother's positive qualities were/are...
21. Three of my mother's negative qualities were/are...
22. This is how I remember my parents' relationship until I was 21 years old.
23. I find it difficult to forgive others for...

**C. How I see myself.**

24. I feel weak and vulnerable when ...
25. The criticism I hear most often from those around me is...
26. Three of my positive character traits are...
27. Three of my weaknesses or faults are ...
28. I find it difficult to forgive myself for...
29. I feel unable to ...
30. I wish I could ...
31. I imagine God to be…
33. I feel God in my life when …. and in this way …
34. My life's purpose is ....

35. Now imagine that you are writing to a very good friend whom you have not seen since grammar school, and you want to describe yourself to him. How would you do it?

Having discovered various experiences, which in the past were painful for us or have programmed us in negative ways, we can go on to analyze each experience separately with the help of the following questionnaire.

## ANALYSIS OF UNPLEASANT CHILDHOOD EXPERIENCES

**a.** Describe an **experience** or **general situation** which was unpleasant, that made you feel fear, sorrow, guilt, rejection, danger, injustice, jealousy or any other unpleasant emotion.
**b.** What were the exact **emotions** you felt **as a child**?
**c.** What **thoughts** did you have, or what **conclusions** did you reach **as a child** because of this experience or situation?
**d.** In what way did you **react** then **as a child**?

**e.** What **effect** did this experience have upon you **later** in life, or even today?

**f.** If you could have been absolutely open and honest at that time, what would you have said to your parents, teachers, God or to others who played a part (or who were with you) in this event or in this situation concerning:

1. What you **felt**?
2. Your **needs** and **desires**?
3. What you **wanted** them to do or not do?

(Write the answers in the second person, as if you were speaking directly to them or writing them a letter).

When you finish with one experience or situation, go on to another and another, answering the same questions.

## EXPRESSING THE EMOTIONS OF OUR CHILDHOOD YEARS

Once we have established contact with some of the unexpressed emotions, needs and beliefs of our childhood years, the next stage is to express and release them **without**, of course, **hurting others**. Some ways in which we can do this are listed here.

**1. Write letters** to the people who played an important role in the unpleasant and pleasant experiences of your childhood (parents, teachers, uncles, aunts, siblings, grandparents, others). We will not necessarily send these letters. We simply need to write them, in order to recognize and express what is hidden within us.

**a.** Communicate totally, **openly** and **honestly**.

**b.** Add new **thoughts** and **feelings** each day.

**c.** Do not concern yourself with chronological order.

**d.** Express how you **felt at that young age** (not how you see it or explain it now).

**e. Release and express** your negative and positive feelings.

**f. Express the needs, feelings, desires and thoughts you had at that time.**
We will also want to express our positive feelings, love and gratitude.

**2. Read these letters** to someone who is experienced in active listening and psychodrama.

**a.** If you find that reading these letters causes strong feelings, take time to express and release those feelings before you continue reading. You may then need to switch to an **emotional release technique**. Do not keep these emotions locked inside you.

**b.** You may need to read these letters **additional times** until the emotional charge is released. You can read it as many times as necessary until you are able to read it without feeling upset about the letter's content.

**3.** Below is a more detailed **questionnaire** that will help with the clarification and expression of exactly what we felt, needed and believed as children. It is best if we write with the **opposite hand** than the one with which we usually write. In this way, we can more easily connect with the weakness, difficulty and vulnerability we experienced in those childhood years. It also stimulates the opposite side of the brain, bringing more memories to the surface.

### Questions which aid in expressing our feelings as children

We imagine that one of the persons who played an important role in our childhood experiences is asking us these questions. We answer the questions **separately for each person** with whom we want to communicate.

It does not matter if the soul we are writing to has left his or her physical body. It does not matter whether the other can fully understand what we are writing. We are not writing this to give it to anyone (although, if we feel that it will help the other, we are free to do so). We are writing this in order to discover, understand and express ourselves more deeply.

We have everything to gain by being as honest as possible by answering from our inner child. If there are matters about which our inner child feels differently from our adult, we can express both sides if we choose, but it is best to place emphasis on the inner child's opportunity to express it self.

**These are the questions we are being asked by this person:**

**a.** Tell me, when you were a child, did I do anything which upset you, hurt you or made you feel fear, rejection, guilt, injustice, bitterness, disappointment, guilt, anger or some other negative emotion?

**b.** Please tell about each occasion, situation or behavior separately. Give me the complete details:

    **1.** What exactly did I do or not do?

    **2.** How did you feel?

    **3.** What did you think then?

    **4.** What conclusions did you draw about yourself?

    **5.** What conclusions did you draw about me?

**c.** Did you feel that I had high expectations of you, that I wanted you to be something special? Please explain to me exactly what you believed I wanted you to be physically, mentally, emotionally, socially, spiritually, etc. Perhaps because I praised you for some things, you believed that I accepted and loved you only if you excelled in those areas?

    **1.** How did you feel about that?

    **2.** What did you think then?

    **3.** What conclusions did you draw about your self-worth and love in general?

**d.** What other emotions would you like to express to me?

**e.** What did you need from me then which I did not give you enough of?

**f.** What would you have liked me to do then which I did not do?

**g.** What would you have preferred that I not do which I did?

**h.** Did you ever feel guilt, shame or self-rejection as a child?

> **1.** At what times and for what reasons? What did you do, say or think?
>
> **2.** What did you believe which made you feel guilty?
>
> **3.** Did I, in any way, cause you to feel guilty in those situations? How?
>
> **4.** Were others also instrumental in causing you to feel guilty? Who, and for what?
>
> **5.** What would you like to say to me or to the others concerning those situations?

**i.** What could I do now, to help you feel better?

**j.** What could you yourself do now in order to feel better?

The above questions help us clarify what we need to express and release. The rest of the questions have to do with the process of **transformation,** and are best left until we feel we are ready to accept what happened, to forgive the perpetrators, and move on with a clean state. We will present them here but they should be used only when we are ready

### Questions which aid in transforming:

**k.** What thought-forms (conclusions, beliefs) were created in you then due to those experiences?

**l.** Which of those thought-forms (conclusions, beliefs) have you totally overcome, and which are still alive in you, even to a small degree?

**m.** What do you think was my inner state, which caused me to behave the way I did then? (Remember that we are imagining that the person who may have hurt us with his behavior is asking us these questions.)

**n.** What do you think were the motives, needs, feelings, and beliefs that caused me to behave the way I did then?

**o.** If the spiritual truth that "life gives us exactly what we need as souls in evolution in order to evolve and develop spiritual virtues," is actually true, what could be the lessons or the virtues which you are being asked to work on here?

**p.** What do you need to learn here in order to be happy?

**q.** Which beliefs do you need to change here in order to free yourself from the false beliefs of the past?

**r.** What do you need to do or believe in order to forgive me and free yourself from my presence in your subconscious?

**s.** What do you need to do or believe in order to forgive yourself and enjoy your purity and goodness?

**t.** What changes do you want to make in your lifestyle in order to find harmony and strength? How and when will you make these changes?

## POSITIVE MESSAGES FOR OUR INNER CHILD

The following is a list of possible messages for our inner child, which can be strengthened internally by:

**a. Writing** them in a letter to the inner child

**b.** Introducing them to the inner child while in the **transformation regression.**

**c.** Replaying them our **daily communication** with the inner child.

**d.** Making a **relaxation cassette** with these messages.

**1.** I accept and love you exactly as you are.

**2.** I appreciate you and respect you.

**3.** I feel affection and tenderness for you.

**4.** You are free to do what you like provided you are not hurting anybody.

**5.** You are capable and strong.

**6.** There is an infinite spiritual power within you that protects you from illness, traumas and dangers.

**7.** Your body is healthy, strong and resistant to illness.

**8.** You live in divine justice which brings to you only what is useful for your development.

**9.** You selected your parents and the events of your childhood, and thus you created the perfect conditions for your development.

**10.** There is a Divine Power that guides you from within.

**11.** There is within you a knowing and wise voice that always leads you correctly in your life. Follow it.

**12.** You have the right and the responsibility to express your inner strength and beauty creatively.

**13.** You deserve love and respect from everyone, regardless of your appearance, social position, profession, knowledge, achievements, or what others think of you.

**14.** Your self-worth is the same as that of every other soul, no more and no less.

**15.** No one else can create or be responsible for your happiness, health or success.

**16.** You cannot create or assume responsibility for the happiness, health or success of others.

**17.** You are an eternal, divine consciousness in the process of developing the ability to express the beauty that exists within you.

**18.** Everything is God. There is no one or thing that is not the expression of the one universal consciousness (God). You are no exception.

**19.** It is not necessary to live your life according to the convictions or expectations of your parents or anyone else. Love, respect and help them, but live according to your own principles, needs and convictions.

**20.** Your "parents" are eternal souls in a process of evolution whom you selected to play these roles in this incarnation. Your only real parent is God.

**21.** You have the same worth, wisdom, strength, and rights as the eternal souls who played the roles of your parents.

**22.** Whatever anyone did to harm you was out of ignorance or fear.

**23.** Your parents were once children who were programmed by their parents.

Having healed the inner child through these truths, we are now ready to begin the process of forgiveness, which is our liberation from the past. If upon working with your childhood years you realize that you need to forgive others or yourself, refer to the chapter on forgiveness.

# CHAPTER 24

# FORGIVENESS AND FREEDOM

Forgiveness is a basic prerequisite for freeing ourselves from the past and its stranglehold on us. As long as we resist forgiving others and ourselves for mistakes or actions of the past, we are bound to that past. When we do not forgive others, we ourselves suffer from the negative consequences those negative emotions have on our body and mind. The same is true concerning not forgiving ourselves.

Feelings of resentment, which sometimes lead to disillusionment, anger and even hate, have a very powerful affect on our nervous, endocrine and immune systems. When such feelings also lead to feelings of weakness, helplessness and hopelessness, then our defense system is even more seriously weakened. Scientific studies show that the defense system is frequently weakened after the unexpected loss of someone or something very important to us. That could be a loved one, a job, our appearance, home, social status or anything else which is very important to us and the loss of which we **cannot** accept. In some of these cases cancer or some other immune weaknesses may develop.

Long standing resentment can be transferred into physical terms as arthritic or rheumatic problems. This transferal of specific emotions into physical phenomena is an extremely interesting field that will gain much more attention in coming years as science will be forced to investigate it.

Thus when we hold on to resentment, anger or hate we harm ourselves. Those feelings exist in **our** body; they affect **our** liver, our kidneys, our heart, our blood vessels, **not** the other's. They inhibit **our** happiness, not the other's. They limit our reality. We are **harming ourselves** with these feelings. When we feel hurt by some life event, such as the loss of a loved one or something else very important to us, what do we gain by holding on to the past, concentrating with bitterness on the injustice of life? Does life suffer or do we suffer?

A natural conclusion to our work on the inner child would be to forgive ourselves and others for all that has happened and move on into the present.

## FIVE STEPS OF FORGIVENESS

Forgiveness, however, should **not be superficial or rushed**. Many, when they start this work, believe that they have nothing to forgive. We may have forgiven consciously but our subconscious may have stored up feelings of which we have no awareness.

We have found that the process of real forgiveness has five stages:

**1.** We must first **get in touch with the feelings** of hurt, bitterness, injustice, anger, guilt or shame still present in our inner child.

**2.** We will then need to **express and release those feelings** in the various ways mentioned in previous chapters. (Letters, psychodrama, catharsis techniques etc.)

**3.** When we have discharged the energy associated with these emotions (which might take from a few days to a few years), then we are ready to move on to the stage of **understanding**. Understanding has two aspects.

    **a.** We need to understand that the **others live in ignorance** of their real divine nature and that their actions and behaviors are based on fear and insecurity and their need for self-affirmation.

    **b.** We also need to understand that we exist and are evolving in a universe with divine laws, that **allow to happen to us only what is perfect for our spiritual growth process**. Thus no one could ever have done anything to us, which was not part of a just and wise system designed for our growth. In the same way, we could not have ever done anything to anyone that was not actually what he or she needed for his or her growth process.

This truth does not prevent us from expecting and asking people to behave towards us with respect. Nor does it absolve us from the basic moral code of doing to others only what we would like them to do to us. It does mean, however, that we can forgive the others and ourselves for the ignorance of our past, from which we are now seeking to free ourselves.

**4.** Having understood, then we are ready to **forgive** others and ourselves.

**5.** The last stage is to feel **love** for that person and wish for his or her best possible growth.

The messages for the inner child listed in the chapter on the inner child are basic spiritual truths which can help in this understanding process.

## LETTERS OF FORGIVENESS

Just as we earlier wrote letters expressing our complaints, hurt and anger, now we can write letters of understanding and forgiveness.

In such letters we release them from every responsibility for whatever may have happened to us, and take total responsibility for our reality, remembering that what has happened is part of a wise and just system of inner growth. We may or may not actually give these letters to the other. This is up to each individual.

This does not mean that we cannot take measures so that whatever happened does not occur again. What this does mean is that we no longer hold negative feelings towards this person, and can comfortably be in his or her company if necessary.

## THE MAIN OBSTACLES TO FORGIVING

We sometimes have difficulty forgiving for the following reasons:

**a.** We still **feel vulnerable** towards this person and fear being hurt again, and thus we want to keep a distance. Not forgiving gives us an excuse for keeping this person out of our heart. Usually, in such a case, we subconsciously need to maintain a negative image of this person, remembering only his or her negative traits and ignoring his positive ones. In this way we can justify holding on to our negative feelings and not forgiving. This is a state is unnatural for our inner self, which seeks unity and love.

**b.** Another obstacle is that we **confuse forgiving someone with admitting that he is or was right** and thus we were wrong. We believe that only one person in a conflict can be right. We believe that if we forgive him, it is like saying, "you were right and I was wrong".

We need to cultivate the truth that there are many perceptions of any situation and that we can forgive someone even when he is clearly wrong. That is what forgiveness is all about. Usually we want the other to admit he was wrong. Real forgiveness does not make that a prerequisite. It forgives even when the other does not see his mistake. Of course, we will protect ourselves from further harm.

**c.** In some cases not forgiving someone is a defense mechanism which we use in order to "cover" ourselves. For example, **not forgiving someone may serve our need to control him**. As long as we do not forgive and he is to "blame", we may be able to get him to do various things that we desire, as he seeks our forgiveness.

**d.** Another case would be that by blaming another we can have an **excuse for not getting our lives together**. The supposed reason why we cannot be creative or productive or take responsibility for our lives is that the "others are to blame". Thus we subconsciously have every thing to gain by keeping the others in the "guilty" verdict.

## TRUTHS WHICH AID FORGIVENESS

Some truths which will help us forgive others are (some are based on various spiritual beliefs or Christian concepts which might not be acceptable to you):

**1.** All events occur according to wise and just divine laws that bring me exactly what I need at every stage of my evolutionary process in order to learn the next lesson.

**2.** Others are simply actors in my life drama, the script of which I write daily.

**3.** Others are the hands of the divine showing me the lessons I need to learn.

**4.** All are souls in evolution, whose negative behaviors are a result of their ignorance and fear.

**5.** Forgiving does not mean saying that what the other did was right, it simply means that I forgive his ignorance and weakness as a fellow soul in the evolutionary process.

**6.** Forgiving does not make me vulnerable. Still needing security, affirmation or love from the other make us vulnerable. Forgiving and loving without needing anything from the other is my real protection.

**7.** I am the sole creator of my reality. I abuse others when I hold them responsible for what I create.

**8.** I have the power to create my life and need not hide behind excuses that I cannot because of something which others have done or are doing.

**9.** As souls in the process of evolution we all make many mistakes. This is natural. What is unnatural is to not forgive ourselves and others for these mistakes.

**10.** All are aspects a divine creation. Although they may not realize it, the divine is functioning through them. Not forgiving them, is a failure to forgive the divine.

And Christ's words:

**11.** "Let he who has not sinned, throw the first stone."

**12.** "Judge not, that you be not Judged."

**13.** "You will be judged with the strictness with which you have judged."

**14.** Peter asked Christ, "How many times should we forgive someone for what he has done, seven times?"

Christ answered, " No Peter, **Seven times seventy times.**"

## FORGIVENESS PSYCHODRAMA

After having worked on forgiving through writing, we can then move on to doing so verbally. We can seek someone experienced in active listening and psychodrama to play the part of the individual who we want to forgive. Our guide listens as we express what we have to say.

If the message is not complete, our guide uses active listening in order to help us give a fuller more complete message. If the facilitator has doubts about the message, he or she can change roles and do **reverse psychodrama**, asking us to play the role of the person being forgiven. Our guide will then simply repeat the message as he or she heard it from us, so we can hear our message from the point of view of the person receiving it. This allows him to determine the purity and humility or not of the message.

This forgiveness psychodrama can also be done with a picture or a wall, or if we are forgiving ourselves, with a mirror.

## FORGIVENESS RELAXATION

**a.** After creating a state of **deep relaxation**, bring to your mind one by one the various negative feelings that you have been having about specific events or problems in your life. **If you are holding negative feelings towards anyone**, then bring that person to your mind and experience those feelings. Imagine yourself expressing to the other how you are feeling. Explain to him or her why you are feeling that way, how you have been hurt and disappointed. Explain how you didn't expect what happened, and how you would really have liked things to have happened differently. Express yourself in your mind as clearly as you can, not only your anger, but also your feelings of hurt and vulnerability.

**b.** Once you have mentally expressed your feelings (or if you no longer have such feelings), move on to the stage of understanding where you realize that these persons have acted out of weakness, fear and ignorance. There is no reason to condemn them. They have made a mistake. We too make mistakes. **Forgive** them and let go of your negative feelings. Forgive them and create if possible positive feelings towards them. Realize that they, like you, are in a process of evolution. They cannot be perfect. They will make mistakes.

**c.** Realize that **you too are a soul in the process of evolution** and that in truth, nothing can really harm you. You are indestructible and self-sufficient. Feel strong, large, safe and secure and forgive the other, realizing that your happiness and security cannot really depend on someone else.

**d.** Realize too that there is a universal law of cause and effect and that **nothing could ever happen to you if you did not deserve it, if it was not useful for your evolutionary process.** Realize that, in fact, no one has ever done you an injustice. For some reason, it had to happen in that way regardless if you are able to understand why.

**e.** Thus while we are in the relaxation, we imagine ourselves forgiving the other and accepting him. We can imagine that we are at good terms with each other. If you feel ready, you can even imagine that you are embracing, making up and experiencing love and harmony between you. If this is difficult, you can at least wish them to be healthy and happy in their lives. Do this for all the people in your family (independent as to whether you feel that you have serious problems with them). Do this with coworkers or anyone else who has been close to you and has had the opportunity to hurt you, or disappoint you.

**f.** Work on each person and each event separately and specifically. When you have difficulty forgiving a specific person, spend some time on him or her in your relaxation on a daily basis until you overcome your inner resistance. This will do wonders for your own health and vitality.

Doing this daily will free us from many negative emotions.

## RETURN TO EXPRESSION & RELEASE

If at any point in our forgiveness process, we discover what we are actually not ready because we are still angry or hurt, then we can revert to the previous stages, giving emphasis to expression and release of negative feelings, until we are ready. This may also happen while writing a letter of forgiveness, or in a psychodrama or relaxation. Just switch gears and start the releasing process for whatever is coming up. Then, when ready, continue with the forgiveness process. We release, however, not on the others, but on our own, crying, shouting, hitting a pillow etc.

## FACE TO FACE

When you are really ready to forgive and love, then you are ready to **communicate directly** with the persons with whom you want to correct your relationship.
**a.** If they are presently living you can write a letter, telephone or visit.
**b.** If they have left their bodies you can write a letter, or communicate with them mentally in a relaxation or meditation technique.
You do not need to actually say the words, "I forgive you for your mistakes" for this may insinuate that they were wrong, something which may not be true for them. We can simply express our **need to recreate our relationship.**

## FORGIVING OURSELVES

This whole process of forgiving others must also be applied to forgiving ourselves if we want to be totally free from the grip of the past. The same steps must be taken.

**1. Remembering** or discovering the **events** which may have caused us to feel guilt, shame or self-rejection.

**2. Expressing and releasing** the emotions associated with those events, which in some cases could be remorse and pain about our mistakes, and in other cases hurt and anger towards others who programmed us in this way.

**3. Understanding** that we are in a process of evolution and that we obviously cannot be perfect and that we are not creating what happens to others. Nothing could happen to anyone that is not a part of his or her evolutionary process.
Of course, that does not free us from the responsibility for our selfish or immoral actions. We are responsible for our actions and must free ourselves from the ignorance and fear, which lead us to those actions. The event, however, could not have occurred to that specific person, if it was not a part of his or her evolutionary process.

**4. Ask forgiveness of others** and / or declare to others that we no longer accept the false social programming which has made us feel shame or guilt until now.
You will remember that we have dedicated a whole chapter to self-acceptance, where we present a list of possible reasons why we might have felt shame or guilt

in the past and especially in the childhood years. These reasons were then broken into two categories, those feelings based on false social programming and those based on an actual conflict with our conscience.

**a.** In those cases where we will discover that our guilt or shame were based on actions in disharmony with our conscience, we ask for forgiveness.

**b.** In other cases where we realize that our self-doubt was created by false social programming, we subsequently declare our freedom from such false beliefs.

**5. We then move on to forgive, accept and love ourselves** as we are at this stage of our evolutionary process.

## RESEARCHING GUILT, SHAME AND SELF DOUBT

The **Research technique**, which was described in chapter on self-acceptance, can be applied here for discovering the moments and situations that trigger our feelings of self-doubt. Two people will be required as described.

Some possible phrases that can be used are: (We use four different words here because each word might bring up different answers for different persons. One can use the four words together or alternately or use one word for a few minutes and then do on to the other words.)

1. **I** feel **guilt, shame, self-doubt** or **self-rejection** when ....
2. **They have programmed me** to feel guilt, shame, self-doubt or self-rejection when ....
3. My **inner child** has been programmed to feel guilt, shame, self-doubt or self-rejection when ....
4. **In the past** I have **felt guilt, shame, self-doubt or self-rejection when...**
5. That which I would like to **hide from others** is ...
6. That which I would like to **hide from God** (imagine that you actually can) is

These six phrases can be used for about five minutes each as they might bring up different revelations.

Remember that, in this technique, the subject should keep repeating the phrase, even when he or she does not have an answer in mind, and allow the answer to flow out by spontaneously. The subject should not be silent for over a minute. Also it is perfectly all right to repeat the same answer more than once. This has significance.

As a result of this exercise we will have a list of reasons why we or our inner child have felt these emotions in the present or past.

We can also go back and check our answers to those questions in the chapters on **Self-acceptance** and **Healing the Inner Child** so as to discover the stimuli of the past and present which cause self doubt, shame or guilt and then move on through the process described below.

# ANALYSIS OF MOMENTS IN WHICH WE FEEL OR HAVE FELT SHAME OR GUILT OR DOUBT OF YOUR SELF-WORTH.

## A.   When we are controlled by social programming.

We select from our **list of reasons** why we or our inner child feel self-doubt those, which we now realize were the results of false social programming?

**1.** Now we write the **letter of declaration** (mentioned in the chapter on self-acceptance) to those who programmed us in this way and explain to them with love that we no longer believe that our self-worth is associated with those conditions, which we learned from them. (Read again the details concerning this declaration.) While writing this declaration we might discover that a particular behavior actually belongs in the second category mentioned below concerning our conscience. In such a case we simply move it to that list and work on it later.

**2.** Now we can make the declaration as a **psychodrama** explaining these same truths to another person, preferably experienced in psychodrama and active listening. We need to express clearly and affirmatively that we do not believe these beliefs which once limited our self-acceptance.

**3.** We can do the same speaking to a picture or the wall, imaging that we are speaking to those from whom we received these beliefs.

**4.** We can also do this psychodrama with a group of people who can play the members of our family.

**5.** Finally we can speak with those persons themselves (if they are still in their physical bodies) and explain with love what we have decided. Remember this does not mean rejecting them, nor does it mean that they need to agree with us.

## B.      When we are in conflict with our conscience.

Now we address ourselves to those situations in which we continue to believe that we were **actually immoral, wrong, ego-centered or in conflict with our conscience.** As we do this analysis, we may actually come to the conclusion that a particular behavior, which we are working on, does not belong to this category, but the one above. In such a case, we add it to the list above and to our declarations.

**1.** What do we actually believe which makes us conclude that we were out of harmony with the divine laws at that moment?

**2.** What needs, emotions or beliefs caused us to act in that way?

**3.** How did we feel then about what we did (or did not do)?

**4.** How do we feel now about what we did (or did not do)?

**5.** Do we believe that we must atone for this behavior? If so, what do we believe we must do in order to finish with this and feel at peace with ourselves?

**6.** Do we want to free ourselves or inner child from these feelings, or do we feel that we must feel guilty, that we shouldn't be allowed to feel okay? Do we believe that we must suffer?

-----------------------

For those who believe in God

**7.** Do we believe in Repentance, Confession and Holy Communion? If so would we like to do that or something similar?

**8.** Do we believe that God's love is with conditions and that we are not worthy of His love? Or do we believe that His love is unconditional and that He loves us with all our mistakes and "sins"? What do we believe about this subject?

-----------------------

**9.** What do we need to do in order to reestablish our feelings of innocence, purity and self worth?

**10.** When, where and how will we do this.

**11.** Would we like to communicate with the others involved and express something to them? What would we like to say or ask?

**12.** Now we can write letters asking forgiveness from those persons whom we believe we might have harmed in some conscious or unconscious way. These letters can be written to:

    **a.** Others

    **b.** God

    **c.** Yourself

## ASKING FOR FORGIVENESS

It is not easy for most of us to ask for forgiveness, even when we know we have behaved egotistically. This is a humbling experience that will require that we realize that we are in a process of evolution that requires greater freedom from our ego and its fears. If we are attached to our ego and how others perceive us, we will never be able to go forward. This is why most religions give so much importance to humility and repentance. This humility is not meant to be a self-rejecting attitude, but simply the realization that we are not these personalities which have so many weaknesses, and that only by seeing and acknowledging their faults and weaknesses, can we ever get free from the dictatorship of our ego.

If we cannot acknowledge our mistakes and weaknesses, and ask forgiveness for them, we will never get free from them. How far each of us wants to go in the process of asking forgiveness is a personal matter. We might ask forgiveness for various reasons. Some possibilities are:

**1.** For any behavior, conscious or unconscious, voluntary or involuntary, which may have caused them emotional, or physical pain or damage.

**2.** For any negligence, omission, indifference or lack of sensitivity which may have caused the same.

**3.** For being superficial or ego-centered.

**4.** For not being there for them when they needed us.

**5.** For not understanding their needs and / or feelings.

**6.** For negative feelings and thoughts we might have had occasionally towards them.

**7.** For caring more about ourselves than for them.

**8.** For not behaving towards them as we would like them to behave to us.

**9.** For forgetting that they are incarnations of the divine and not behaving towards them with the appropriate love and respect.

Some of these reasons might seem exaggerated, but some of us actually feel guilty about these behaviors.

## COMMUNICATING

Now that we have established the reasons why we feel less than totally pure and lovable, we can ask forgiveness in the following ways.

**1. Letters** asking for forgiveness from others, God and ourselves

**2. Psychodrama** in which a psychologist or facilitator plays the role of the person we want to ask forgiveness from and does active listening while we ask for forgiveness. The person doing the active listening should verify that the questions in the above questionnaire **Analysis of Moments in Which We Feel or Have Felt Shame, Guilt or Self-doubt**, are been answered as well as possible.

**3.** The same **psychodrama** can be done with a picture or a wall.

**4.** We can then go **directly to that person** and ask forgiveness verbally or if we feel more comfortable with a letter.

**5.** Repentance, Confession and Holy Communion can be very healing for those who believe in it.

## FORGIVING OURSELVES

The next stage is to understand and forgive ourselves.

**1.** This can be done through **reverse psychodrama** in which the facilitator plays us and we play the role of those from whom we are asking forgiveness. The facilitator asks forgiveness from us explaining all that we had expressed earlier. We then forgive the facilitator, or in other words, ourselves.

**Remember** that **we do not need the other's forgiveness**, we need only to be able to **ask** for forgiveness. If we have asked for forgiveness and the other is not ready to forgive, this is no problem for us. We have done our work and we are free and with a clear conscience. He has the right to suffer, holding on to it if he wants to.

**2.** We can do what ever we can on the practical level **to correct any wrong** that we have caused. We might need to return some money or help someone in some way.

**3.** We may decide to **do something selfless** so as to counter our self-centeredness such as serve the poor, the orphans, the blind, the elderly etc. It is best if we do this as anonymously as possible.

Remember that we are not doing this to gain merit points with God, so that we can get into heaven. We are doing this because we will then **be freer from the main source of all our problems** and the main obstacle towards happiness and evolution - our self-centeredness.

**5.** We can **write a letter to our inner child** explaining to him the various truths concerning his divine origin and divine destination.

**6.** We can remind ourselves frequently through written affirmations, deep relaxations and signs and note of the following **logical and spiritual truths.**

### TRUTHS FOR SELF FORGIVENESS

### Warning

The following truths can be misunderstood, misapplied and used as excuses for egotistical behavior. No truth should lead us to become indifferent to how our actions might affect others. Nor should they allow us to behave towards them in ways in which we would not like them to behave towards us.

These truths are there to help us get free from the guilt, shame and doubt of the past, not to give license to do whatever we like in the future.

**1.** All happens according to a divine plan, which brings to all exactly what we need at every stage of our evolutionary process in order to learn the next lesson. I may, in some cases, have been the instrument for that learning process for others. Thus, I am not the creator of their reality, but I can ask forgiveness for any selfish behaviors or negative emotions that I have had towards them.

**2.** Others are simply actors in each person's life drama, the script of which each of us writes daily for ourselves.

**3.** I, as all others, am a soul in evolution, who occasionally acts negatively out of ignorance and fear.

**4.** Asking forgiveness does not mean that I am evil, but that I recognize my ignorance and want to get free from it. Admitting it is the first step towards that freedom.

**5.** Asking for forgiveness does not demean me, but rather, frees me from the illusion on my ego.

**6.** Each is the sole creator of his reality. I create no one else's reality.

**7.** Each has the power to create his life and need not hide behind excuses that he cannot because of something that I or others have done or are doing. I refuse to be emotionally blackmailed by such situations.

**8.** As souls in the process of evolution we all make many mistakes. This is natural. What is unnatural is to not forgive ourselves and others for these mistakes.

**9.** I am a divine creation. The divine is functioning through me. Not forgiving myself, is to not forgive the divine.

**10.** Let he who has not sinned, throw the first stone. Who is there to judge me?

**11.** God's love for me is unconditional. I am loveable as I am, with all my mistakes.

**12.** God has created me with my weaknesses. I cannot be judged for what has been divinely created. My destiny, however, is to free myself from my selfishness and ego-centeredness which are based on illusion.

**13.** Peter asked Christ, "How many times should we forgive someone for what he has done, seven times?" Christ answered, " No Peter, Seven times seventy times." This also applies to ourselves.

**14.** I love and accept myself exactly as I am.

**15.** I appreciate and respect myself.

**16.** There is within me an all-wise voice that leads me.

**17.** I have the right and the responsibility to express my inner beauty and creativity.

**18.** I deserve everyone's love and respect, regardless of my appearance, social position, profession, knowledge, achievements and of what others think of me.

**19.** My self worth is the same as that of every other soul, no more no less.

**20.** I am an eternal, divine consciousness in the process of developing the ability to express the beauty that exists within me.

**21.** Everything is divine. There is no one or nothing that is not the expression of the one universal consciousness (God) - I am no exception.

**22.** It is not necessary to live my life according to the convictions or expectations of my parents or of others. I can love, respect and help them, but live according to my principles, needs and convictions.

**Remember not to misuse these truths**, but do use them properly to free yourself from the past and from the illusion of the ego.

## ALIGNING OUR BEHAVIOR WITH OUR CONSCIENCE

**Another basic aspect of self-forgiveness is to make adjustments in our behavior so that it is in harmony with our conscience. This means discovering the emotions, beliefs and needs which have caused in the past to behave in ways, which we ourselves do not condone. We then need to move forward and transform those beliefs and their subsequent behaviors.**

We all have so much to gain by freeing ourselves from the past through forgiving others and ourselves, and moving on.

# CHAPTER 25

# COPING WITH THE DEPARTURE OF LOVED ONES

The emotions which we experience upon the death of a loved one or in any major loss such as divorce, loss of job or a part of the body, have an intensity and power of their own. For this reason we are attending to this in a separate chapter.

Without a doubt, the most painful experience in life is the loss of a loved one. The most devastating for most people is the loss of a child or a spouse. Over the years, I have had the fortune to conduct seminars on death and immortality, and also support groups for those who have recently lost loved ones.

I am very grateful to all those who have attended and taught me by sharing their emotions, experiences and insights through the various stages of coping with this extremely painful and often totally overwhelming event.

I would like to share with you here some thoughts about what I learned about coping with the death of loved ones throughout these years.

## EMOTIONS FREQUENTLY EXPERIENCED

Before discussing these emotions, I would like to clearly state that I respect the depth and strength with which they can flood our being. Thus, when I point out other ways of looking at what is happening, it is not because I do not recognize the power of these emotions nor do I claim that we can easily change perspective. The fact, however, is that our evolutionary process demands that we begin to perceive ourselves, life and death in ways more aligned with the truth of our immortal nature. We need to transcend the limits created by our exclusive identification with our bodies and minds.

**1.** The **pain** of losing a loved one is similar to losing a part of our body. It hurts. We feel a part of our own selves is missing. It is simply inconceivable to us that our loved one simply does not exist anymore - as a body. We expect at any moment to hear or see him or her again.

What can we do? At first, there is not much that we can do but simply observe, experience and express what we feel. The more we allow ourselves to express this pain, the more quickly it will exhaust itself.

We hurt. This is the truth. Nothing can change this except for a strong belief in the truths of life. If we do not already have this deep faith, it will be difficult for us to suddenly acquire it now. Thus, we are left with experiencing and expressing our pain.

We could find someone professionally trained to listen to and facilitate our emotional expression and externalization. Meeting with him or her once a week can help us acknowledge and release our feelings. In addition to pain, we may feel fear, anger, guilt, jealousy, bitterness, etc. As we discuss each of these feelings, we need to accept them before they can pass on.

We can express them verbally, in written form, through movement or crying, or perhaps by emoting sounds or hitting a pillow. It is best not hold back our tears or our pain at this point.

In this way, the storm of emotions will pass much more quickly so we will be ready to accept what has happened and get on with our life.

In each case, there will be specific spiritual and emotional lessons or opportunities, but we cannot gain from these until we first discharge our emotions, pain, hurt and anger.

Once that is done, our loss becomes our gain. Our pain becomes the triggering process that opens the door toward spiritual dimensions. We now feel the need to learn the truth about life and ourselves; the truth that relieves all pain, all fear; Christ's Truth "which will set you free."

**2.** We can **fear** that we will not be able to continue living without the person whom we've lost. This applies especially to widows who have been programmed to believe they are weak and need a husband in order to be safe, secure or socially accepted. It also applies to all situations in which we feel that we need that other person emotionally, physically, socially, mentally, economically or in any other way.

The truth is that losing a loved one is an excellent spiritual opportunity to develop inner strength, security, worthiness and self-respect. It may take some time to overcome the fear, but as it gradually subsides, we will be much stronger because of this loss. Each loss of external support is an opportunity to find inner strength.

**3.** We might feel **injustice** and **bitterness** that "Life" or God took our loved one. This is more intense when the departed one was young, a child or a spouse in the prime of life.

We cry, "WHY? Where is the justice? Why my child? Why my beloved spouse?

Why has this happened to me? What have I done to deserve this? What did my loved one do to deserve this? What am I being punished for? I have done nothing to deserve this!"

Such an experience is obviously a very trying test of our faith in God and in the wisdom of Divine Justice. Many of us have lost our faith in and love for God in such moments. Remembering how Job and Abraham handled their tests may help us cultivate that faith which we are often lacking.

When we cry "WHY?" and rightly so, let us do it with all our might, demanding an answer! Then afterwards, let us then sit quietly alone with our eyes closed and **be willing to hear the response**. If we shout "WHY?" as an accusation, then we, in all fairness, must give the accused party the chance to answer and explain. Thus, after each "WHY?", let us sit quietly and be receptive, allowing our minds to be open so we may hear the answers. There **are** answers if we want to hear them. They may not come at the moment we are sitting. They may come after some time when we are watching a TV show, listening to the radio, talking with a friend, reading a book (perhaps this book), walking in nature, taking a bath, envisioning a dream, meditating, praying, or doing nothing at all.

They may come after many years, when our pain and anger have subsided enough to allow the truth to rise up from within. The truth is always there. We may not be ready to see it, because no one has ever helped us to be ready, because we live in a death denying – non-believing society.

Thus, our loved one's death will eventually become an avenue toward greater understanding of the nature of reality and the laws of the universe. Our pain becomes a motivating force, pushing us toward the realization that **there is a perfect and just divine plan governing birth, death and all between**. We will then realize that our loved one's death was no accident, nor an injustice, but exactly what we both chose as souls in order to grow spiritually.

That does not mean that our loved one sacrificed his or her life so we could wake up spiritually. He or she got out of the "game of life" early and is the lucky one who had fewer lessons to take. We are staying, suffering and absorbing the lessons. What has happened was perfect for our mutual evolution.

We can believe this through faith or understanding of the Universal Laws.


**4.** We might experience **depression** and **disillusionment** that life has no meaning without our loved one. This again is especially true when we have lost a child or spouse who was the "purpose of our lives", who was our main occupation.

We identify with these roles of parent, spouse or child and thus learn to find our identity and meaning in life through them. When the person or persons who played those roles with us suddenly disappears we are left with depression unless we can find a new identity and meaning in life.

This, of course, is a great spiritual opportunity in that we now have the chance to grow and evolve into new and hopefully more universal roles. We have found through the years that four basic goals help people to move forth with their lives more quickly.

One is the goal of **evolution** or self-improvement. Life is meaningful and interesting when we are working on improving ourselves.

The second is **creativity**. We experience joy when we create. Creativity can emerge in all areas of life from drawing, singing, dancing and writing to gardening, cooking, developing a business or bringing up children.

The third is **service**. We feel that our life has meaning when we can be of use to others, when we can make their lives happier or more comfortable in some way.

The fourth is **relationships**, which give our lives meaning, allow us to feel love, share and serve.

We encourage all persons to align their lives with these basic life purposes: evolution, creativity, service and relationship. This is especially important for persons who are in a state of depression.

**5.** We might feel **Guilty** that we did not sufficiently express our love to that person. We might think, "I did not show him enough love. I scolded him too much. I complained too much. I was negative and unpleasant. I never told him how much I loved, respected and appreciated him. I was unpleasant and nagging."

All this may be true, although it is probably not as true as we now imagine it to be. Our loved one may not have experienced us as negatively as we imagine. If, however, we do harbor guilt, there are some solutions.

We can bring that person to mind and imagine that he or she is standing in front of us. (This may require some practice in relaxation, positive projection, or meditation techniques.) We can then communicate mentally with this person, expressing our remorse and regret, and ask for forgiveness. (This can also be done in **written** form.)

I did this with my Father who was murdered. It helped me overcome guilt I felt about not showing him the love and respect I always had for him.

We can also express our hurt, anger, disappointment and any other feelings. We can settle accounts. They hear us, and thus, we can simultaneously forgive and ask forgiveness.

Such an exercise will bring us peace of mind. If we are accustomed to the sacraments of Confession and Holy Communion, we can partake in them as well.

Then let us forgive ourselves and be over with these useless emotions of guilt which do not help anyone at all - not our loved one and certainly not ourselves.

**6.** We might feel **guilty** thinking we could have done more to keep him or her alive. We might think, "I should have taken him to another doctor, to another hospital. If only we had done this other operation. If only I had been there when he died, I could have prevented it. It is all my fault. I am to blame for his death."

Such feelings are common. Let us, however, take a closer look at them. This is like playing God. Am I so godlike that I can keep someone alive? Such thoughts are totally in contradiction with the laws of the universe, which state that each soul (in collaboration with his own self-created divine plan) decides the moment of physical birth and death. No one can create or prevent someone else's death.

I do not believe that the person who shot my father was the cause of his death. I believe that he was simply the means by which my father's death was manifested. I believe that my father, as a soul, had chosen to die in this way on that day, although his conscious mind was totally unaware of this fact. The only thing he said after being shot, as he looked into the eyes of his assailant was, "WHY?"

Yet three days earlier, my mother heard him call out in his sleep, "Ray, Ray watch out he has a gun". Ray was the other professor who was shot by the same student five minutes earlier. The student shot Ray (whom my father was warning in his sleep) and then my father. My father knew in his subconscious mind that he would die on this day, but this remained unknown to his conscious mind.

If we believe in a divine law that dictates that each soul, in collaboration with the Divine, creates its own destiny, how can we believe that someone else is responsible for another's death, even he who pulls the trigger. Thus, how much more unreasonable it is for us to believe that someone died because we did not take him or her to one more doctor, do one more operation, or because we were not there when he or she left the body.

This, of course, does not mean that we should not do whatever we can to save every life. Nor does it mean that we allow those, who harm or kill others, free from justice. It is simply important to remember that when the soul departs, it has nothing to do with us or our presumed negligence. We are obliged to do whatever we can, but then we must accept and offer to the Divine all results. As St. Paul declared, "not a hair moves on the head of man, without His will".

**7.** Some of us might experience **sorrow, disappointment, disillusionment and bitterness** that we do not have the emotional support we expected from friends and relatives. The days immediately after the funeral are filled with numerous mind-distracting activities. Many come to express their condolences. Perhaps they may offer various types of help. There are many official papers to be filled out, as well as many matters, economic and otherwise, to be addressed.

Then suddenly one day, all this passes and we are alone perhaps for the first time since our loved one departed. There are no more papers to fill out; no more matters to arrange.

Our friends have their lives to live, with their responsibilities, jobs, families and social engagements. They may feel uncomfortable in our presence, because they do not know what to say or do to help us feel better. They may even feel guilty that they still have their loved ones and are happy. Also, our pain might trigger their fear of losing loved ones, or their pain about the same or other matters.

As a result, they might not enjoy being with us, not because they do not love us or care for us, but because they are unable to face the pain and suffering which permeate our environment. This is especially so when we ourselves are obsessed with talking exclusively about the death of our loved one. The others may sit with us a number times, but eventually they will not be able to hear anymore about something which they have no power to change.

Such a situation may be an opportunity to cultivate understanding toward the others and their difficulties in the face of pain and suffering. It may be an opportunity to overcome the belief that we need others to feel well, to be happy or secure. We can overcome the belief that because we have passed through this terrible misfortune that others are obliged to pay attention to us and to help us, even if we ourselves are not ready to let go of our pain.

If we see people pulling away, it may be that the time has come for us to release our pain and perhaps start helping others. They, too, have their problems. Loneliness can be healed by others reaching out to us or by our reaching out to them.

Gradually, we will get on with our lives and connect with other people. Then our loneliness will disappear. Getting involved in service toward others who are lonely or need some type of selfless service will help considerably.

**8.** We may feel **loneliness**. We may think, "It is difficult to connect with other people. They are not open, not friendly. I have no one to talk to, to share with, to be myself with."

It is natural to feel lonely when we lose a loved one. We experience an emptiness which that person helped to fill. We have learned to fill our emptiness through others or through various stimuli such as TV, newspapers, stimulants, tranquilizers, and activities in general.

That which fills us most, however, is a deep unconditional love relationship. This is healing, supporting and verifying. It gives us a feeling of security and self-worth. It is natural to feel lonely when a person who offered us all that disappears, even if our relationship wasn't perfect.

Loneliness is the «dis- ease» of our times. It has nothing to do with being alone. We could be surrounded by many persons and feel lonely because we cannot be ourselves with them. Likewise, we can be alone in seclusion and feel connected with others, nature or the Divine.

If we can accept loneliness and face it, we might find that we can also feel well alone, or that we can feel comfortable and be ourselves with other persons who we do not know so well.

Another important aspect of facing loneliness is developing a relationship with ourselves. This we can do by actually spending time alone and learning to occupy ourselves and enjoy our solitary moments.

Focusing on our relationship with God through prayer, meditation and other forms of awareness of and communication with the Divine can also be very fulfilling.

Walks in nature can fill that emptiness as we feel our connection with the universe through nature.

And finally, by serving others who are lonely - the poor, the homeless, orphans and the elderly, we fill our emptiness as we fill theirs.

Remember: our loneliness can disappear when others reach out to us, or when we reach out to them.

**9. We could likely feel jealous** that others still have their loved ones and we do not. We have all felt jealousy when someone has something we do not have. Although jealousy is natural, it will not bring our loved one back and we often feel guilty about experiencing those emotions.

Accepting that we are jealous and perhaps allowing ourselves to express it, to confess it to someone we trust, will help us release these feelings.

It is amazing how our feelings gradually deflate when we confess them and share them with someone who can understand. This is an important phenomenon; that when we acknowledge our emotions and express them, that they gradually dissipate.

We often do the opposite. We are afraid to admit our emotions even to ourselves. We fear that if we admit them to others, they will reject us. Such suppression does not work as others sense our emotions anyway.

**This is true of all the emotions we are discussing in this section.** We have everything to gain by recognizing them, admitting them and sharing them with someone who will understand. Also, our feelings will subside as we **get on with our lives** and learn to **enjoy** people and events, having nothing to envy in the others.

In addition, as we learn to believe in the universal rule that "we are given exactly what we need in order to evolve and learn life's lessons," we will be able to accept and be happy with what we have.

If we look objectively, we will see we are better off than a good 80% of our brothers and sisters on this planet.

**10.** It would be natural to feel **anger** toward those who were in some way connected with or "responsible for" our loved one's death. Perhaps a doctor made a mistake, or someone was driving recklessly, and now our loved one is dead.

Our pain demands that we find who has committed this wrong? Who has made this horrible mistake? Who is to blame? Feeling anger, in some cases, serves to divert us from our pain and fear.

This anger might also be directed toward God, who allowed this to happen, and may lead to rejection of God and all which has to do with Him. We think, "If there was a God, He would not have let this happen." We are angry and hurt.

In the case where some human was possibly at fault, we may even feel the need for revenge. We might want to make this person feel the same pain we feel. We think this might lessen our hurt. We cannot think clearly. We simply feel that someone must pay for what has happened here.

In such a case, we must to find someone whom we trust to listen to us and acknowledge our feelings. We need help to see more objectively. We must be careful not to be carried away by the desire for revenge, for it will not remove our pain, nor make our loved one happy where he or she is. For the truth is that no one was responsible for his or her death. That moment and event were chosen by the soul which has left.

As for God, we have already mentioned that this is an opportunity to cultivate real faith. To stop believing in God because He did not do what we wanted Him to is like denying that a person exists because he or she refuses to give us something we ask from him or her.

Our children ask things from us which we choose not to give because we believe or know that it is best for them not to have those things at the present. Should they hate us for this or claim that we do not exist because we do not do what they want?

Our requests are heard, but often losing a loved one is much better for our spiritual evolution and development. It is illogical to say that God does not exist simply because we do not understand what is best for our evolution and want things to remain as they always were in order for us to feel secure and happy.

**11.** We might also feel **anger** toward or **rejection** of our loved one who "chose" to leave the earth plane at this time, leaving us here alone. We may interpret this as a form of rejection, abandonment and lack of love.

We need to recognize, accept, admit and express all these **emotions**. We would do well to seek help in doing so. Then, we need to move on to the next step, which is to investigate and discover the specific **beliefs** that create our pain and other emotions.

We will then be ready to move on to study, believe and employ the **truth** in our lives. The truth is that we are immortal spirits that have temporarily incarnated in the material plane in order to continue our evolutionary process. We lose nothing by leaving. It is also possible that we have agreed that this would happen even before we incarnated into this material plane, that we agreed that he or she would leave and we would stay so we both could learn our respective lessons.

## NEGATIVE THOUGHT FORMS
## ABOUT THE DEATH OF A LOVED ONE

These emotions are the result of various beliefs, programmings or thought-forms that have been instilled into our conscious and subconscious minds. As long as the beliefs are there, the emotions will come forth.

Let us look at some of these beliefs which generate these emotions within us.

**1.** I cannot live without him / her.
**2.** I am not secure without him / her.
**3.** No one else but he or she can give me joy or security.
**4.** My life has no meaning without him / her.
**5.** I want to die; I want to be with him / her.

We have been programmed to believe we must have specific persons close to us who will make us feel secure, happy, worthy, etc. We give these persons the «keys» to our happiness and security. Very likely, there was a time in our lives when we didn't even know them, when we were not with them. Now we cannot imagine ourselves happy without them.

The truth, however, is that we can. The fact that many **billions** of people have lost their loved ones in the past proves this. Each has struggled with these thoughts, but each has moved on to live a normal life when these feelings naturally subsided and the need to continue prevailed. We will eventually move on, just as all those before us have.

We will all lose everyone we know, either through our death or theirs. Each and every one of us will die within the next 70 to 90 years (taking into consideration the small children we know). We will lose everyone and they will lose us. **This is the nature of the physical universe.**

**6.** Death is a bad, painful experience.

This does not seem to be true. All who have died momentarily and returned report that leaving the body is a wonderful and very enjoyable experience. Very few actually wanted to return to the body. We who remain in life continue to suffer and learn lessons. Those who have left are on "vacation" from the school of life.

**7.** I don't have the right to be happy since my loved one has died.
**8.** I will betray my loved one if I allow myself to be happy.
**9.** I will betray my loved one if I love someone else as much as I loved him / her.
**10.** I will betray my loved one if I find a different purpose and meaning in my life.

Our loved ones are immortal spiritual beings who have played various roles with us in various life times in order that we all continue our evolution. Which loved one would we be betraying if we love another one from this life or the previous thousand lives? Have we not then betrayed all our loved ones from previous lives by loving those of this life?

**How can love betray?** Can love be promised to only one aspect of the Divine, or is it for all aspects of the Divine? I am not talking about sex or free sex, but about **love, service and unity.** Can loving or serving another aspect of the Divine ever betray my loved one who has moved on to another dimension? I would simply be loving and serving another aspect of my loved one.

**11.** I have been treated unjustly.
**12.** I am unlucky.
**13.** I am the most miserable person I know.

Every day, 40,000 parents are forced to witness their children's death, because they do not have the means to keep them alive. Yesterday 40,000 children. Today 40,000 children. Tomorrow 40,000 children. The day after tomorrow 40,000 children. This week 280,000 parents will see their children die. This month 1,112,000 parents will suffer their children's deaths. This year 13,440,000 parents will suffer their children's deaths. And next year? And in the 70 years of a normal life, 938,000,000 parents? Here we are not counting all the deaths of those other than children and those caused by wars, accidents, suicides, etc. Need I say more?

This may not soften our pain, but it should remove the false belief that we are unlucky, being treated unjustly or feel the most miserable. Yes, we have pain. No one can deny that, but we are not being treated differently than the rest of creation. Life in the physical body is temporary.

**14.** The other's death is a punishment for him or me.
**15.** I am a sinner; otherwise God would not have punished me in this manner.
**16.** God does not love me since He allowed my loved one to die.
**17.** There is no God; otherwise He would not have allowed my loved one to die.

My perception is that there is no punishment in the universe. There are only **lessons**. God is love. He gains no pleasure in punishing. We create our **evolutionary curriculum** in cooperation with the Divine. It is unfortunate that we interpret opportunities for growth as punishment.

If, as students, we decide to become doctors, we set ourselves up for a number of years of suffering in terms of expenses, limited freedom, and exhausting hours of study and examinations. We do not interpret these as punishment, for we remember that he have chosen this so as to develop the qualities we need in order to become doctors.

It the same way, we, as souls with the goal of manifesting our unlimited divine potential here on earth, program various tests and lessons through which we will be given the opportunity to develop those divine attributes. One of the most difficult, and yet most potentially liberating tests, is the loss of a loved one. It has nothing to do with punishment, neither for us nor for our loved one.

**18.** It is my fault he died. I could have done something more.

We have already mentioned that this thought is in direct violation of the Law of Creation. We create our own physical birth and death. No one can do this for anyone except himself or herself. If our time had not come, not even the greatest mass murder in the world could have touched us. Everyone else would be touched except for those whose hour had not come. We are not in a position to change these events.

**19.** I did not have the chance to correct my relationship with him or her. I feel guilty. I was not entirely correct.

We can still correct this relationship by communicating with our loved one now. When we say communicate, we do not mean go to a medium and have a conversation with him or her. We do **not** recommend that this as a good idea. First of all, many «mediums» are not exactly what they say they are. Secondly, we may not be communicating with our loved one, but rather with some low-level spirit hovering around the earth rather than proceeding on in its evolution. Thirdly, we hold our loved one back by such communications. We call his or her attention toward the Earth level. It is a totally different thing to close our eyes and communicate with our loved one during those first days after his or her departure, and totally another to badger him or her with mediumistic contacts for years after because of our inability to let go.

We can close our eyes, bring our loved one into our awareness and express our feelings. We can forgive and ask for forgiveness, then let go and get on with our lives.

This can be done a few times in the beginning, and then after a few months if we notice that we still have suppressed feelings. After a year or so, we would best let that soul get on with its work, and we with ours.

**20.** He / she deserted me. He / she left me alone.

We do not choose death as a way of deserting another. We have mutually chosen this event for our mutual spiritual benefit.

### Note:

I repeat that I in no way underestimate the pain and strength of emotions we feel when we lose a loved one. This is **completely natural**. Please do not be offended when I encourage us all to let go and move on.

If you are not ready for some of the messages in this chapter or this book, that is perfectly natural. These emotions need time to dissipate. Come back to these pages again after some time; you may perceive them completely differently then.

### POSITIVE THOUGHT FORMS

There are some beliefs or thought forms, which can be very supportive in our effort to cope with the death of a loved one. If you find any of these helpful, write them down with large letters and place them where you can see them often. Feel free to alter them to apply more appropriately to your own specific needs.

You could also make a record with these messages to play while in deep relaxation or as you fall asleep.

**1.** I am an eternal soul and have the power to live an abundant and meaningful life. All is within me.

**2.** My loved one is an eternal, immortal soul who continues to live in another dimension more beautiful than the one in which I currently exist.

**3.** Since my loved one is very well and far closer to his or her true nature and to God, I can be glad for him / her and can give joy to myself and to those around me.

**4.** God is within and around me, so I always feel secure, protected and tranquil.

**5.** Everything happens according to a perfect and just Divine Plan that gives to each of us what he or she needs for his or her evolution as a soul. For some reason, it was best for my loved one to move on to another level of existence. As for my own evolution toward God, it is best that I continue on here, even without him or her.

**6.** Everyone on this earth has lost loved ones (not only me). Also, we will all eventually lose all the people we know because we are only temporarily on this earth and our departure is perfectly natural.

**7.** The departure of the soul from the restrictions of the temporary physical body is a beautiful liberation from a very limited incarnated state.

**8.** The loss of my loved one is a great opportunity for spiritual development through the cultivation of inner power, tranquility, security and self-acceptance.

**9.** I accept the perfection of the Divine Plan, and I forgive God and everyone for what is happening to me. I release all from any responsibility for my reality.

**10.** My loved one would want me to be happy and to continue my life creatively and beautifully.

**11.** I am acceptable, lovable and interesting because of what I am not because of my relationship with someone.

**12.** The loss of a loved one is not related to punishment, but is instead a great opportunity for spiritual development and inner growth.

**13.** I am a pure child of God and He loves me unconditionally.

**14.** No one can be responsible for someone else's death. Each person has selected the hour and the place when he or she will leave. Others are simply the instruments we use for our departure.

**15.** I can, even now, correct my relationship with my loved one with inner concentration and prayer.

**16.** We are all evolving souls, all children of God. I open myself to my brothers in the family of humanity who are now with me on this planet. My loved one would want me to do so.

**17.** I share with others my sorrow and joy. We are one big family of humanity.

**18.** I find meaning in life by serving, creating and evolving. This is why I have come on this Earth.

**19.** Life is a gift of God, and it is my duty to use it for my benefit and that of others.

**20.** Today, 40,000 parents have lost their children. Tomorrow, another 40.000 parents will lose their children. I am not alone in pain. The soul's departure from the physical body is a natural part of life on earth.

**21.** There is only one universal life force, which expresses itself through all beings. The same consciousness that expressed itself through my loved one is now expressing itself through everyone around me. Loving and offering to others, I love and offer to him / her.

### STEPS WE CAN TAKE

**1.** We can **study the spiritual truths** related to the following topics:
    **a.** What is a human being?
    **b.** What is the relationship between the soul and the body?
    **c.** Why does a soul take on a body?
    **d.** What happens when the soul leaves the body?
    **e.** What is the relationship between man, nature and God?

**2.** We can **express our feelings openly** to those who can respect and understand them, even if that means finding a "professional listener" (A priest, minister, psychologist, spiritual teacher or a good friend).

**3.** We can **pray for our loved ones' development** and growth as souls on the dimensions where they are now residing. We can light a candle for them as frequently as we feel the need, sending them energy and love. We do not need to go to the grave. Our loved ones are not there. During the first days, they are most likely wherever we are. They are not attracted to the discarded body, but to those they love. We can ask others to pray for them also. This is important for the first forty days and then less so for another year.

**4.** We can gradually free ourselves from excessive concentration on those who have left this plane and **pay more attention to those who are here** with us. It might be best eventually to remove belongings that remind us of him or her. We can give them to charity or to those who need them or would appreciate them. Their presence around the home will obstruct our gradual detachment and the ability to move forward with our lives (which is what our loved ones would want).

**5.** We can occupy ourselves with meaningful activities four of which are: **a.** Service **b.** Creativity **c.** Evolution - Self knowledge **d.** Conscious Love Relationships

**6.** We need to **be patient with ourselves** and those around us. Overcoming such a shock will usually take time.

**7.** We can **cultivate faith in God** and in ourselves.

**8.** We can **join a group of people** dedicated to the process of growth where we can mutually support each other in this process.

Books by the same author which deal with this subject are:
  **a)** *"The Mystical Circle of Life"*
  **b)** *"Universal Philosophy"*
  **c)** *" Miracles of Love and Wisdom"*

# CHAPTER 26

# HOW TO BECOME REALLY BEAUTIFUL

Everyone wants to be beautiful, to be attractive to others. We also want to be surrounded by beauty, to look at it and enjoy it. What makes something beautiful and how can we ourselves become beautiful?

## OBJECTIVE BEAUTY VS. SUBJECTIVE BEAUTY

We say that **"beauty is in the eyes of the beholder"**. This is certainly true in most instances. We are attracted to some object or person because of a personal subconscious programming which interprets that particular sight as pleasant and beautiful. On the other hand, there also seem to be some cases of objective beauty in which over 90% of the world's population would agree on the beauty of a particular sight.

For example, there are scenes in nature, which few people, if any, would not find beautiful. Most of us find small children, kittens, puppies and young offspring in general attractive. Flowers create the same sense of awe and inner movement for most of us. What do scenes in nature, children, kittens, puppies and flowers all have in common? There are two basic factors.

**1. They are freshly formed from the creative power of the universe.** They are like the young shoots of the plants which come forth in the spring; soft, tender, smooth to the touch and pure, innocent, full of vitality and spontaneity. The life force within them is still radiating externally. It is not yet hidden behind various defense mechanisms. Even thorns, when they first come out of the rose bush, are soft, pliable and pleasant to the touch. But eventually, like all defense mechanisms, they become hard because their purpose is to **repel**. While the rose attracts with its beauty, its protective mechanism, its thorns, repel.

**2. They have no ego defense mechanisms to cover their beauty yet.** The child, kitten and puppy have not yet developed the mechanisms of self-protection or survival. They are still being protected by their parents and feel safe and secure. Nature, of course, does not have an ego in the way man does. **Thus the beauty of the universal creator is still apparent and easy to perceive.**

Nature also exists within **us**. We, too, are products of nature, of the same creative power. But we have separated ourselves. We do not cooperate with the natural flow of nature. We live for ourselves and not for the whole.

In our separateness we feel vulnerable, insecure and alienated from nature, the elements and the people around us. Thus we are forced to build up a protective wall around us in the form of various ego "self-protective" mechanisms. In doing so, we completely cover our **natural inner beauty**. We start to lose our innocence, simplicity, openness, love and thus, our inner natural beauty. We lose contact with these wonderful qualities, which always existed and still exist within the center of our being.

Because we have lost contact with our inner peace, security, love, beauty, and contentment, we pursue these qualities outside of ourselves. We seek security in accumulating money, forming relationships and succeeding professionally and socially. We seek love and approval through doing what we believe others want us to do in order for them to love us. We seek contentment through achieving the goals and prerequisites of success established by society, i.e. money, houses, cars, food, sex, etc. We seek to reestablish our lost attractive power with special exercises to loose flesh from one part of the body and put it on in another. We attempt to restore our lost inner brilliance with creams, colors, powders, jewelry, and fancy clothing.

## SUPERFICIAL BEAUTY vs. INNER BEAUTY

If the love that others have for us is conditional upon our changing and camouflaging ourselves internally and externally, do they love us or a mask that we are creating?

Making ourselves beautiful by changing our appearance chemically or technically is in a way the result of our inability to recognize and externalize our inner natural beauty. We are seeking enhance the appearance of a being which is an expression of the same source which has created millions of breathtakingly beautiful flowers, oceans, mountains, sunsets and sunrises?

Why does Nature's beauty affect us so deeply? Why do we feel such peace, excitement, love, joy, such a need to stay on and absorb it, enjoy it, become one with it, to share it with someone else, to come into erotic union with it? Why?

The **answer** is that we are **reminded of our own natural inner beauty.** We are reminded of our own **Self**.

**We recognize our true Self in absolute beauty, and that is why we are attracted to it.**

But we have buried this real self and our inner beauty under many layers of ego defense mechanisms that imprint themselves on our body and face. Then we are forced to cover these defense mechanisms with artificial means.

## HOW TO BRING FORTH OUR INNER BEAUTY

**1. Re-establish the vitality of the body through natural means.** We are attracted to bodies and minds that are vital and energized. We can understand this by comparing our feelings towards freshly cut flowers as opposed those towards the same flowers a week later after the vital energy has gone out of them.
Our life energy shines out through our eyes, face and skin creating an aura that is felt and enjoyed by all. It is much more pleasant to be with an energized person than it is to be with someone who is tired physically and mentally.

**How can we increase the vitality flowing though our being?**

**a.** We can eat a **pure diet** with as much **live food** as possible. Live food still has vitality, life force in it. Dead meats, fish, white flour, white sugar, white rice, white pastas, canned foods, preserved foods and food cooked days before eaten are all **dead** foods. Fresh vegetables, fruits, nuts, whole grains, sprouts, beans and yogurt are live food. They make us body strong, vital, pure and attractive.

**b.** By **exercising the body** on a daily basis we facilitate the removal of toxins, which cause the body and skin to age more quickly. **When a body is functioning well on the inside it shines on the outside**. Daily exercise also releases accumulating physical and emotional stress, allowing our inner beauty to shine forth, something which is impossible when we are tensed. And, of course, extra flesh is worked off.

**c.** Regular practice of **deep breathing techniques** generates greater flow of vitality throughout all the body ensuring proper functioning of all organs and a glow in the face and eyes.

**d.** Daily practice of **deep relaxation** techniques brings us into contact with the **inner peace,** which is always present in the center of our being. Peace is beautiful to all beings, just as love is beautiful to all beings because it is something which we have great need for, and in truth something which reminds us of the peace and love which exist in the center of our being.

**2. We need to accept our body and personality exactly as they are**. We can begin by realizing that we are acceptable and worthy of love and respect exactly as we are. We have all seen people who, by external superficial standards, are not at all «beautiful» but in spite of that, they attract the love, attention and acceptance of all those around them? These are probably people who have accepted themselves as they are and feel okay about themselves.

**Our beauty does not depend on our external appearance. It depends on how true we are to who we are.** When we seek to alter our appearance it like saying, «I don't feel beautiful, I don't feel my inner beauty, I am not beautiful, I must change myself in some way in order to become acceptable and attractive to others».

The same is true about our personality, which we try to make look more intelligent, more important, more fancy with various lies and half-truths. We need to be ourselves. We are beautiful just as we are.

**Honesty** and **simplicity** are beautiful to all beings. To whom do we feel more attracted? To one who is simple, honest and comfortable to be with, or to one who is trying to be constantly something other than what he or she is and is constantly on guard, playing ego games?

Accepting and loving ourselves exactly as we are allows our natural inner beauty to appear from within. If we are afraid of losing someone's love or attention in the event that we stop altering our appearance, then we need to ask ourselves, "Is that the kind of love I want"? If the other person's love or attention would be affected by your physical appearance, then it is probably not the love that we are looking for and deserve.

**3. We can become pure and innocent like children.** Purity and innocence are beautiful and attractive to all beings. People feel safe, comfortable, at ease with innocence and purity. Purity is both physical and mental. Physical purity means **cleaning the body regularly** on the outside and the inside. Just as we clean our skin every day, the inner organs must be kept clean through pure nontoxic food and occasional fasting with water or juices.

Mental purity means letting go of slyness, bitterness and ulterior motives. It means **forgiving** others for whatever they may have done to us, just as a child forgives and forgets. It means being **honest** and direct in our communications, saying exactly what we feel, think or need and not being indirect or cunning in our attempt to fulfil our needs.

**4. We are beautiful when we are happy, positive and smiling inside and out.** For most people, a smile is beautiful and a frown is ugly. Why? Because happiness is a reflection of contact with our inner self - the source of all happiness. Unhappiness is he result of being lost in the ignorance and pain of the ego. When we smile, we are beautiful, we offer beauty to the world, we allow our inner beauty to flow into the room and world around us. No artificial substance could simulate the power of this natural beauty, which flows from the center of our beings when we are happy and smiling.

**5. Developing contact with our inner Self is essential.** The inner self or soul within each of us is the same Universal Soul, which is the source of beauty in all of nature and in all beings. Through prayer, concentration or meditation we let go of the thoughts and anxieties. We allow our consciousness to experience the peace, bliss and beauty of the inner self, which are then externalized in our body and personality.

This also creates eventually an inner sense of security and self-acceptance which allows us to accept ourselves and let go of the various defense mechanisms which smother our inner beauty and cut us off from our inner peace.

**6. We can cultivate feelings of oneness and love with people and nature.** Everyone loves a lover. Love is beautiful. Unity is beautiful. Beauty is a result of oneness. The oneness we feel in nature is the result of the lack of fear and alienation we experience. When we begin to feel a oneness with the people around us, we manifest the beauty of the truth, that we are all one being in reality.

Obviously making such changes in our lives so as to become more attractive to others would not be the highest possible motive. However, if this is important to us, such a natural solution based on our inner self will be preferable external artificial solutions.

What then, in conclusion, are the ways in which we can make our bodies and personalities manifestations of absolute beauty?

1.      Maintain our **vitality** and **health**.

2.      **Accept** ourselves exactly as we are

3.       Become **pure** and **innocent** like children.

4.      Be **positive**, **happy** and smile inside and outside.

5.      Develop **contact** with the **inner self**.

6.      Develop a feeling of **oneness** and **love** with people
         and nature.

CHAPTER 27

# KEEPING OUR ENERGY
# HIGH AND HARMONIOUS

The quantity and quality of our energy flow deeply affect our emotions, thoughts and reactions. The quality of our relationships, productivity, creativity and health all depend upon creating a high level of harmoniously flowing energy.

As methods for creating a positive energy flow are explored in depth in other books by this and many other authors, we will briefly mention here a few factors that affect our energy flow.

The following techniques and ways of life will aid us in building a freer and more positive energy flow.

You can find much more information on all these subjects on our web site *www.HolisticHarmony.com*.

**1. PROPER DIET:** Few of us realize the powerful effect of a proper diet not only on our physical health, but also on our emotional, mental and spiritual states. A pure diet can create greater health, more positive emotional states, clearer mental functioning, and increased spiritual attunement.

This personal harmony leads to more harmonious relationships, as well as greater effectiveness, creativity and productivity in all endeavors.

**2. VITAMINS:** Our way of life, in conjunction with the depletion of the soil, leaves many of us deficient in essential vitamins and minerals. Although I do not believe in regular consumption of supplements, I have seen periodic intake do wonders in rebuilding the psychosomatic system. More specifically in the case of emotional problems, the B-complex vitamins help strengthen a weakened nervous system. If we suspect our emotional state may also be the result of our worn down nervous system, we might benefit from a strong multivitamin and mineral supplement for one month. In some cases, this provides immediate first aid, which then leads to an optimistic feeling that the problem can be solved.

**3. FASTING:** Fasting is not the most popular solution for emotional disturbance. In some cases, however, where we suspect that our negativity may also be associated with a toxic body or food allergy, we can dramatically improve how we feel with short one-day fasts, or a mono-diet in which we eat only one type of food, such as only apples, watermelon or grapes. Some of us may experience an increase of symptoms as a healing crisis is produced. A beginner in this process should be assisted by an experienced guide.

**4. HERBS or FLOWER ESSENCES:** Some herbs can be very calming and / or invigorating, offering an extra boost which may give us the needed optimism we need to make internal changes. Bach Flower Essences, as well as other essences, have proven especially beneficial to those who need help in overcoming emotional mechanisms.

**5. DAILY PHYSICAL EXERCISE:** The body is a **live machine**, and like all machines, it needs to move or it will begin to develop problems. Exercise is essential not only for a healthy muscular, skeletal and circulatory system, but also for a relaxed nervous system and balanced endocrine system. This systemic harmony is necessary for emotional and mental peace. I have seen many negative emotional states greatly reduced, or even completely removed, due to daily exercise.

Especially important in our attempt to strengthen the nervous system are those exercises that increase the blood supply to the brain.

**6. BREATHING TECHNIQUES** are essential for the abundant flow of vital energy throughout the body and mind. Bioenergy is the basis of all physical and mental functions. When this energy is low or not allowed to flow freely through the body-mind structure, the results include illness, disharmony, and negative emotional and mental states.

Breathing exercises are one of the most effective ways to increase our energy level and keep it steady and harmonious so we will be less susceptible to low emotional states or illness. We should, however, have the guidance of person experienced in breathing techniques before we begin.

**7. DAILY DEEP RELAXATION** will calm the muscles, nerves and all other bodily systems, and thus rejuvenate the body and the mind. Our hectic lifestyle makes us vulnerable to a wide variety of psychosomatic illnesses that result from our lack of inner peace, agitated nervous systems and worn out immune systems. Deep relaxation, in conjunction with the above-mentioned techniques, contributes to the development of strong and healthy immune system as well as a form of self-therapy from psychosomatic illnesses.

We all have much to benefit from stopping at least once per day, lying down on our backs (or sitting straight in a chair), and **consciously relaxing all parts of our body and minds.** This simple technique allows our healing energies to restore the harmony in the nervous, endocrine and immune systems required for health and vitality in the body and mind.

In deep relaxation, we are able to mentally **direct our body's healing energies** to the areas we would like to more specifically affect. Thus, if we have a problem with our liver, we can send healing energy there by imagining light, peace, or positive healthful vibrations or feelings flowing into the liver. This can be done with any part of the body.

The same technique of positive imagery or feeling can be applied to all aspects of our lives. We can **imagine** ourselves with **greater self-acceptance, self-confidence, self-love, peace of mind** and ease and confidence in our social and professional contacts. We can visualize ourselves in harmonious and loving relationships. We can imagine ourselves as healthy, energetic and happy.

This is not self-deception. **We are simply directing our mind's energies toward the eventual creation of positive realities.** Changes in our thoughts and mental images eventually lead to changes in our lives, including our health.

A number of relaxation techniques are described on our web site.

**8. CREATIVE SELF-EXPRESSION** is much more important to our physical, emotional and spiritual health and harmony than most people imagine. Man is a creative being. Our purpose on earth is to create in some way. We might create a family, a business, a farm, a painting, a piece of music, a dance, etc. Creative self-expression is essential for our health, harmony and happiness.

**9. MEANINGFUL ACTIVITY** is necessary for us to feel that our life is worth living. If we do not see what we are doing as meaningful, useful or helpful in some way, we lose our reason to exist, and our health and happiness gradually deteriorate. We must discover the type of work and lifestyle that suits us so our lives can be lived with joy and inspiration.

**10. MASSAGE:** Some of us are unable to overcome our negativity without help. We are so tense that we cannot even begin a regimen of simple exercises or breathing techniques, or even basic analysis. Various types of massage and energy healing can greatly benefit us in such situations. Shiatsu massage, polarity massage, spiritual healing and Reiki can be especially effective in relaxing the nervous system and reducing negativity. The mind becomes clearer and more positive so we may begin to see what is happening more objectively.

**11. CLEANSING TECHNIQUES:** There are various methods for cleaning the body, thus producing a beneficial effect on our overall energy flow. One simple method is to increase the number of showers or baths. Contact with water can be healing and calming, especially if we are subject to insomnia or intense ups and downs in energy flow which cause us to have too much nervous energy at one moment, and no energy at all the next. Contact with water is a form of first aid in these cases.

We can also benefit by cleaning the body systems with enemas and other internal cleansing techniques. These techniques greatly affect the mind as much as the body.

**12. EMOTIONAL RELEASE:** We might need to partake in a program of emotional release under the guidance of an experienced professional, who can help us release pent up emotions which undermine our health and energy level, and cause us to become emotionally vulnerable.

**13. SOCIAL HARMONIZATION:** Our inner harmony is deeply affected by our relationships with those around us. The opposite is even truer: our relationships with others will simply mirror our relationships with ourselves. This is an aspect of our lives we must address when seeking to create health and harmony. We need to discover and overcome any fears or beliefs that prevent us from feeling comfortable with others.

**14. SPIRITUAL ORIENTATION:** Each of us has his or her own personal relationship with the universe. Some believe in God. Many adhere to a religion that has specific concepts of what God is. Whether or not we adhere to any particular religion, it is important for our inner balance that we feel and cultivate our relationship with the whole as humanity, as nature, or as God.

**15. SELF-KNOWLEDGE** means to understand the various aspects of our being: physically, emotionally, mentally, socially and spiritually. We need to comprehend our own inner mechanisms, needs, desires, fears, expectations, beliefs and subconscious workings in order to free ourselves from the negative emotions, mechanisms or which undermine our health, happiness and relationships. Only then can we create the life we desire.

**16. ENLIGHTENING THE SUBCONSCIOUS:** This aspect of self-improvement usually requires a psychologist or other experienced professional who can help us reprogram the subconscious with positive, more objective beliefs and perceptions of ourselves, others and the world.

I hope you will benefit from some, if not all, of these aspects of creating a healthy, harmonious, productive and happy life.

# ABOUT THE AUTHOR

American born, Robert Elias Najemy is presently living in Athens Greece, were he has founded and is directing the **Center for Harmonious Living** since 1976 which serves 3500 members with classes and workshops designed to aid each in the improvement of his or her body, mind, relationships and life in general.

Robert has 18 books published in Greek, which have sold over 90,000 copies.

He is the author of hundreds of articles published in magazines in England, Australia, India and Greece.

He has developed a program of seminars for Self-Analysis, Self-Discovery, Self-Knowledge, Self-Improvement, Self-Transformation and Self-Realization.

This system combines a wide variety of well-tested ancient and modern techniques and concepts

His teachings come from what he calls "Universal Philosophy" which is the basis of all religions and yet beyond and not limited by religions.

### His seminars include a variety of experiences including:

**1.** Basic **psychological** and **philosophical teachings.**

**2. Self analysis** through specially designed questionnaires.

**3.** Methods of **contacting** and **releasing** the contents of the **subconscious** in a safe and gentle way.

**4. Exercises**, breathing, movement, **singing**, chanting and **dance** for expression and release.

**5.** Methods for **discovering and releasing** through **regressions** (in relaxation) the events of the past, which have programmed our minds negatively and thus, are obstructing our happiness and effectiveness in the present.

**6.** Techniques for **solving inner conflicts** and also for **solving conflicts with others**.

**7.** Methods for **calming the mind** and **creating positive mental states.**

**8. Experiences for feeling greater unity** with others and breaking through feelings of separateness.

**9.** Opportunities to **share with others** that which one is feeling and experiencing.

**10. Emotional release techniques**.

**11. Methods of meditation** and transcendence of the mind for those who are ready.

### Some titles of his books are:

| | |
|---|---|
| *Universal Philosophy* | *Contemporary Parables* |
| *Miracles of Love and Wisdom* | *Our Universal Self* |
| *The Mystical Circle of Life* | *Relationships of Conscious Love* |
| *The Art of Meditation* | *Saram - Adventures of a Soul* |

## About Our Web Site
## www.HolisticHarmony.com

We have 30 years of experience in
helping people clarify and improve their lives

### YOU MAY BE ABLE TO USE US TO:

1. Create **emotional harmony**
2. Improve your **health**
3. Develop inner **peace**
4. **Resolve** inner conflicts
5. **Communicate** more effectively and Harmoniously
6. Open your heart to **love**
7. **Accept** and love your self more
8. Develop **self confidence**
9. Cultivate **higher virtues**
10. Obtain greater **self-knowledge**
11. **Deal** with challenging tests
12. **Understand** what Life is asking you to learn
13. Develop your own **personal philosophy** of life
14. Clarify your **value system**
15. Make **decisions**
16. Strengthen the **truth** within
17. Increase your **creativity**
18. Become a **happier** person
19. **Overcome** fears
20. **Remove blockages** towards manifesting dreams
21. Improve your **meditation**
22. **Deal with death**, yours or loved ones
23. **Free** yourself from old emotional games
24. **Let go** of the past and future
25. **Accept your life** as it is
26. Develop your **relationship with the Divine**
And many others ways you might think of.

### WHO ARE WE?

We are a group of life-management facilitators working for the **CENTER OF HARMONIOUS LIVING** a non profit organization based for the last 25 years in Athens, Greece. We have aided over 10,000 people in clarifying their life issues through lectures, seminars, group work, books, cassettes, videos and personal appointments.